Red Flag Wounded

Ronald Grigor Suny is the William H. Sewell Jr. distinguished professor of history at the University of Michigan and emeritus professor of political science and history at the University of Chicago. He is the author of *The Soviet Experiment*; *Red Flag Unfurled*; and *"They Can Live in the Desert but Nowhere Else": A History of the Armenian Genocide*.

Red Flag Wounded

Stalinism and the Fate of
the Soviet Experiment

Ronald G. Suny

VERSO

London • New York

For Val Kivelson,
colleague, critic, comrade

First published by Verso 2020
© Ronald G. Suny 2020

1 3 5 7 9 10 8 6 4 2

Verso
UK: 6 Meard Street, London W1F 0EG
US: 20 Jay Street, Suite 1010, Brooklyn, NY 11201
versobooks.com

Verso is the imprint of New Left Books

ISBN-13: 978-1-78873-074-7
ISBN-13: 978-1-78873-073-0 (LIBRARY)
ISBN-13: 978-1-78873-076-1 (US EBK)
ISBN-13: 978-1-78873-075-4 (UK EBK)

British Library Cataloguing in Publication Data
A catalogue record for this book is available from the British Library

Library of Congress Cataloging-in-Publication Data
A catalog record for this book is available from the Library of Congress
Library of Congress Control Number: 2020937946

Typeset in Minion Pro by MJ & N Gavan, Truro, Cornwall
Printed in the UK by CPI Group (UK) Ltd, Croydon, CR0 4YY

Contents

Introduction

Lessons of October: The Fate of Democracy and Socialism in the Age of Revolution and Counterrevolution

The year 1917 was a turning point at which the world certainly turned.[1] The revolutions in Russia both destroyed and made worlds, upended one understanding of historical motion and set out another, shattered the expectations of many and inspired new longings, ambitions, and opportunities of countless others. Unlike political revolutions in a single country that replaced one government with another, or nationalist revolutions that appealed to a single people and its diaspora, the Russian Revolutions, like the American and French Revolutions of the eighteenth century, resonated internationally, boldly proclaiming a new historical era and new political possibilities. The year 1917 was marked by a euphoria of popular power and democracy, a dream of utopia that soon would devolve into civil war and terror, eventuating in the nightmare of Stalinism.

Lost in much of the popular imagination of 1917 is its radical commitment to democracy of a new type, something beyond the formalism of "bourgeois democracy." Beyond universal suffrage, parliaments, and civil rights, the maximalist revolutionaries of 1917 envisioned the guarantee of social rights that would make the democratic exercise of power by ordinary people possible. But the imperatives of holding onto power in a civil war undermined the elemental democracy that emerged after the fall of tsarism. Particularly incompatible with democracy was the use of terror, for a terrorized people is unable to deliberate freely.

---

1 This chapter was originally prepared as a talk for presentation at various universities and conferences during the centenary of the Russian Revolution in 2017–18. An earlier version of a part of this introduction was published as "Lessons of October" in *Science and Society* LXXXI, 4 (October 2017), pp. 587–94.

At the same time, the revolutionaries were deeply committed to anti-imperialism and national self-determination, some (like Vladimir Lenin) more fervently than others. Even before the Bolsheviks took power in October, the socialist leaders of the post-February Petrograd Soviet held a vision that rejected the norms of the imperial powers. Both moderate and more radical socialists were determined to end the war without reparations, annexations, and rewards to the victors. The Petrograd Soviet's idea of a "democratic peace" was in line with (but more radical than) that of Woodrow Wilson and from the first weeks strained the Soviet's uneasy relationship with the Provisional Government and its more conventional war aims: "war to a victorious conclusion." Once the Bolsheviks took charge in October, they sought to expose the intimate connection of the war with the foundations of capitalism and bourgeois democracy and to turn the world war between nations into a civil war between classes. Their challenge to the established order and the prevalent assignment of property, privilege, and power, and their hostility to bourgeois society, capitalism, parliamentary democracy, and colonialism presented an immediate threat quickly grasped by European and US elites. Thus, from day one of Soviet power, Lenin and his comrades presented the rest of the world with an international security dilemma. Their rhetoric and practice propelled the Western powers to use whatever means they had at hand to destroy the Communist menace. Both an international civil war and the future Cold War were already inscribed in the western, Ottoman, and Japanese interventions in the Russian civil war.

Soviet power and the inspiration generated by the revolution went hand in hand with the international opposition to Bolshevism and revolution more generally. The anti-imperialism of Moscow was met by anti-imperialism from US president Woodrow Wilson but more forcefully by a renewed commitment to empire by the major European colonial powers. In the interwar period, European imperialists were not about to give up their overseas colonies, and anti-colonial nationalist movements were inspired by (if not directly linked to) the Comintern. In the two decades before Hitler and Stalin's war against Poland initiated the cataclysm of World War II, the major conflicts in the world took place in colonial and semi-colonial countries. Civil war in Russia was reflected in an international civil war between the forces of radical change and the forces of order.

One of the great paradoxes of the Soviet experience is that as anti-imperialist as the Soviet Union was rhetorically and in its support of anti-colonial movements, its internal structure—a pseudofederal structure that left the bulk of decision-making and a monopoly of sovereignty in Moscow—and its legitimizing discourse—its Marxist *mission civilisatrice,* that a vanguard party would lead a worker-peasant country to socialist civilization—were imperial. The USSR was a self-denying empire, never willing to consider itself imperial, indeed thinking of itself as the principal foe of imperialism on the globe; the Comintern and Communist parties around the world were in fact leading forces in the anti-colonial movements in the colonized world.

A related irony or paradox of Communist imperialism was that, like few other empires, the Soviet Empire was intentionally engaged in two forms of nation-building within its own territory: nation-building on the ethno-territorial level of republics and other institutional formations (such as autonomous regions) and on the all-Soviet level where efforts were made to create a "Soviet People" (*sovetskii narod*), an imagined and affective community of all Soviet citizens. The Soviet federation was in reality a "pseudofederalism" with little delegation of real power to the constituent units; it can be theorized as a particular form of empire.[2] Like other imperial formations, the Soviet Empire was marked by institutionalized differences and inequalities as well as authoritarian rule in the form of dictatorship or autocracy. While nation-states with their notions of representation of the nation and sovereignty of the people have a potential affinity with liberalism and democracy, the history of empires, from antiquity to the present, is replete with the usurpation of sovereignty by the metropole, a small elite, or one person.

A key question, then, arises for students of the Russian Revolution and the Soviet experience: why did the radically democratic, anti-imperial, and anti-nationalist revolution of 1917 so quickly devolve into an authoritarian imperial state, formally federal but hypercentralized, and committed to the formation of nations within its borders? The answer offered in this book is that the process of revolutionary empire-breaking and postrevolutionary empire-making was connected primarily to the political and strategic imperatives that the Bolsheviks encountered that, combined with their own vision of their preferred and anticipated future, led them rapidly away from participatory, bottom-up forms of Soviet power to a political system monopolized by a single party with sovereign power centered at the top ranks of the Communist Party in Moscow. Another contributing factor was the fatality of different languages and

---

2   For a discussion of the nature of the Soviet Union as an empire, see Valerie A. Kivelson and Ronald Grigor Suny, *Russia's Empires* (New York: Oxford University Press, 2017).

already formed ethnic communities that compelled the Bolsheviks to make fateful concessions to the principle of national self-determination that after seven decades would shatter the union itself. And yet an essential part of the answer, as I have argued in *Red Flag Unfurled* and others have suggested as well, lies with the choices made by Bolsheviks, most importantly by Lenin, choices in the heat of war and civil war that moved the country toward dictatorship.[3] "In the end," Terry Eagleton writes, "the Bolsheviks were simply too fearful to trust the working class as they might have done, and their relentless vanguardism helped to destroy soviet democracy and lay the ground for Stalinism."[4] The Bolshevik understanding of who their friends and enemies were and their conviction that history was moving in a predictable and favorable direction for them—their sociology as well as their eschatology—led them to make decisions that steered them away from popular participation to direction from above. A combination of pragmatic adjustment to an existential crisis and political and ideological preferences was key to the slide toward empire and authoritarianism.

The Fate of Soviet Democracy

The year 1917 was the second great cataclysm of the twentieth century, the first being the outbreak of World War I. The angry crowds that gathered in gloomy, frigid Petrograd were initially motivated by hunger, cold, and resentment at the callousness and incompetence of the tsarist government. Women were the first into the streets, on International Women's Day (February 23 by the Julian calendar, March 8 by the Gregorian), and they shamed the men in the factories to come out and join them. The inchoate rebellion became a revolution when the soldiers, including the imperial guards regiments, refused to fire on the crowds. The tsar abdicated; Duma politicians set up the Provisional Government; and the workers and soldiers elected their own representatives to the soviets. The first lesson of the revolution was that ordinary people with only the most perfunctory leadership could make history, topple a three-hundred-

3   Ronald Grigor Suny, *Red Flag Unfurled: History, the Russian Revolution, and the Soviet Experience* (New York: Verso, 2017); see also Suny, *The Soviet Experiment: Russia, the USSR, and the Successor States*, 2nd ed. (New York: Oxford University Press, 2011).

4   Terry Eagleton, "Lenin in the Postmodern Age," in Sebastian Budgen, Stathis Kouvelakis, and Slavoj Žižek (eds.), *Lenin Reloaded* (Durham and London: Duke University Press, 2007), p. 57.

year-old dynasty, and initiate radical social change with unpredictable consequences.

In the eight months that followed, Russia experienced a festival of democratic experimentation. Every constituency in the city, and through-out the country, formed committees, held meetings, elected delegates to congresses, passed resolutions, and expressed directly their fears of counterrevolution and hopes for a more just, egalitarian, and participatory political system and social order. But civil war was in the air from the very first days, with the city and country divided between the lower classes organized in soviets and increasingly becoming more radicalized and gravitating toward the Bolsheviks and the middle and upper classes rapidly losing faith in democracy and turning to strong men and the remnants of the army to reverse the gains of the workers, peasants, and soldiers. The second lesson of the revolution was that no shared consensus on the future united Russia's polarized society. Lenin and the Bolsheviks understood the impossibility of a coalition of the "vital forces of the nation" advocated by their former comrades, the Mensheviks, and called for "All Power to the Soviets," that is, a government excluding the middle and upper classes, what was known as *tsentsovoe obshchestvo*, and limited to what in Russian was called the *demokratiia*, the people who worked with their hands or served with arms. Class conflict in major cities made the victory of the Bolsheviks possible, but Soviet power was at the same time a declaration of civil war.

With the Bolshevik overthrow of the relatively democratically elected Constituent Assembly in January 1918 and the emasculation of worker and soviet institutions, the democratic institutions and practices of 1917 eventually atrophied. In the next four years of fighting against White counterrevolutionaries, anarchist and peasant armies, foreign interventionists, separatist nationalists, and more moderate socialists, terror replaced persuasion; military discipline and the prohibition of factions within the Communist Party eliminated the rough and tumble infighting of the Bolsheviks before 1921; bureaucracy burgeoned; and political decision-making narrowed to the Central Committee, then to Politburo, and ultimately to one man, Joseph Stalin.

Imperialism and National Self-Determination

The Russian Revolution and the early years of building the Soviet state occurred at a historical conjuncture—World War I and the restoration of bourgeois power in its aftermath—when Western colonial powers still considered empire and colonialism as a viable, even enviable, progressive form of governance over backward, benighted non-Europeans. Although the three great contiguous landed empires—Romanov Russia, Ottoman Turkey, and Austro-Hungary—had failed the test of war and given way to nationalist movements, independent ethnonational states, and colonial mandates, Britain, France, Belgium, the Netherlands, and Portugal all were prepared and willing to crush opposition to their imperial holdings and maintain European dominance in Africa and Asia. The United States was more ambiguous about empire, and its wartime president Woodrow Wilson had proposed national self-determination, at least for the peoples of Europe and the Ottoman Empire. The principal voice against colonialism was the Soviet Union for both ideological and strategic reasons.

Lenin had condemned imperialism in his famous polemic, *Imperialism, the Highest Stage of Capitalism: A Popular Outline* (1916), as the cause of devastating wars and a principal impediment to the progress of socialism. He proposed that capitalism had reached a new stage of maturity "in which economic competition and geopolitical rivalries were tending to merge together." This imperialist stage required "an anti-imperialist alliance between the working class in the advanced countries and national liberation movements in the colonies."[5] Strategically, he calculated that, if the great European powers were threatened and weakened by revolts in their colonies, the international revolution against capitalism would succeed far more easily.

For Lenin, "the war of 1914–18 was imperialist (that is, an annexationist, predatory, war of plunder) on the part of both sides; it was a war for the division of the world, for the partition and repartition of colonies and spheres of influence of finance capital, etc."[6] He expected that the elimination of imperial oppression would result in the spontaneous and irresistible attraction of small nations to the socialist nations and that in the long run the state would wither away and nations would merge together. The "inevitable merging of nations" would only occur, however, with the socialist revolution and "only by passing through the transition period of complete liberation of all the oppressed nations, i.e., their freedom to secede."[7] He carried this vision into the Kremlin and

5   Alex Callinicos, "Lenin in the Twenty-First Century?: Lenin, Weber, and the Politics of Responsibility," in Budgen et al. (eds.), *Lenin Reloaded*, pp. 36–7.

6   "Preface to the French and German Editions," *Imperialism, the Highest Stage of Capitalism*, (1920), marxists.org.

7   V. I. Lenin, "Sotsialisticheskaia revoliutsiia i pravo natsii na samoupravlenie

argued that the national and colonial questions were linked tightly to the future existence of the Soviet state and the possibility of building socialism in the former Russian Empire. Consistently opposed to what he labeled "Great Russian chauvinism," he accused non-Russian comrades like Stalin and Orjonikidze of such attitudes. "No nation can be free if it oppresses other nations," he quoted Marx as saying. Yet, in the interests of economic development and therefore of socialism, he privileged the interests of large nations over smaller nations and thereby left a large loophole by asserting that international, even global, concerns outranked narrow national interests.

Lenin's Marxism was genuinely pragmatic. One of his favorite and repeated remarks was "Facts are stubborn things. You can't beat facts by gossip."[8] Rather than deducing what had to be done from the writings of the masters, concrete situations had to be analyzed and the correct tactics induced from the particular historic conjuncture. A movement for a republic in one country might have to be opposed if it proved to be "merely an instrument of the clerical or financial-monarchist intrigues of other countries."[9] The flexibility that he proposed in 1916 would two years later, with the Bolsheviks at the head of the Soviet government, have enormous consequences for non-Russian nationalities in a time of civil war and foreign intervention. Subordinating the particular to the general interest caught the Soviets in a contradiction that would only be resolved in specific cases: the contradiction between favoring national self-determination and subordinating that noble aim to the general interest. In a prescient and dark warning, he emphasized what Engels had suggested in a letter to Kautsky: "*the victorious proletariat can force no blessings* of *any kind upon any foreign nation without undermining its own victory by so doing.*"[10]

Once the Bolsheviks took power in Petrograd in October 1917, Russia began to fragment into independent states. Like the liberals and moderate socialists, the Bolsheviks wanted to preserve the great state, but, given their prerevolutionary commitment to national self-determination

---

(Tezisy)" ["The Socialist Revolution and the Right of Nations to Self-Determination, Theses"] *Vorbote*, no. 2 (April 1916); *Sbornik "Sotsial-Demokrata,"* no. 1 (October 1916), in *Polnoe sobranie sochineniia*, 5th ed. (Moscow: Gosudarstvennoe izdatel'stvo politicheskoi literatury, 1962), vol. XXVII, p. 256 (Henceforth, *PSS*).

8   See, for example, this sentence in a letter to Nikolai Bukharin, October 14, 1916, *PSS*, XLIX, p. 308.

9   V. I. Lenin, "Itogi diskussii o samoopredelenii," *Sbornik "Sotsial-Demokrata,"* no. 1 (October 1916); *PSS*, XXX, p. 39.

10   Ibid., p. 51 (emphasis in original).

including separation from Russia, as well as their isolation in the major cities and weakness in imperial peripheries, they were willing to support, for a time, the aspirations of non-Russians for autonomy or even independence. The pragmatic versus the doctrinal was nowhere more evident than in Lenin's dealings with Ukraine. In June 1917 Lenin accepted the Ukrainian Rada's Universal Act, issued in Kyiv, which essentially declared Ukraine's autonomy and right to issue its own laws governing Ukraine while recognizing Russian laws through the entire space of the Russian Republic.[11] No other major political party in Russia was willing to make such a concession in 1917 to national self-determination.

At the beginning of December, a congress of soviets in Kharkiv declared a Soviet republic in Ukraine. With two antagonistic governments functioning in Ukraine, each claiming to be the legitimate sovereign power in the country, the Soviet Council of People's Commissars in Petrograd recognized the Soviet republic and "its right to secede from Russia or enter into a treaty with the Russian Republic on federal or similar relations between them."[12] As if to reassure his audience that his government remained faithful to the principle of national self-determination, Lenin declared in the same manifesto that the Soviet government has "not taken a single step, in the sense of restricting the Finnish people's national rights or national independence, against the bourgeois Finnish Republic, which still remains bourgeois, nor shall we take any steps restricting the national independence of any nation which had been—or desires to be—a part of the Russian Republic." But he complained that the Ukrainian Rada was disarming Soviet soldiers in Ukraine, had refused to convene a congress of soviets, and was supporting the Cossack revolt against the Soviet government in southern Russia. Petrograd demanded that the Ukrainian Rada cease its actions against the Soviets: "In the event that no satisfactory answer is received to these questions within 48 hours, the Council of People's Commissars will deem the Rada to be in a state of open war with Soviet power

---

11   V. I. Lenin, "Ukraina," *Pravda*, no. 82, June 28, 1917; *PSS*, XXXII, p. 342. "We do not favour the existence of small states. We stand for the closest union of the workers of the world against 'their own' capitalists and those of all other countries. But for this union to be voluntary, the Russian worker, who does not for a moment trust the Russian or the Ukrainian bourgeoisie in anything, now stands for the right of the Ukrainians to secede, *without imposing* his friendship upon them, but *striving to win* their friendship by treating them as an equal, as an ally and brother in the struggle for socialism" (emphasis in original).

12   V. I. Lenin, "Manifest k ukrainskomu narodu s ultimativnymi trebovaniiami k ukrainskoi Rade," December 3, 1917, *PSS*, XXXV, pp. 143–5.

in Russia and the Ukraine."[13] But after a report from Prosh Proshian, a Left Socialist Revolutionary member of his coalition government, Lenin softened his position and agreed to open talks with representatives of the Rada.[14]

Toward the end of 1917 Lenin defined the situation as a civil war declared by the enemies of the Soviet state. Rather than choosing to engage in democratic negotiation and compromise, a different logic would soon prevail, the logic of war. "Recent events in the Ukraine," Lenin wrote,

> (partly also in Finland and Byelorussia, as well as in the Caucasus) point similarly to a regrouping of class forces which is taking place in the process of the struggle between the bourgeois nationalism of the Ukrainian Rada, the Finnish Diet, etc., on the one hand, and Soviet power, the proletarian-peasant revolution in each of these national republics, on the other .... [T]he civil war which was started by the Kadet-Kaledin counter-revolutionary revolt against the Soviet authorities, against the workers' and peasants' government, has finally brought the class struggle to a head and has destroyed every chance of settling in a formally democratic way the very acute problems with which history has confronted the peoples of Russia, and in the first place her working class and peasants ....[15]

But the Rada's commitment to break with the Cossack revolt was not convincing to Petrograd, and, within a month, the Bolsheviks in Russia sided with their comrades in Ukraine, in the hope that their allies would prevail in the contest over Ukraine. They considered the Rada "fully responsible for the continued civil war which the bourgeois classes of the various nations have launched and which is absolutely hopeless, because the over-whelming majority of the workers, peasants and soldiers have come down solidly on the side of the Soviet Socialist Republic." The Soviets reassured the Ukrainians, "As for the national demands of the Ukrainians, the independence of their people's republic, and its right to federate, these are all recognized by the Council of People's Commissars and are not in dispute at all."[16] In an environment in which it was not

---

13 Ibid., p. 145.

14 "Rezoliutsiia Soveta narodnykh komissarov o peregovorakh s Radoi," December 19, 1917 (January 1, 1918), *PSS*, XXXV, pp. 182–3.

15 V. I. Lenin, "Tezisy ob uchreditel'nom sobranii," *Pravda*, no. 213, December 13 (26), 1917; *PSS*, XXXV, p. 164.

16 "Postanovlenie SNK ob otvete Rady Sovetu narodnykh komissarov," December 30, 1917, *PSS*, XXXV, pp. 211–12.

clear which side, the Soviets or the Rada, would emerge victorious in Ukraine, Lenin decided to let the question of who represented the nation be decided on the battlefield.

In January 1918, the Bolsheviks forcibly dissolved the democratically elected Constituent Assembly and did not permit it to reassemble; in so doing, they essentially declared war not only against the liberal and conservative forces in the country but also against their former comrades on the Left, the moderate socialists, the Mensheviks and the Socialist Revolutionaries. The situation was further complicated by the intervention of foreign powers. The Germans supported, indeed propped up, the anti-Bolshevik governments in Ukraine, Georgia, and the Baltic republics; the Ottoman Turks overthrew the Soviet in Baku and backed an independent, anti-Soviet Azerbaijan. With the defeat of the Central Powers and the end of World War I, the British became the major force behind the anti-Soviet opposition. For the three years from 1918 to 1921, the Red Army was engaged in a simultaneous battle against "bourgeois nationalists" and "foreign interventionists." The Bolsheviks hoped that Soviet power would survive until allied revolutions in Europe and Asia could come to the aid of the Russian revolution. Their anti-imperialism merged in their view with the drive to "liberate" the former subject peoples of the Russian Empire. Speaking to the Third Congress of Soviets in January 1918, Lenin was pleased to report that his government had outlasted the last workers' government, the Paris Commune, by five days. The lesson Marxists had learned from the French experience, both Jacobin and Communard, was that "there is no other road to socialism except the dictatorship of the proletariat and the ruthless suppression of the rule of the exploiters."

> We must not depict socialism as if socialists will bring it to us on a plate all nicely dressed. That will never happen. Not a single problem of the class struggle has ever been solved in history except by violence. When violence is exercised by the working people, by the mass of exploited against the exploiters—then we are for it! [*Stormy applause.*] And we are not in the least disturbed by the howls of those people who consciously or unconsciously side with the bourgeoisie, or who are so frightened by them, so oppressed by their rule, that they have been flung into consternation at the sight of this unprecedentedly acute class struggle, have burst into tears, forgotten all their premises and demand that we perform the impossible, that we socialists achieve complete victory without fighting against the exploiters and without suppressing their resistance.[17]

17   V. I. Lenin, "Doklad o deiatel'nosti Soveta narodnykh komissarov, 11 (24) ianvaria," *PSS*, XXXV, pp. 264, 265.

With little real ability to impose its will in the borderlands, the Soviet government made a strategic shift in response to the growing number of autonomies and accepted by January 1918 the principle of federalism. As they launched an attack on Ukraine, the Bolsheviks announced that they recognized the Central Executive Committee of Soviets of Ukraine as "the supreme authority in Ukraine" and accepted "a federal union with Russia and complete unity in matters of internal and external policy."[18] The Third Congress of Soviets resolved: "The Soviet Russian Republic is established on the basis of a free union of free nations, as a federation of Soviet national republics."[19] Both federalism and national-territorial autonomy were written into the first Soviet constitution, adopted in July 1918.

Until his last active days, Lenin continued to advocate caution and sensitivity toward non-Russians, whereas many of his comrades, most notably Stalin and Orjonikidze, were less willing to accommodate even moderate nationalists. The Bolshevik *mission civilisatrice* involved the building of a federated state that would both nurture the nations within it, raise the borderlands up to the cultural and economic level of the center, and thus forge new loyalties to the ideals of the socialists. The pragmatic gradually won out over the purely aspirational. Perhaps most ominously, in the light of a resistant reality in which the inevitable movement toward communism appeared stalled, the gap widened between the actual practices of Bolsheviks and the inflated rhetoric that disguised them. The language of national liberation and anti-imperialism remained a potent discursive cloak under which an empire of subordinated nations was gradually built.

The harshest lessons of the revolution were, first, that war and civil war polarize politics and undermine democratic choices; and, second, that they give well-placed elites enormous discretion to shape the nature of the political regime. Without strong institutions to constrain the actions of those in positions of influence and power, however humane and progressive their ambitions and goals, the will of the people will be compromised, even jettisoned. That second lesson would be made even more starkly with the final crisis of the Soviet Union. Resisting the gradual and inconsistent reforms of Mikhail Gorbachev, more radical reformers attempted to hasten the overthrow of Communist rule only to weaken the entire polity. Once the self-proclaimed democrats around

---

18   Richard Pipes, *The Formation of the Soviet Union: Communism and Nationalism, 1917–1973*, Revised edition (Cambridge, MA: Harvard University Press, 1997), p. 111.

19   Ibid.

Boris Yeltsin secured power, they then carried out their own coup d'état in 1993 against an elected parliament and imposed a powerful presidency that eventuated in the authoritarianism of Vladimir Putin. The people cannot stay mobilized forever, and those in or near the seats of power usually prove to be more durable political players.

Journalists and even scholars have often facilely explained the failure of Russians to achieve more democratic and representational politics in 1917–21 and 1989–93 as the fault of ordinary Russian and Soviet people, a people, it is said, with a deep, authoritarian streak, who possess a political culture or even a genetic propensity to love slavery, disregard the value of human life, and yearn for strong men to rule them. Such fantasies of national character and embedded culture are much more revealing of their authors than of the actual experience and history of the largest country on the globe. Generalizing about Russian character or history is a pernicious practice that leads more easily to distortion and confusion than to enlightenment.

Human beings, Karl Marx wrote, make their own history but not under circumstances chosen by themselves. History constrains as well as enables. A crucial lesson learned from looking at the Russian Revolution is that opportunities were missed, though they were fleeting; risks that might have altered outcomes were not taken; choices were made that sent the revolution down a tragic track. In October 1917, Lenin had boldly and purposefully convinced his closest comrades that it was time for the soviets to take power. He spurred them to action when many of his closest associates were hesitant. His shrewd strategic sense, his perceptive reading of the social dynamics of the moment, brought his party to power in a few days with minimal losses at the time. Four years later, in March 1921, he faced another moment of decision. As the civil war wound down, the central party leaders experienced new threats: strikes in Petrograd and other cities; the mutiny of the Kronstadt sailors calling for soviets without Communists; massive peasant revolts; and within the party ranks opposition to the policies of War Communism, *embourgeoisement* of the party, and undemocratic and authoritarian practices. Lenin tacked toward moderation on the economic front and introduced the state capitalist New Economic Policy (NEP). But he made no compromise with the actively rebellious sailors, workers, or peasants and sanctioned a major campaign against the insurgent sailors of Kronstadt and the peasant rebels in Tambov province and elsewhere. And at the Tenth Party Congress, against the Workers' Opposition led by Aleksandra Kollontai and Aleksandr Shliapnikov, he pushed through the plank forbidding organized factions within the party. The party leaders chose economic liberalization, on the one hand, and political tightening on the other. NEP worked well; factories began to whirr again; peasants produced more now that they were allowed to keep part of their output after paying a tax in kind to the state. But, in the political sphere, internal party democracy rapidly withered. Oppositions fell one after the other, as dominant factions led by Stalin steadily defeated his enemies and consolidated his power. By the twentieth anniversary of October, a one-man dictatorship based on police terror and the strictest control of public media and education turned on the party ranks itself and murdered hundreds of thousands of Communists, including Lenin's closest comrades. Nearly 700,000 people were shot in 1937–38 alone. Millions of ordinary citizens were deported, exiled, imprisoned, or executed. As Leon Trotsky, then himself in foreign exile, put it, a river of blood separated Lenin and Stalin.

A Russian historian at a prestigious West Coast university once told me with great conviction that nothing good came out of the Soviet Union. There was nothing redeemable or praiseworthy. Taken aback by so categorical a condemnation, I asked, what about the victory over fascism? The Soviets, after all, took on three quarters of the Nazi forces, as well as allied Finns, Romanians, Hungarians, and others. They liberated Auschwitz and other death camps in the east and essentially brought the Holocaust to an end. Ironically, it was the Red Army that saved the world for democracy and capitalism. What about industrialization of a vast peasant land, forced to be sure, inefficient, chaotic, and haphazard in many ways, but adequate enough eventually to raise the standard of living of tens of millions, turn the country from 80 percent rural to 80 percent urban, and create an educated population that after a half century of paternalistic rule no longer in any way required domination by the superannuated Communist Party?

A lesson of studying Russian and Soviet history ought to be that black-and-white images hide more than they reveal, that complexity and nuance, anomalies and contradictions must be recognized. Considering what the Soviets proudly called their *dostizheniia* (achievements) does not require whitewashing the horrors of collectivization and the Ukrainian famine (*Holodomor*) or ignoring the wasted lives of Stalin's Great Purges or the thousands of petty absurdities that characterized everyday Soviet life.

The Russian Empire was one of the most backward states in Europe in 1917, considered the "prisonhouse of nations," a colonial power that competed with the great European overseas empires for its place in the sun. The October Revolution turned Russia into the leading anti-imperialist, anti-colonial country in the world. While its practices would never quite live up to its grandiose promises, the Soviet Union was the defender of national liberation movements around the world at a time when the United States was sending its troops near and far to suppress anti-imperialisms that appeared to be favoring Communism. Within the Soviet state, which, in its own way, was a peculiar empire in which goods and services flowed from center to periphery rather than the other way round, hundreds of ethnic and national groups were given cultural, educational, and political institutions while their sovereignty was usurped by Moscow. Leninist programs made nations within the body of the empire, not perhaps under circumstances chosen by themselves, but promoting ethnonational development to the point that by 1991 Soviet nations were ready to jump the sinking ship and declare themselves independent of the Kremlin. Soviet nationality policies kept the peace between ethnicities for seven decades and even forged a transnational identification with the USSR as a whole. Kazakhs and Ukrainians, along with Armenians and Azerbaijanis, fought against fascism in World War II for both their national homelands, their own survival, and the Soviet state. Whatever ethnic hostilities they held in the postwar period were embedded in discriminations favoring the titular nationalities of certain republics or sublimated in football rivalries.

After the death of Stalin, a similar reversal of economic exploitation with many of the states in East Central Europe occurred as well. "Goulash Communism" created higher standards of living in Hungary and Poland than in the USSR itself. Deviation from the Soviet Bloc, however, could result in the unwelcome, harsh suppression by the Soviet Army, as in 1953 (East Germany), 1956 (Hungary), and 1968 (Czechoslovakia). The Soviet Union was, like many empires, a developmentalist state. It changed itself and those nations and states subordinated to it without agreeing to grant them sovereign power until the Gorbachev years. Its *mission civilisatrice* was hampered by its own underdevelopment and overstretched ambitions, yet colonized peoples around the globe studied in Moscow and looked to the Soviets as a viable alternative to capitalism.

The Soviet Empire proved to be an exception among many empires in many ways. It never achieved the longevity of most of its predecessors. The historical sociologist Karen Barkey, who in her work on the Ottoman Empire set out to answer the question of why empires lasted so long, noted that the Roman, Byzantine, Ottoman, Habsburg, and Russian Empires were political formations that endured for centuries. Such durability was remarkable, although also explainable. Rome as an empire lasted from 31 B.C. to A.D. 476. Byzance after the rise of the Eastern Empire continued from 527 to 1453. The Ottoman Empire formally existed from 1300 to 1918. The Habsburgs ruled nearly 400 years, and the Romanovs ruled from 1613 to 1917.[20]

Yet the Soviet Empire, which represented the end of empire even as a new empire was founded, disintegrated after only seven decades. Collapse and disintegration certainly testify to failure but at the same time, in many ways, the Soviet Empire actually succeeded in achieving its civilizing mission—developing an urban, educated, mobile population from an archaic society of peasant villages, people ready for self-government. Its very successes doomed the empire to irrelevance. Who needed the vanguard, the Communist *nomenklatura*, that aging imperial elite as the age of empire came to an end in 1991?

Trotsky wrote his famous essay "Lessons of October" in 1924 in the belief that too little was known about the October Revolution and that other countries needed their own October. We might also consider what October might teach us today about the future of socialism (and democracy, which is so intimately connected to socialism), but only by appreciating the ambiguous legacy of Soviet "socialism." A central irony of the Soviet experiment is that what it did in the name of Marxism in many ways crippled Marxism itself. To Western liberals and conservatives, what Stalin built *was* socialism, and it looked pretty unattractive to those living in the developed West. Democratic socialists, neo-Marxists, and Social Democratic parties attempted to carve an independent space for non-Communist socialism with notable results in many cases, but to large publics Marxism was seen as a descent into dictatorship evidenced by the cases of one-party Leninist states. At the turn of the twenty-first century, socialism, in most of its historic forms, appeared to be discarded on the trash heap of history, while racism, authoritarianism, xenophobia, and religious fundamentalism competed against an increasingly embattled liberalism.

The basic takeaway from October and the Soviet experience is that there is no real socialism without democracy, while the fundamental

20   Karen Barkey, *Empire of Difference: The Ottomans in Comparative Perspective* (New York: Cambridge University Press, 2008), p. 15.

takeaway from Russian and US politics today is that there is no real democracy without socialism. That is, there cannot be polarized inequality; great sums of money or an overweening government distorting elections, the media, and education; lack of opportunity to advance; no secure basis on which to live and raise one's family, and still have a truly democratic society and politics in which ordinary people can make meaningful decisions about their lives and leaders. As in 1917, so a century later, we are living in a moment of global crisis, both economic and political, but now the greatest challenge for the Left is to find a way to move beyond the limits of bourgeois democracy toward a sustainable democratic socialism.

The picture looks bleak as I think about both Russian and US politics. A clueless, narcissistic real estate tycoon was elected president of the most powerful and influential country in the world; political discourse was reduced to vicious politically incorrect, racist sound bites; mass media collaborated with a political system in which money is speech, corporations are people, and justice and elections are decided by how much money one can raise—these are fundamental characteristics of bourgeois democracy. Perhaps the proverbial Russian optimist might be right. When the pessimist complained that things cannot get any worse, the optimist declares, yes, they can.

It is always easier to state the nature of a problem than to find a solution. Perhaps the tentative first step would be to think clearly about the history of the twentieth century, what missteps were made and what successes were achieved. Understanding the past and how the present was constructed may lay the ground for rethinking how to make a future worth living in. Dark times may lie ahead, but progressive discourses, like history, are powerful enablers and constraints. A new more positive, perhaps even utopian, discourse about democracy and socialism will provide a light at the end of a dark tunnel. Right now, the task is to find that tunnel.

Part I

Stalin and Stalinism

1

Making Sense of Stalin: His Biographers

What is exceptional about the life of an exceptional individual is the location of that life in a particular historically organised milieu and the interactional patterning of the series of experiences through which individuation is then achieved—in fact, the meshing of life-history and social history in a singular fate. Individual lives are indeed unique but their uniqueness, I suggest, is not a matter of some elusively private personal factors but of the diversity of movement available to historically located individuals within historically located social worlds. ... The problem of the individual can, I conclude, be made manageable in historical sociology by treating it as itself genuinely a problem of history.[1]

Stalin continues to fascinate—the central mystery within the riddle inside the enigma that was the Soviet Union. If you Google "Stalin, biography," about a half million web sites come up. Amazon offers thousands of titles with his name in it, many of which qualify as biographies, whole or partial. The man who toward the end of his life arguably was the most powerful individual in the world had at various earlier times been seen as a "grey blur," "the man who missed the revolution," "a non-entity hooked by history," "the marvelous Georgian," "Generalissimo," and "History's villain."[2] A person such as Stalin is not easily put aside by the dismissive phrase "of interest only to historians."

---

1   Philip Abrams, *Historical Sociology* (Ithaca, NY: Cornell University Press, 1982), pp. 297, 299.
2   The Menshevik-Internationalist Nikolai Sukhanov called Stalin a "grey blur" in his brilliant account of the Russian Revolution [N. N. Sukhanov, *The Russian Revolution, 1917: A Personal Record* (New York: Harper Torchbook, 1962), I, p. 230]; historian

The Stalin industry has been booming for quite a long time. To understand the mystery at the center of the Soviet enigma and create an organic narrative linking his Georgian boyhood to his mature tyranny, analysts have used methods from psychohistory to sensationalist recreations of a Caucasian bandit to explain what fragmentary sources cannot deliver. Though less crude than those familiar childhood accounts on which many of us broke our historical teeth—"Christopher Columbus, Boy Explorer," "Florence Nightingale, Girl Nurse," "John Wanamaker, Boy Merchant"—the first chapters of the various lives of Stalin are an almost ritualistic search for signs of the paranoid revolutionary-from-above of the 1930s. The usual practice of historians who "know" the autocratic Stalin of totalitarian Russia is to read back the characteristics of the General Secretary into the prerevolutionary Stalin, emphasizing what fits (violence, paranoia, arrogance, the need to dominate) and rejecting what does not (romanticism, literary sensibility, love for his homeland, revolutionary idealism). In the absence of biographical data, other paths are taken—excursions into Georgian culture, the heavy burden of Orthodox beliefs, whether Christian or Marxist, or speculation that Stalin must have been an agent for the tsar's secret police (*Okhrana*).[3] The imaginative portraits by Alexander Solzhenitsyn, Vasilii Grossman, Anatolii Rybakov, and others help us to sense what the mind of the dictator might have been like, but we accept them as fictions and do not require the precision and evidence of historical argument.[4] With *glasnost'*

Robert M. Slusser referred to Stalin "as the man who missed the revolution" [*Stalin in October: The Man Who Missed the Revolution* (Baltimore: Johns Hopkins University Press, 1987); Vladimir Lenin wrote to Maxim Gorky in late February 1913 about a "marvelous Georgian" [V. I. Lenin, *Polnoe sobranie sochineniia*, 5th ed. (Moscow: Gosudarstvennoe izdatel'stvo politicheskoi literatury, 1958–1966) [Henceforth, *PSS*], XLVIII, p. 162]; Stalin took on the rank of Generalissimo in World War II; and countless historians have seen him as a villain in history.

3   One of the first psychoanalytic discussions of Stalin was by Gustav Bychowski, "Joseph V. Stalin: Paranoia and the Dictatorship of the Proletariat," in Benjamin B. Wolman (ed.), *The Psychoanalytic Interpretation of History* (New York and London: Basic Books, 1971), pp. 115–49. For the theory that Stalin was a police agent before the revolution, see Isaac Don Levine, *Stalin's Great Secret* (New York: Coward-McCann, 1956); Edward Ellis Smith, *The Young Stalin: The Early Years of an Elusive Revolutionary* (New York: Farrar, Straus and Giroux, 1967); and H. Montgomery Hyde, *Stalin: The History of a Dictator* (New York: Farrar, Straus and Giroux, 1972).

4   Aleksander Solzhenitsyn, *V kruge pervym* (New York: Harper & Row, 1968); Aleksander Solzhenitsyn, *The First Circle*, trans. Thomas P. Whitney (New York: Harper & Row, 1968); Vasilii Grossman, *Zhizn' i sud'ba* (Moscow: Knizhnaia palata, 1988); *Life and Fate*, trans. Robert Chandler (New York: Harper & Row, 1985); Anatolii Rybakov, *Deti Arbata* (Moscow: Sovetskii pisatel', 1987); Anatolii Rybakov, *Children of the Arbat*, trans. Howard Shukman (Boston: Little, Brown and Co., 1988).

and the opening of the Soviet archives, the possibility of entering the inner sanctum of Stalinist politics has certainly enriched our appreciation of the intricacies of his despotic rule.[5] A rich harvest of memoirs and published documents filled in blank spots, even though *perestroika* politics, as well as the turbulent post-Soviet landscape, placed historical imagination in service to a specific politics of eroding the Stalinist inheritance. Since the Thaw of the early 1950s and Khrushchev's "Secret Speech," dismantling Stalin and Stalinism has been part of frustrated attempts at liberalization and democratization in the USSR and Russia. Discoveries by historians have only confirmed the horrors of the Stalin years and allowed conservatives in the West to enjoy a "told you so" schadenfreude as they watch those who in the past were more equivocal about Communist rule in Russia squirm.

For roughly thirty years, from about 1923–24 until Stalin's death on March 5, 1953, the life of Stalin and the political history of the Soviet Union merged so completely that leading historians chose biography as the appropriate form to chronicle the central three decades of the Soviet experience. The successive lives of Stalin have reflected the shifting political contexts at the moment of writing. The first biographies were partisan accounts by players in the colossal drama then unfolding in the 1930s—Henri Barbusse's hagiography, Boris Souvarine's disillusionment, and especially Lev Trotsky's final combat with his rival, cut off when he was murdered by one of Stalin's agents. In the throes of the Cold War, two former Communists, Bertram Wolfe and Isaac Deutscher, told Stalin's story from opposing points on the political spectrum—one to condemn to oblivion the Soviet alternative, the other to redeem another form of socialism. Wolfe, who ended his days at the Hoover Institution, saw the Soviet experiment as fatally flawed from the beginning, the product of a built-in authoritarianism originating in ideology, personality, and particular principles of party organization.[6] Deutscher, who remained a Marxist and a leading figure in the Trotskyist movement, strained

---

5   Important contributions to our understanding of the inner workings of the Stalinist dictatorship and Stalin's court politics include Yoram Gorlitzki and Oleg Khlevniuk, *Cold Peace: Stalin and the Stalinist Ruling Circle, 1945–1953* (Oxford and New York: Oxford University Press, 2004); and Sheila Fitzpatrick, *On Stalin's Team: The Years of Living Dangerously in Soviet Politics* (Princeton, NJ: Princeton University Press, 2015). For the larger social and cultural context of Stalinism, see the idiosyncratic and revealing reconstruction by Karl Schlögel, *Moscow 1937*, trans. Rodney Livingstone (Cambridge and Malden, MA: Polity Press, 2012).

6   Bertram D. Wolfe, *Three Who Made a Revolution: A Biographical History of Lenin, Trotsky, and Stalin* (New York: Stein & Day, 1948).

to be balanced, contrasting the horror with the achievements. "Stalin undertook, to quote a famous saying, to drive barbarism out of Russia by barbarous means. Because of the nature of the means he employed, much of the barbarism thrown out of Russian life has crept back into it."[7]

> The whole structure of Russian society has undergone a change so pro-
> found and so many sided that it cannot really be reversed. It is possible
> to imagine a violent reaction of the Russian people itself against the
> state of siege in which it has been living so long. It is even possible to
> imagine something like a political restoration. But it is certain that even
> such a restoration would touch merely the surface of Russian society
> and that it would demonstrate its impotence vis-a-vis the work done by
> the revolution even more thoroughly than the Stuart and the Bourbon
> restorations had done. For of Stalinist Russia it is even truer than of any
> other revolutionary nation that "twenty years have done the work of
> twenty generations."[8]

Biographies proliferated with the rise of academic Sovietology, and the general outlines of a master narrative fell securely into place with the accounts by Roy Medvedev, Robert C. Tucker, Adam B. Ulam, Ronald Hingley, Robert Slusser, and Robert McNeill.[9] More popular and sensationalist versions were produced by Robert Payne, Edward Ellis Smith, H. Montgomery Hyde, and Alex De Jonge.[10] The story of the abused boy from Gori who rose to become one of the three principal power brokers on the world stage was unified around a single motivation, an all-consuming and uncompromising drive to power, that integrated the fragments of his life into a unified narrative. The answers to the central mystery—why did he do what he did the way he did it—were sought by some with the aid of psychoanalysis, but, ultimately, they returned to the irreducible, the drive for power. The very thing that needed explanation

7   Isaac Deutscher, *Stalin: A Political Biography* (New York: Oxford University Press, 1966; original edition, 1949), p. 568.

8   Ibid., p. 569.

9   Roy A. Medvedev, *Let History Judge: The Origins and Consequences of Stalinism* (New York: Alfred A. Knopf, 1972; revised edition: New York: Columbia University Press, 1989); Robert C. Tucker, *Stalin as Revolutionary, 1879–1929: A Study in History and Personality* (New York: W. W. Norton, 1973); Adam B. Ulam, *Stalin, the Man and His Era* (New York: Viking, 1973; 1989); Ronald Hingley, *Joseph Stalin: Man and Legend* (New York: McGraw-Hill, 1974); Slusser, *Stalin in October*; Robert H. McNeal, *Stalin, Man and Ruler* (New York: New York University Press, 1988).

10   Robert Payne, *The Rise and Fall of Stalin* (New York: Avon Books, 1966); Smith, *The Young Stalin*; Hyde, *Stalin*; Alex De Jonge, *Stalin and the Shaping of the Soviet Union* (New York: William Morrow, 1986).

became the source of the explanation and was itself beyond further examination. The disjunctures and anomalies of human experiences, of radically different contexts, were smoothed away, as often is the case in biographies, in service to a literary imperative to give meaning and recognizable shape to the life as a whole.

By the 1970s, the limitations of biography for explaining the complex social phenomena that tore apart Soviet society were widely recognized, and interpretations largely from personality and politics were displaced, at least for a while, in the general move by scholars toward social history. The professional study of Stalinism bifurcated between those who concentrated on the dictator himself and those who sought to ground the political in a more deeply textured social landscape. Monographic studies of the peasantry and collectivization (Moshe Lewin, R. W. Davies, Lynne Viola), social mobility (Sheila Fitzpatrick), and workers (Vladimir Andrle, Donald Filtzer, Hiroaki Kuromiya, Anne D. Rassweiler, Lewis H. Siegelbaum) appeared along with new treatments of the intelligentsia (Kendall E. Bailes), the party (Gábor T. Rittersporn), and cultural production (Katerina Clark, Vera Dunham). Stalin himself, however, proved irresistible and irreducible to the social, and with the collapse of the system he created and the breakup of the pseudofederal state he had forged, the new context of the ultimate failure of his project—and the appearance of new sources, new witnesses—led investigators back into the darkest recesses of Stalinism.

The stakes in telling Stalin's story are high, for they become a battleground for attack or defense of the Soviet experience. Where Stalin is concerned, the need to know has very often taken precedence over what we can know. For all the extraordinary revelations about his years in power, the fruits of *glasnost'* and the archival revolution have not yet helped much to fill in the outlines of Stalin as a personality, particularly in his prerevolutionary years. Methodologically, Stalin biographers have divided between a majority restrained by traditional approaches to evidence and unwilling to engage in attenuated interpretations and a bolder minority ready to borrow from the arsenal of psychoanalysis to find the hidden meanings beneath Stalin's actions and utterances.

Stalin on the Couch

Psychohistory has long existed in a penumbra in the discipline of history, on the fringes of respectability, suspect in the minds of mainstream practitioners, and refused the respectful acceptance granted to social and cultural historians. Russian and Soviet studies in particular has not been hospitable to psychohistorians, though a few, like Arthur Mendel, Philip Pomper, and Robert C. Tucker, have contributed major biographical studies.[11] Psychohistory has been attacked within the historical discipline almost as much as it has been employed. It has been accused of "present-mindedness," neglect of social and cultural context, too great a focus on the individual, reductionism, insufficiently cautious use of evidence, and a host of other sins. Responding to charges that their methods are ahistorical and neglectful of social and cultural context, many psycho-historians reacted against the exclusive focus on the internal life of their subjects and placed them more fully in their social and cultural environments. Yet the emphasis on deep-seated psychological determinants, particularly irrational and unconscious impulses, continues to render the socio-cultural context less important than internal drives. Cultural mediation is often not considered as the psychohistorians impose psychological insights from their own society on actors in very different cultures. And politics is often seen as sublimation of other, more pathological impulses.[12]

In his eloquent defense of psychohistorical practice, Peter Gay writes that historians are amateur psychologists whether they admit it or not and

11   Among Russianists who have used psychohistorical methodologies one might mention Patrick P. Dunn, "Fathers and Sons Revisited: The Childhood of Vissarion Belinskii," *History of Childhood Quarterly* I, 3 (Winter 1974), pp. 389–407; Patrick P. Dunn, "Belinskii and Bakunin: A Psychoanalytic Study of Adolescence in Nineteenth-Century Russia," *The Psychohistory Review* VII, 4 (Spring 1979), pp. 17–23; Arthur P. Mendel, *Michael Bakunin, Roots of Apocalypse* (New York: Praeger, 1981); Arthur P. Mendel, "Fantasy and Revolution: A Russian Tragedy in Three Acts," *The Psychohistory Review* XII, 2/3 (Winter 1984), pp. 45–60; Nigel Moore, "The Myth of Stalin: The Psychodynamics of Its Utopian Ideals," *Russian History* XI, 2–3 (Summer–Fall 1984), pp. 283–97; Philip Pomper, *Peter Lavrov and the Russian Revolutionary Movement* (Chicago: University of Chicago Press, 1972); Philip Pomper, *The Structure of Mind in History: Five Major Figures in Psychohistory* (New York: Columbia University Press, 1985); Tucker, *Stalin as Revolutionary*; Robert C. Tucker, "A Case of Mistaken Identity: Djugashvili-Stalin," *biography* V, 1 (Winter 1982), pp. 17–24; Richard Wortman, "Power and Responsibility in the Upbringing of the Nineteenth Century Russian Tsars," *Group for the Use of Psychology in History Newsletter* IV, 4 (March 1976), pp. 18–35. See also the essays by Baron, Wortman, and Tucker in Samuel H. Baron and Carl Pletsch (eds.), *Introspection in Biography: The Biographer's Quest for Self-Awareness* (Hillsdale, NJ: The Analytic Press, 1985).

12   See, for example, the work of historian Anna Geifman, who employs a psychological approach to her studies of violence in tsarist Russia: *Thou Shalt Kill: Revolutionary Terrorism in Russia, 1894–1917* (Princeton, NJ: Princeton University Press, 1995); and *Death Orders: The Vanguard of Modern Terrorism in Revolutionary Russia* (Santa Barbara, CA: Praeger ABC-CLIO, 2010).

that their enterprise is not so different from that of psychoanalysts. Unhesitatingly they attribute motives, study passions, analyze irrationality, and make predictions about human behavior based on an understanding of certain stable and discernible traits.[13] Furthermore, they have borrowed psychoanalytic vocabulary, largely that of Freud, as part of the ordinary discourse of historians—usually without acknowledgement or serious study—and his insights have been widely misunderstood, abused, and oversimplified. For example, Gay notes, while Freud consistently stressed inherent drives like sexuality and aggression, he remained open in his own work to the importance of environmental influences.[14]

Gay chides historians for their use of unexamined conceptions of human nature. "If, for psychoanalysis, man is the wishing animal, he is, for the historian, the selfish animal. The two are not identical: the first struggles to reduce his tensions under the unremitting impress of his unconscious; the second lives under the sway of conscious egotism."[15] Historians would prefer, he claims, to deal with human beings as basically rational, self-interested creatures but are forced to recognize that optimal ends are disguised, that people do not always know what is best for them, and that passions and ignorance distort rational desires. Here, says Gay, psychoanalysis has a unique role to play, for it can illuminate the limits on the ego, on self-interest, and the centrality of instinctual drives. "Self-interest, to put it into psychoanalytic language, is a product of the reality principle, serving, while it affronts, the pleasure principle."[16] Gay's project is to bring the historian and the psychoanalyst together to enlarge both their historical and psychological senses of reality.

Given the still tentative and often conflicting interpretations in the study of human psychology, the skepticism of most historians is directed less at psychology in general than against a specific psychology with claims to universality. As Gay acknowledges, historians dealing with the behavior of crowds, periodic episodes of witch-hunting, or the general problem of ideology have recognized the nonrational side of human activity and thought. Even Marxist historians, perhaps the most hostile to psychoanalysis of the past, have argued that self-interest and rational economic choices are compromised by the lack of full consciousness of the ends and means to achieve them as well as by the disguises employed in class society to mask real social relations. Marx's concept

---

13 Peter Gay, *Freud for Historians* (New York: Oxford University Press, 1985), p. 6.
14 Ibid., p. 25.
15 Ibid., p. 100.
16 Ibid., p. 110.

of "the fetishism of commodities" or Lenin and Gramsci's elaboration of bourgeois social hegemony are correctives to the kind of rationalism that accompany liberal and classical economic understandings of human nature under capitalism. But Marxists are here talking about the difficulty or impossibility of knowing and therefore making fully rational choices, rather than the psychoanalytic notion of repressing unendurable experiences.

Historians in our own time tend to be eclectic in their analytical approaches and suspicious of reductionist or monistic explanations. The professional culture in which they write and test their conclusions encourages selective borrowing. Perhaps certain fundamentals of Marxism (the theory of surplus value, for example) will be rejected by the same writer who uses concepts of class or imperialism indebted to Marx. A historian may have no problem with psychological repression or sublimation while avoiding the Oedipus complex, the death instinct, or penis envy. Indeed, ideas from both Marxism and Freudianism have become so integral a part of twentieth-century social thought that any serious historian, anthropologist, or sociologist (or perhaps even political scientist) is unlikely to avoid completely their pervasive vocabulary. As Gay puts it (and we might supplement his thought), many of us have "been speaking Freud [and Marx] without knowing it."[17] Though the partial integration practiced by most historians will satisfy neither the committed Freudian nor the "orthodox" Marxist, both might take comfort in the fact that a discipline that has traditionally abhorred theorizing and often been content to limit itself to a simple empiricism has already been transformed by its encounter with these universalizing theories.

The major Stalin biographers of the 1930s, Boris Souvarine and Lev Trotsky, specifically rejected the crude psychoanalysis that reduced Stalin's initial political formation to relationships within his family. Rather than probe into an inaccessible inner life, Souvarine concluded, "Stalin's character is comprehensible without a knowledge of its early indications; his work can be estimated without knowing his childish impressions, his early desire for knowledge or any precious ideas he may have had."[18] He considered the reminiscences of Ioseb Iremashvili (1878–1944), Stalin's boyhood friend, "too suspect to be accepted by serious persons without

17   Ibid., p. 169.
18   Boris Souvarine, *Stalin: A Critical Survey of Bolshevism* (New York: Longmans, Green & Co., 1939), p. 5.

confirmation of the contents."[19] Yet Iremashvili's text contains the key reference to the young Stalin being beaten by his father, the principal childhood source (for psychohistorians) of his later aberrant behavior.

Although he, too, avoided psychoanalysis, Trotsky considered Iremashvili generally reliable. In his unfinished work, he repeatedly emphasized social environmental factors in Stalin's development, like the "social gradations" in school "where the children of priests, petty gentry and officials more than once made it clear to Joseph that he was their social inferior."[20] Trotsky's unique perspective was sharpened by his intimate knowledge of the revolutionary milieu in which Stalin operated, and he was able to make subtle psychological judgments about Stalin and his actual role in the early years because of his personal acquaintance with him and familiarity with the internal life of Social Democracy. Yet his portrait of Stalin is colored by his political struggle with Stalin and Stalinism and the particular condescension that many Russian intellectuals display toward less extraordinary people. "I was repelled by the very qualities that would strengthen him," Trotsky wrote, "namely, the narrowness of his interests, his pragmatism, his psychological coarseness and the special cynicism of the provincial who has been liberated from his prejudices by Marxism but who has not replaced them with a philosophical outlook that has been thoroughly thought out and mentally absorbed."[21]

In the latter part of the book, not fully reworked when he was murdered, Trotsky loses his usual balance and engages in extravagant charges, accusing Stalin of poisoning Lenin, but these excesses do not lessen the general value of this extraordinary portrait.[22] Trotsky's Stalin is a psychopath, marked by viciousness and vengefulness. He is also no intellectual, which for Trotsky appears to be the most damning accusation. As Peter Beilharz has pointed out, Trotsky refuses to allow Stalin "any kind of power of initiative" and fails to recognize that his intellectual limitations were more than compensated by his political acumen.[23] Trotsky's portrait

19   Ibid., p. 3. Joseph Iremaschwili [Ioseb Iremashvili], *Stalin und die Tragödie Georgiens: Erinnerungen* (Berlin: Volksblat Druckerei, 1932).

20   Leon Trotsky, *Stalin: An Appraisal of the Man and His Influence*, ed. and trans. by Charles Malamuth (New York: Harper & Brothers, 1941), p. 9.

21   From Trotsky, *Moia zhizn'*, II, pp. 213–14, quoted in Dmitri Volkogonov, *Stalin: Triumph and Tragedy*, ed. and trans. by Harold Shukman (New York: Grove Weidenfeld, 1991), p. 57.

22   Trotsky, *Stalin*, pp. 372–83.

23   Peter Beilharz, "Trotsky as Historian," *History Workshop Journal 20*, 1 (Autumn 1985), pp. 46–7.

of a mediocre small-time provincial endured as a powerful template for many future biographers.

A decade later, Trotsky's political disciple, Isaac Deutscher, quite deliberately set out to "study the politics rather than the private affairs of Stalin."[24] Deutscher's biography, at one and the same time a monumental history of the formation of the Soviet Union, soon became the interpretation most influential on the post-Stalin generation of Soviet specialists. This work by "an unrepentant Marxist" challenged the liberal and conservative orthodoxies of the Cold War years and sought to rescue socialism from its popular conflation into Stalinism.[25]

Though reduced as an explanatory factor, the personality of Stalin was in no sense eliminated. Using the same sources as the psychohistorians, Deutscher extracted only what a commonsense reading would allow: "His defences against his father's heartlessness were distrust, alertness, evasion, dissimulation, and endurance. Life was to teach him, early, lessons—and some *ruses de guerre*—that would be useful later on."[26] It was less his personal talents or evil machinations than the postrevolutionary slump in revolutionary enthusiasm that guaranteed Stalin's fortune. Deutscher laid out a law of revolution in which

> each great revolution begins with a phenomenal outburst of popular energy, impatience, anger, and hope. Each ends in the weariness, exhaustion, and disillusionment of the revolutionary people ... The leaders are unable to keep their early promises ... [The revolutionary government] now forfeits at least one of its honourable attributes—it ceases to be government by the people.[27]

The revolutionary party splits between those who deplore the new situation and those who accommodate to it. Stalin linked up with the actual, rather than the preferred, direction of the revolution. He became "both

24   Deutscher, *Stalin: A Political Biography* (New York: Vintage, 1960; second edition: New York: Oxford University Press, 1967), p. xv. (Page references to Deutscher are from the second edition. Deutscher's Stalin biography was originally published in 1949.)

25   The phrase is that of one of Deutscher's most severe critics, Leopold Labedz. See his two-part article, "Deutscher as Historian and Prophet," *Survey* VIII, 41 (April 1962), pp. 120–44, and "Deutscher as Historian and Prophet, II," *Survey* XXIII, 3 (Summer 1977–1978), pp. 146–64; as well as "Stalin and History: Perspectives in Retrospect," *Survey* XXIII, 3 (Summer 1977–1978), pp. 134–46; and "Isaac Deutscher's 'Stalin.' An Unpublished Critique," *Encounter* 52, 1 (January 1979), pp. 65–82.

26   Deutscher, *Stalin*, p. 3.

27   Ibid., pp. 173–5.

the leader and the exploiter of a tragic, self-contradictory but creative revolution."[28]

For Deutscher, Stalin was a Janus-like figure, representing both the backwardness of Russia's national environment and the progressive aspects of its transformation. The Russian Revolution had occurred without the prerequisites for socialism as defined by most Marxists, and the subsequent disappearance in the Civil War of a coherent and conscious working class prepared the way for its substitution by the Bolshevik Party and state bureaucracy. Stalinism was a "historically determined evil," the product of isolation and backwardness. His critics, like the liberal philosopher Isaiah Berlin who accused him of historical falsification, were quick to pounce on Deutscher's apologia for the necessity of collectivization, even though he noted that there were more optimal ways to carry out the shift in agricultural policy than the disastrous dekulakization that Stalin ordered. And Deutscher was rightly taken to task for believing that the leading military strategist in the Soviet Union, Mikhail Tukhachevskii, was guilty of leading a conspiracy to overthrow Stalin. Even though he modified his argument in the later (1967) edition, Deutscher still argued that a coup was being plotted. We now know the accusation was fabricated and a confession beaten out of the general.[29] He was right, it seems now, to reject the accusation that Stalin had been behind the murder of Sergei Kirov in December 1934, which was widely believed at the time to have been the dictator's handiwork.[30] In both Trotsky's and Deutscher's treatment, Stalin had been hooked by history and pulled upward. Yet the deliberately anti-psychological approach of the work and its rationalization of many of Stalin's policies left the field open for more critical, psychologically based interpretations.

In the late 1940s, the temptation to make sense of the seemingly senseless brutality of the Stalin era led Gustav Bychowski, a clinical professor of psychiatry in New York City, to make the first explicitly psychoanalytic reconstruction of Stalin's early life. Basing his analysis on Iremashvili, Bychowski argued that Stalin's reach for power was the "struggle of the

28   Ibid., p. 569.
29   The battle over Deutscher's biography is discussed at length in David Caute, *Isaac and Isaiah: The Covert Punishment of a Cold War Heretic* (New Haven, CT: Yale University Press, 2013), pp. 70–8.
30   For opposing views, see Amy Knight, *Who Killed Kirov?: The Kremlin's Greatest Mystery* (New York: Hill & Wang, 1999), who blames Stalin, and the definitive rebuttal by Matthew E. Lenoe, *The Kirov Murder and Soviet History* (New Haven, CT: Yale University Press, 2010).

son against the father," a repetition of the kind of succession struggles that go on in "primitive tribal societies."[31]

> The only surviving son of a crude and tyrannical peasant shoemaker, Stalin, the boy, learned early how to hate and how to suppress hostility until the opportune moment…. Undeserved, frightful beatings made the boy as grim and heartless as his father. Indeed, his suppressed hatred against his father transferred itself to persons in power and to all authority.[32]

Added to the personal humiliations suffered at the hands of his father were the social humiliations of Russian rule in Georgia. "Stalin transferred all the pain and resentment of his miserable childhood from his native land to the vast area of the tsarist empire. He, representative of a minority persecuted by the tsarist regime, behaved as if he identified himself with the old aggressor and, once in power, carried out the old imperialistic policy."[33] Totalitarianism is explained as the "desire to perpetuate unlimited power and to suppress the anarchistic and rebellious impulses unleashed by the revolution with its shattering of the old ego ideal."[34]

While his analysis of Stalin's drives were plausible given what he had read, Bychowski did not pretend to be a historian, and his psychological portrait made no attempt to deal with the real political imperatives with which Stalin had to deal both as revolutionary and as ruler. Basically, he was analyzing the Stalin he found in Iremashvili and Trotsky. His Stalin was a man driven by a deep pathology, an identification with his native land's enemy, and a thirst for flattery, whose inner impulses were shaped by the violence of the revolution. A toxic "cooperation of historical and sociological factors with the personality of a fanatic leader" created the monolithic negation of Western civilization of Cold War imagination.[35]

₭

31   Gustave Bychowski, "Joseph V. Stalin: Paranoia and the Dictatorship of the Proletariat," in Benjamin B. Wolman (ed.), *The Psychological Interpretation of History* (New York: Basic Books, 1971), pp. 123–5.

32   Ibid., p. 125. Bychowski uses the quotation about "beatings" from Iremashvili in the exact phrase used by Trotsky's translator, Charles Malamuth; see Trotsky, *Stalin*, p. 7.

33   Ibid., p. 131.

34   Ibid., p. 146.

35   Ibid., p. 139.

About the time that Bychowski was writing, a young American diplomat stationed in Moscow was himself engaged in psychological investigation. Though an American official, Robert C. Tucker was in a real sense a prisoner of Stalin, for he was not permitted to leave the Soviet Union with his Russian bride. While still in the USSR, he repeatedly read Karen Horney's *Neurosis and Human Growth* and was impressed by her concept of the "neurotic character structure."[36] Adverse emotional experiences in early life, wrote Horney, may lead to formation of an idealized image of oneself, which may then be adopted as an *idealized self*, which has to be realized in action, in a search for glory. The real empirical self threatens failure, and repressed self-hatred is projected as hatred of others. Walking down Gorky Street sometime in 1951, Tucker began to wonder "if the idealized image of Stalin appearing day by day in the party-controlled, party-supervised Soviet press was an *idealized self in Horney's sense*?"[37] The cult of Stalin, which was all around him in Moscow, reflected Stalin's own "monstrously inflated vision of himself."[38] Here was a way to penetrate the secrecy of the Kremlin and reveal the dictator. Through the cult, Stalin "must be the most self-revealed disturbed person of all time. Finding out what was most important about him would not require getting him onto a couch; one could do it by reading *Pravda*, while rereading Horney! I began to do just that, and in the process grew more and more convinced of my hypothesis."[39] Tucker found little support for his hypothesis of Stalin as neurotic and paranoid among his State Department colleagues. His academic associates would prove more receptive. In the years after Stalin's death, he elaborated his views (first as a researcher at the Rand Corporation and later as professor of politics at Princeton University) on the importance of the personality of the dictator in totalitarian systems and eventually embarked on a multivolume biography of Stalin from a psychohistorical point of view.

Tucker's Stalin wanted political power in order to become the "acknowledged leader of the Bolshevik movement, a second Lenin." His rise to power and his autocracy are to be understood as the outcome of four major influences—Stalin's personality, the nature of Bolshevism, the Soviet regime's historical situation in the 1920s, and the historical

36   Karen Horney, *Neurosis and Human Growth: The Struggle toward Self-realization* (New York: W. W. Norton, 1950), pp. 18, 22, 62, 154, 188, 212, 222, 277.

37   Robert C. Tucker, "Memoir of a Stalin Biographer," *University: A Princeton Magazine* (Winter 1983), p. 2.

38   Robert C. Tucker, "A Stalin Biographer's Memoir," in Baron and Pletsch (eds.), *Introspection in Biography*, p. 251.

39   Ibid., pp. 251–2.

political culture of Russia ("a tradition of autocracy and popular acceptance of it"). The rough treatment by his father and the great love of his
mother created a psychological tension in the young Stalin, simultaneously "the feeling of a conqueror, that confidence of success that often
induces real success" and "anxieties and threats to self-esteem." "Uncon-
ditionally admired by his mother, he grew up taking such admiration
as his due, expecting to be idolized and to be worthy of it. Encouraged
by her idealization of him, he started idealizing himself, and showed it
by a number of identifications with hero-figures ..." A compensatory
fantasy life, a self-idealization, acquired from reading Georgian romantic literature became "psychologically indispensable." In the short novel
"Patricide" by Aleksandre Qazbegi, the young Jughashvili found his role
model, his "idealized image of the hero as avenger," and the excited prose
of the story prepared his mind for "a vision of the hero as revolutionary."
During his years at seminary in Tiflis, the repressive atmosphere of the
school and the rebelliousness of the students deepened his childhood
"predisposition to rebel against paternalistic authority.... By the time
he left the seminary in 1899 he was a committed revolutionary, in revolt
against that great punitive system of paternalistic authority known as
tsarism."[40]

The choice of Marxism was a natural one, for it already held sway
among the radical Georgian intelligentsia. "But it was not only as a philosophical system that Marxism exerted its appeal. What may have been its
most magnetic feature for this rebel against established authority was the
grand theme of class war." As a "gospel of class war," Marxism not only
"legitimize[d] the young man's resentment against the various forms
of established authority, it identified his enemies as history's, bestowed
higher meaning on his urge to live a life of combat against forces of evil,
and sanctioned his quest for vindictive triumphs along the way." It was
only a short step to the militant Marxism of Lenin and to a psychological
identification with his new hero. "Lenin was for Djugashvili everything
that a revolutionary leader ought to be, and that he too would like to be
insofar as his capacities permitted." Whatever the power of Lenin's idea,
Tucker argues,

clearly Djugashvili did not become an ardent Leninist solely because of
the persuasive force of Lenin's political arguments. Becoming a Leninist
also involved, in this case, a rebellious young man's emotional need for

40   Tucker, *Stalin as Revolutionary*, pp. xv, xvi, 76, 81, 82, 115.

psychosocial identity …. Leninism confirmed him as Koba the heroic people's avenger while offering membership in the select fraternity of professional fighters against the existing order that Lenin called "the party."

The final step in Jugashvili's metamorphosis into Stalin was the shedding of his Georgian ethnic identity and the acceptance of a Russian national identity. "Via Bolshevism, Djugashvili joined the Russian nation," and by doing so abandoned "a losing for a winning side in history."[41]

Rather than a psychoanalysis of Stalin, Tucker's work used psychoanalytic insights to discover Stalin's deepest motivations. Not content simply to record his behavior and thought, suspicious that underneath this restrained figure lay a kind of monster, Tucker used Horney's model to reconfigure the bits and pieces of reminiscences that have come down to us. Given that the very lack of data did not permit a deep reading of what Stalin said, psychoanalytic method became in places the substitute for data. On the whole, the work is redeemed by the care and tentativeness of the psychological speculation and the more traditional reliance on other factors. But, at times, one has the feeling that Tucker suffers from some of the same tendencies as other practitioners of psychohistory. In the words of Thomas A. Kohut:

> Too often, when employing the psychohistorical method the historian comes to the past with an understanding and explanation already in hand; the understanding and explanation do not emerge from the past itself but are the products of a theoretical model. In short, it is often less accurate to say that the model is applied to the past than that the past is applied to the model.[42]

ॐ

Far more extreme than Tucker in his deployment of psychoanalysis, literary critic Daniel Rancour-Laferriere employed the tools of psychoanalysis to illuminate Stalin's darkest sides and wrote a short, unconventional "psychoanalytic investigation of selected, attested behaviors in Stalin, from childhood to old age."[43] Building on the work of Bychowski, Pomper, and

41   Ibid., pp. 119, 120, 134–5, 137, 140, 142.
42   Thomas A. Kohut, "Psychohistory as History" *American Historical Review* XCI, 2 (April 1986), p. 338.
43   Daniel Rancour-Laferriere, *The Mind of Stalin: A Psychoanalytic Study* (Ann Arbor, MI: Ardis, 1988), p. 7.

especially Tucker, Rancour-Laferriere presents a Stalin marked by mega-
lomania, paranoia, sadism, vindictiveness, and the need to control others.
The victim of an abusive, alcoholic father, Stalin remained for life a very
insecure man with deep feelings of inadequacy who required the adulation of others. Over time, he developed an arsenal of defense mechanisms
—an idealized self-image, projection of his faults and failures onto his
enemies, rationalization, and identification with the aggressor. This
son of a cobbler had a special fondness for feet, for boots and kicking,
and a homosexual affection for Hitler. "When confronted by Hitler, an
aggressor who took out his aggression on homosexuals, Stalin behaved
irrationally. He not only identified with that aggressor, he was attracted
to him sexually."[44]

Like many historical approaches, psychohistory has suffered from its
most extreme practitioners. In Tucker's now canonical account, psychoanalysis is only part of the explanation, and context, particularly in the
form of political culture, is maintained, as well as the particular conjunctures of historical events; in Rancour-Laferriere's much bolder (or
reckless) and avowedly subjective engagement with Stalin, however, all
distance is lost as the author melds the figure of Stalin into that of his own
disabled, crutch-wielding father. Transference, the author's own dreams,
and Staliniana are all interpreted freely within the broad framework
of psychoanalytic general laws. A distinct person of a distinct foreign
culture, of another time and place, is interpreted as if his understanding
of parenting, family life, friendship, loyalty and betrayal, ambition, and
self-identity were the same as ours. In fairness, Rancour-Laferriere does
not claim to have written history or a biography but rather a historical
psychoanalysis. In such a pure psychohistory, it seems, there is no need
for conventional history at all. Given the right psychological theory, a full
psychopathology may be deduced from a few anecdotes, and the usual
mediation of politics, society, and culture evaporates entirely.

The tendency of practicing psychohistorians of Stalin to derive his
mature behavior unproblematically from his childhood trauma has been
questioned by a number of theorists of psychohistory. Proposing a more
complex motivation that would at one and the same time include the
socio-political and cultural structuration of the world of the subject as
well as inner needs and drives, T. G. Ashplant suggests use of the psychoanalytic principle of overdetermination.

---

44   Ibid., pp. 109–10.

Looked at from the point of view of the actor, any single action in the external world is posited as the outcome of a range of different, perhaps even conflicting, drives or motives; while a single drive or motive can underlie a range of different, sometimes conflicting, actions. (Conversely, any one external event can give rise to a wide range of internal responses, depending on the previous experiences and resultant patterns of coping and responding of the various individuals affected. This understanding is very valuable as a corrective to the rather mechanical psychology which underpins much historical writing, assuming in effect that an external event evokes an identical response across a wide population.)[45]

In their own practice, says Kohut, psychoanalysts use multicausality and a kind of empathy to understand their patients, methods quite similar to those used by good historians to understand the past.

Just as the historian appreciates the complexity of the past, so the psychoanalyst recognizes the complexity of his patient, the many factors that influence him, the many different motives he may have. Just as the historian understands an event of the past as being the product of a multitude of causal factors, historically comprehensible only from many different perspectives, so the psychoanalyst understands his patient in many different ways, from many different points of view, offering literally hundreds of different interpretations during the course of an analysis. And, just as the historian focuses on a particular past event and seeks to understand it in depth and on its own terms, so the psychoanalyst focuses on the experience of his particular patient and seeks to understand him in depth and in terms of his own unique language and experience.[46]

Regrettably, Kohut continues, examples abound of seasoned and gifted psychoanalytic clinicians who, when trying their hand at history, do not apply the rich repertoire of interpretation that they use in their practices and instead impose theory where data is lacking and reduce explanations to a single interpretative formulation. Even Erik Erikson in his *Young Man Luther*, often acknowledged as the most successful psychohistorical recreation, turned "to theory to provide from the present what is missing in the past."[47] Summing up, it seems that the actual practice of

45   T. G. Ashplant, "Psychoanalysis in Historical Writing," *History Workshop Journal*, no. 26 (Autumn 1988), p. 106.

46   Kohut, "Psychohistory as History," p. 343.

47   Ibid., p. 341. Erik Erikson, *Young Man Luther: A Study in Psychoanalysis and History* (New York: W. W. Norton, 1958).

psychotherapy in historical writing, then, rather than its potential for explanation, can be faulted for reducing the complexity of the subject to a single explanatory key.

Beyond Psychohistory

While psychology cannot be avoided in a biography, most Stalin biographers leave Freud, his disciples, and psychoanalysis out of their analysis. In his sprawling biography of Stalin, political scientist Adam Ulam rejects a specific model of psychoanalysis and, instead of psychopathology, emphasizes rational choices. Tsarist oppression rather than a craving for power or a revolt against parental authority was Stalin's stimulus to joining the revolutionary movement.[48] Shaped by "years of conspiracy, with its suspicions and betrayals," as well as "the notion of historical forces so deeply ingrained in Marxism-Leninism," Stalin became "a man who operated as a conspirator throughout much of his life, even when dictator."[49] Ulam elevates politics and ideology as explanatory factors, resisting "the temptation to read into the personality of the young Georgian socialist and agitator all and already full developed characteristics of the dictator."[50] How does one explain all the "little Stalins," like Sergo Orjonikidze, Viacheslav Molotov, and Anastas Mikoyan, who did not have the brutalized childhood of their leader? The "natural rhythm of human existence" must be wedded to "the politics of the time and the movement" in order to explain the unique path that led to Stalin and Stalinism. The particularly noxious combination of absolute power with faith in Marxism-Leninism corrupted an already ruthless politician, creating a monstrous tyrant. The real villain in Ulam's story is not Stalin's father, or even Stalin himself, but the particular view of history as a constant struggle between the forces of light and darkness that endowed the Bolsheviks with the sense of historic mission and enabled them to stifle their scruples and protect their power. "The terror was necessary, not only to keep men obedient, but even more to make them believe."[51]

About the same time that Ulam published his Stalin biography, an intrepid Soviet historian was gathering materials for a mammoth volume on Stalin and Stalinism. Roy Medvedev, one of the Soviet *shestidesiatnikii*

---

48   Ulam, *Stalin*, p. 33.
49   Ibid., pp. 12, 9.
50   Ibid., p. 13.
51   Ibid., p. 740.

(Sixties generation), was a dissident voice in Leonid Brezhnev's USSR without ever breaking fully from the system. Remaining what might be called a "Leninist humanist," Medvedev worked under the threat of arrest, operating on the fringes of permissibility. He published a dissident journal, was twice searched by the KGB, and was thrown out of the Communist Party. His apartment became a repository for the unpublished memoirs and secreted archives of dozens of political activists. Begun in 1962 in rough outlines and first published in the West in the early 1970s, this huge volume of reminiscences, analyses, judgments, and documents unavailable elsewhere was fundamentally shaped as much by the Khrushchev "Thaw" as by Brezhnev's retrenchment when conservatives attempted to resurrect a sanitized Stalin.[52] At once an unconventional work of historical synthesis and a political act, part of a renewed offensive against the legacy of Stalinism, Medvedev's rich and rambling portrait of the dictator does not differ significantly from the portraits drawn by Western historians like Deutscher or Tucker, but the sheer volume of new material adds fascinating detail to the story of the crude and vicious manipulator who rose to dominate and distort the Communist movement. As the revised edition appeared, Medvedev emerged, along with other *shestidesiatniki*, as a respected public figure, an elected deputy to the short-lived Congress of People's Deputies, and a major player in the Gorbachev revolution.

Medvedev's sources are varied and often quite tenuous. Rumors and second- and third-hand stories are interwoven with the written memoirs of participants and victims. One story, for example—that Stalin told an Armenian delegation that the poet Eghishe Charents should not be touched just months before his arrest—comes to us from the artist Martiros Saryan, who told it to writer Ilya Ehrenburg. Medvedev valiantly attempts to separate fact from fiction, but an uncertainty about many of the incidents remains even as he painstakingly paints in a shocking landscape of arbitrariness, inhumane torture, senseless waste of human lives, and the corruption of the original ideals of socialism.

Medvedev's contribution to the debate over Stalinism is both unique and so specific that ordinary academic conventions seem overly restrictive when evaluating his labors. Throughout he appears restrained, balanced, and critical, in contrast to the more polemical accounts of Solzhenitsyn or Vladimir Antonov-Ovseenko, but, at the same time, he remains a Bolshevik, attempting to make sense of the incomprehensible and to

---

52   Medvedev, *Let History Judge.*

salvage what he can of Lenin's project. His lodestone is Lenin, invariably the corrective and moral measure against which the excesses of the Stalinists are to be condemned. He often talks about policies being "correct" or "incorrect" and does not doubt the necessity and rightness of the revolution itself. His Marxism is expressed through his sympathies, rather than in his methodology, and the work is largely a political history focused on the state and party rather than an analysis of broader social dynamics.

Medvedev accepts that the Bolsheviks failed to realize their ideals but not because the ideals were unrealizable. Insufficient moral and cultural development and a "failure to comprehend the contradictions in the new social system" ran the revolution off its tracks.[53] "It was not the struggle with the autocracy, not jail or exile, that was the real test for revolutionaries. Much harder was the test of power, having the vast and powerful resources of the state at one's disposal."[54] He argues that Stalinism was a pseudo-socialism that existed alongside "truly socialist relations," state capitalist, and even semi-feudal forms. Stalin may have been an heir of Lenin, but he squandered Lenin's legacy and created a system "profoundly alien to Marxism and Leninism."[55] Cut off from the people, the heroes of the revolution turned into a party bourgeoisie. The dominant emotion of the book is regret, and for all its narrative power and engaged energy and his compelling indictment of Stalin and Stalinism, Medvedev ultimately leaves historians much to ponder about the deeper causes, the hidden dynamics, and the seeds of destruction that lay within the Stalinist system.

A decade after the fall of the Soviet Union, Medvedev joined forces with his twin brother Zhores and produced a slimmer volume on the same subject.[56] Zhores, a biologist and science writer (who was named after the martyred French socialist Jean Jaures), wrote a chronicle of the tragic experience of Soviet geneticists in *The Rise and Fall of T. D. Lysenko* and was expelled from the USSR in 1973. He continued his critical opposition to the Brezhnev regime from London. Both brothers aimed toward what they understood to be a "return to Leninism," a more democratic socialism with a more serious regard for "socialist legality." When, after the crushing of the Prague Spring in 1968 the social democratic wing of the intelligentsia withered (to be replaced largely by Westernizing

53   Ibid., p. 719.
54   Ibid., p. 692.
55   Ibid., p. 872.
56   Roy Medvedev and Zhores Medvedev, *The Unknown Stalin: His Life, Death, and Legacy* (New York: The Overlook Press, 2003).

liberals like Andrei Sakharov from one side and Slavophilic conserva-
tives and nationalists like Aleksander Solzhenitsyn from the other), the
Medvedevs continued writing as lonely witnesses better known in the
West and in Sovietological circles than among their own countrymen.

Made up of discrete essays by one or the other brother, *The Unknown
Stalin* is a hodge-podge of bits and pieces about Stalin, primarily about
science and foreign policy, with something here about Bukharin, something there about Stalin's mother. It has much interesting material, culled
from memoirs, personal experience, and published materials, but there
is no consistent theme or compelling organization of its material. This
well-written text is easy reading, but it adds little to what is available
elsewhere, though for a Stalin buff, it has its own fascination. Chapters
cover episodes like the making of the Soviet atomic bomb, Khrushchev's
"secret speech" of 1956, and Stalin's intentions to make Mikhail Suslov his
heir. There is an exploration of the "riddles" surrounding Stalin's death
that concludes that there was no plot to kill him. Again, interest in the
subject is greater than the content of the volume.

The further the world moved away from the Stalin period, the more
Stalin was seen in the West as a rational actor and, in some accounts,
quite intelligent, at least by the standards and requirements of the brutal
world of Soviet politics. The historian Robert H. McNeal spent more
than a quarter century investigating the world his subject inhabited.[57]
He diligently recovered the existing sources, travelling to Georgia and
Russia in search of detail, and wrote a cool, dispassionate narrative in a
readable single volume. Fascinated by the private Stalin, he lingered over
whatever material opened up his family and emotional life. He did not
incorporate much of the new social history on Stalinism that divided
the Sovietological profession in the West, nor did he benefit from the
archival revelations that were just appearing in the USSR as he was completing his work. With few allusions to other Stalin biographers, except
Trotsky, he carefully weighed variant accounts and cautiously stated his
own conclusions—that Stalin was neither mad nor deluded that he was
an infallible super-hero; rather, he was a cynical realist prepared to use
the most extreme violence to bring his Marxist vision of humanity in line
with actual human nature.

Yet Trotsky's marginalization of Stalin before he emerged as a major
player in the mid-1920s continued to shape biographies through the

---

57   McNeal, *Stalin.*

1980s. In a detailed study of Stalin's role in 1917, Robert Slusser argues that Stalin's personal qualities prevented him from becoming a major presence in the revolution.[58] After his arrival in Petrograd in mid-March, Stalin quickly replaced younger activists, like his future foreign minister, Molotov, as one of the two paramount leaders (along with Lev Kamenev) of the local Bolshevik organization. Active in the party infrastructure, he quickly shifted from his more accommodating views to accept Lenin's militant opposition to the Provisional Government and the more moderate socialist parties. With Lenin in hiding and the newly minted Bolshevik Trotsky in jail, Stalin made the key reports to the Sixth Party Congress in July. Not a public speaker nor a personality known to the broad masses, he nevertheless appears here to have been a very large cog, a driving wheel in fact, in the machinery of the party—at least until the fall of 1917. With the reemergence of Kamenev and Georgii Zinoviev and "the meteoric rise of Trotsky," Stalin was suddenly eclipsed. He avoided involvement in the direct planning and execution of the October insurrection, was rebuffed in the Central Committee when he tried to defend the defectors Kamenev and Zinoviev, and even offered to resign as an editor of *Rabochii put'* (Workers' Way) just days before the uprising.

Slusser claims that Stalin was a "slow learner" who misunderstood what was happening around him, and since the Bolshevik seizure of power was "a team effort, and Stalin was not a team player," he "missed the great, never-to-recur, moment of truth."[59] Though his is not primarily a psychological study, Slusser barely sketches the revolutionary context. He holds a steady focus on Stalin, grading him poorly for his Marxism, better for his organizational skills; he adds little to the psychological profile given by Trotsky and Tucker but speculates throughout about the motivations of a man who is seen as having no fixed principles and a boundless opportunism and ambition. Here, as in Ulam, politics is substituted for psychology, and the revolution itself, its massive upheavals, social polarization, and economic disintegration are left largely invisible.

Slusser shares the evaluation of the Menshevik Nikolai Sukhanov, who dismissed Stalin as "a grey blur." Yet the effect of reading this assembled account does not confirm that Stalin "missed" the October Revolution, but paradoxically illustrates the weight and importance of the man. In Slusser's own telling, Stalin seems to have continued to be an important, if not central, player in October. He was senior editor of the principal

58   Slusser, *Stalin in October.*
59   Ibid., pp. 248–9.

Bolshevik newspaper in the capital at the moment when Alexander Kerensky launched his fatal attack against the party's press; he was a member of several key committees, including the Military Revolutionary Committee and the Political Bureau of the party, and attended almost all of the Central Committee sessions that discussed the insurrection, including one in the wee hours of the morning of October 25 (November 7). Thus, the rather bizarre thesis of the last fifth of the book, that Stalin missed the revolution, simply does not hold. Nor does it follow, as Slusser suggests, that Stalin's need to show he could make his own revolution led to the "revolution from above" of the 1930s and that explanations for the Great Purges must include the "urge to destroy and silence awkward witnesses" to his failure in 1917. Here, Slusser echoes the last lines of Tucker's first volume where psychology rather than politics explains the ferocity of the Great Terror:

> He was under stringent inner pressure to keep the idealized Stalin-figure steadily and clearly in focus and to shut out everything in himself or his past that marred it … In the terror of the thirties, untold thousands of loyal party members and other Soviet citizens would have to be condemned as covert enemies of the people so that Djugashvili could prove to himself and Russia that he was really Stalin.[60]

After the Fall

Despite the best efforts of modern tyrants, conscious of public and historic opinion, the traces of the last century's political crimes are daily being uncovered. New witnesses to the sheer vastness of the holocausts of the twentieth century—the Ottoman genocide of the Armenians and Assyrians, the Nazi murders of Jews and political "deviants," and Stalin's wars on his own people—are finding voice. The dead refuse to stay buried. Recovery of the past does not bring with it reconciliation but rage at the betrayal of what might have been and the need to settle accounts. A boy growing up in the village of Agul in western Siberia, his family exiled after the execution of his father as an "enemy of the people," watched in 1937–38 as "some soldiers turned up in our little village, followed by columns of prisoners. They started cordoning off zones, and in some six months camps were established in Agul and a number of neighboring

---

60   Tucker, *Stalin as Revolutionary*, p. 493.

settlements. Barbed wire appeared; so did high fences behind which one could just make out the huts, the armed sentries on watchtowers, and the guard dogs."

> The locals soon began seeing long columns of exhausted people constantly arriving on foot from the railhead sixty miles away. It seemed the camps must be infinitely expandable. Later they understood what was happening…. Boris Frantsevich Kreshchuk, who was living then in Agul and whose father, a blacksmith and elder brother had been shot, told me of the time he and some other boys were out looking for pine nuts when they suddenly heard the crack of gunfire nearby, "just like the sound of a large canvas being ripped apart." They ran to the place and from behind some bushes watched as the firing squad threw some twenty executed prisoners into a ditch. "I remember one of them was clinging to the grass, obviously he wasn't dead. We ran away."[61]

That son of the people's enemy grew up to become, first a loyal Stalinist and a graduate of a military academy, later still general of the army, head of the Institute of Military History, and eventually a key advisor to Boris Yeltsin. In 1978, before Gorbachev and *glasnost'*, he began writing a multivolume biography of Stalin. With his unprecedented access to archives, General Dmitri Volkogonov unraveled the triumphal epic that older Soviet citizens had been told about the victor of the war against fascism and began to fill in the "blank spots" of Soviet history. In what would emerge as the first critical biography, he retold the story of Stalin as a tragedy in three acts: the first covered the failure of the party leaders to heed Lenin's warnings about Stalin's character; the second, the deadly rivalry between Stalin and Trotsky; the third, the war. All through the book Volkogonov recovered the silenced voices of the victims. From the archives of the party and the army, examining Stalin's own marginal comments on documents, he showed conclusively the centrality of Stalin's initiative and direction of the purges. This was a history with a purpose: to seek justice for those who perished.

As the book unfolds, a man of limited intelligence but great cunning and an infinitive capacity for cruelty maneuvers himself into control of the only political party in the USSR. "Stalin," Volkogonov writes,

---

61   Volkogonov, *Stalin*, p. 563. First published as *Triumf i tragediia: Politicheskii portret I. V. Stalina*, 2 vols. (Moscow: Novosti, 1989).

was a great actor. He acted a host of parts with consummate skill: the modest leader, the fighter for the purity of party ideals, and later the leader and father of the people, great commander, theorist, connoisseur of the arts, prophet. But, more than anything, Stalin tried to play the part of the dedicated pupil and comrade-in-arms of the great Lenin. All this gradually brought him popularity in the party and the country as a whole.[62]

His vision of socialism was bereft of any humanism—in Volkogonov's words, it was "sacrificial socialism"—and was blind to "the outlines of a conception of socialism" in Lenin's last articles "that embodied a link between industrialization and voluntary cooperative farming, a powerful rise in the culture of the broad masses, an improvement in socialist relations and the unconditional development of democratic principles in society."[63]

> In my opinion, Stalinism is synonymous with alienation of the working people from power, the installation of a multi-faceted bureaucracy and the inculcation of dogmatic formulas in the public mind. The exercise of autocracy resulted in a specific kind of alienation which in turn gave rise to general apathy, a weakening of the real meaning of socialist values and a dampening of the movement's dynamism.[64]

Volkogonov goes on: "Genuine socialism occurs when the center of attention is man, and where democracy, humanism and social fairness are intrinsic properties. Such an approach has no room for violence, for distancing the people from power, for demigod leaders."[65] Instead, Stalin's paradoxical achievement was of another order: "No other man in the world has ever accomplished so fantastic a success as he: to exterminate millions of his own countrymen and receive in exchange the whole country's blind adulation."[66]

Like the reformers led by Mikhail Gorbachev who initiated the radical transformation of the USSR from the very top of the Communist Party, Volkogonov posited early on a kind of democratic Leninism as the original goal of the Bolsheviks that was deformed grotesquely by Stalin. By

62   Ibid., p. xxvi.
63   Ibid., pp. 121, 105.
64   Ibid., p. xxvii.
65   Ibid., p. 121.
66   Ibid., p. 188.

the time he reached his final few chapters, however, his thinking had clearly evolved along the lines traversed by many of the Moscow intelligentsia of the Gorbachev years. Now, he saw Stalin's practice, not as the necessary outcome of Marxism or Leninism, but certainly

> one way—one extremely negative way—of realizing the ideas contained in Marxist doctrine. ... But well before the revolution, Lenin attacked other Marxists who interpreted the doctrine in their own way as heretics and revisionists, with the result that any "unauthorized" view became stigmatized as "hostile." Russian Marxism thus acquired the character of a political doctrine that sought not to adapt itself to changing conditions but to adapt conditions to fit its postulates. Much too late in the day, Lenin tried to put the party into reverse, to make the Bolsheviks of the early 1920s take a practical view of the situation that had arisen in the overwhelmingly peasant country they were ruling. They were not up to the task and the dogmatic tendency was left to flourish.[67]

Volkogonov denied that writing this book was his "way of avenging the wrongs done to my family."[68] Rather, like many of his contemporaries, he wrestled with what Stephen F. Cohen called "the most tenacious and divisive issue in Soviet political life—a 'dreadful and bloody wound.'"[69] Since the fall of "Communism," the "Stalin Question" has deepened from evaluating the positive and negative in Stalin's regime to grappling with whether "socialism" in any form is any longer retrievable or whether the wound was so deep or the cancer so intrinsic to the system that its death was inscribed at its birth.

No one in the West has spent more time chronicling the Great Terror than Robert Conquest; among his nearly thirty books, he wrote half a dozen on various aspects of the purges of the 1930s. Stalin stands at the center of the Terror, the first cause and the final arbitrator. Terror, in Conquest's view, is as natural to the Soviet system as it was necessary and stemmed from the unpopularity of the October Revolution ("an almost purely military operation") and the consequent illegitimacy of the Soviet regime. Whereas Volkogonov wrestled with the problem of popular despotism, Conquest dismissed the idea that Stalin enjoyed

---

67   Ibid., p. 547.
68   Ibid., p. 564.
69   Stephen F. Cohen, *Rethinking the Soviet Experience: Politics and History Since 1917* (New York: Oxford University Press, 1985), p. 93.

widespread support.[70] Rejecting the so-called "revisionist" accounts (by J. Arch Getty, Roberta Manning, Gábor T. Rittersporn, and others) that propose social and systemic explanations for the Great Purges, Conquest located the motivation for the killing squarely with Stalin, whose aim was "to destroy or disorganize all possible sources of opposition to Stalin's progress to absolute rule."[71] With the so-called "archival revolution" of the late 1980s and early 1990s, when it became possible in an unprecedented way to mine Soviet archives and uncover buried memoirs, Conquest, Volkogonov, and Tucker (among others) produced thousands of pages of numbing episodes of arbitrary cruelty and pointless brutality that lead to the unavoidable conclusion that Stalin was the architect of both the system and its excesses.

But recording and retelling, as indispensable as they are for the preservation of historical memory, is not a satisfactory substitute for the hard work of analysis. In his breezy, condensed biography of Stalin, Conquest himself disclaims analysis. "In these pages," he concludes, "the character of Stalin has been displayed, rather than dissected. And this summing up, if such it can be called, is not an analysis. It is a broad description of the image of Stalin as it appears to one observer."[72] Yet, throughout his work, the author is frank about his own politics, his contempt for much of Western scholarship on Stalinism, and his utter dismissal of Marxism, which he sees as a pseudo-science parallel to phrenology. Stalinism, coming out of Marxism, was a particularly dangerous version of a nineteenth-century scientism that held that all social and human actions can be calculated, considered, and predicted. Conquest's Burkean vision of an organic, natural, true path of human development that Marxism, Bolshevism, and Stalinism attempted, to their own detriment, to shortcut paralleled the conservative historiography of Martin Malia and Richard Pipes. They are unconcerned by the fraught questions over which their adversaries on the Left agonized: Was Stalin the only possible fulfillment of the revolution? Was the tragedy of Stalinism the result primarily of the ideological precepts of Marxism, the structures laid down by Leninism, or the particular agency of Stalin himself?

ဆ

---

70   "There is little reason to accept a view now found almost solely in certain Western circles, that Stalinism enjoyed broad, let alone warm, popular support." Robert Conquest, *Stalin, Breaker of Nations* (New York: Viking, 1991), p. 167.

71   Robert Conquest, *The Great Terror: A Reassessment* (New York: Oxford University Press, 1990), p. 445.

72   Conquest, *Stalin, Breaker of Nations*, p. 327.

While Conquest's biography eschews some of the conventions of scholarship, like footnotes, the second volume of Robert C. Tucker's Stalin
biography, appearing fifteen years after his influential psychological study
of the young Stalin, grounds his prodigious reading and research on full
documentation.[73] Unlike Conquest, Tucker engages the central questions
of historiography of the Soviet period. Muting to a considerable degree
the psychobiographical approach of his first volume, Tucker develops
here a radical version of the "continuity thesis," that Stalin's revolution
"was basically a reversion to a developmental mode that had existed
in earlier Russian history," state-sponsored revolution from above.[74] A
voracious reader of Russian history, Stalin was especially intrigued by
the figures of Ivan the Terrible and Peter the Great and envisioned "the
construction of socialism with state building in an historical Russian
sense."[75] Tucker sees the effects of the Stalin Revolution as analogues to
prerevolutionary forms. Collectivization was a second serfdom, at least
in the eyes of the peasants; the "proletarian dictatorship" was the forging
of a renewed autocracy; the security apparatus was Stalin's own private
oprichnina (Ivan IV's loyalist troops that terrorized his enemies), whose
actions cleared the way for a new "service nobility."

Tucker's sense of continuity appears centered in the personality-
driven choices made by Stalin. Though Russia was not necessarily fated
to repeat its autocratic and repressive past, that political environment
and culture were an available context in which Stalin, as a pragmatic
and power hungry politician, was able to consolidate his own strength
and implement his own vision. Stalin's "inner world" was constructed of
fantasies of heroism, the need to fulfill his own self-identity as the second
Lenin. His own political and psychological insecurities required the
physical elimination of his enemies. His political orientation was toward
a Russian national Bolshevism that offered his people "a Soviet Russian
nationhood as a collective identity to be proud of, and [presented] the
socialism-building enterprise as a Russian mission in world history."[76] He
required his own revolution and turned his back on the reformist road
to socialism implied in Lenin's New Economic Policy and the program
of Nikolai Bukharin and the "Right" in the Communist Party.

The Stalin of Volkogonov, Conquest, and Tucker appears much more
purposeful and radical in his aims and methods than the opportunistic

---

73   Robert C. Tucker, *Stalin in Power: The Revolution from Above, 1928–1941* (New
York: W. W. Norton, 1990).

74   Ibid., p. xiv.

75   Ibid., p. 65.

76   Ibid., p. 41.

centrist of Trotsky's earlier imagination. He was a consummate actor, whose inner thoughts were kept well hidden even from his closest associates. For thirty years, he staged an elaborate drama with himself as protagonist. The public role he chose for himself was of a modest man, hard and rude toward the enemies of socialism, but moderate and accommodating toward potential allies, particularly abroad. He was skillful enough to convince tough-minded journalists, like Walter Duranty of *The New York Times*, that even his most destructive policies, like collectivization and the purging of the top cadres in the party and the army, were the necessary means to the desired end. Duranty, who became infamous for his unwillingness to reveal all he knew about the man-made famine in Ukraine in the early 1930s, employed the phrase "You can't make an omelet without breaking eggs" to justify the violence that accompanied the social transformations in the USSR.[77] No one, apparently, pointed out to these apologists and rationalizers that successful cooks do not smash the eggs with their fists, mixing shell with yoke.

Two major studies of Stalin appeared in the second decade after the Soviet collapse by the journalist and novelist, Simon Sebag Montefiore. Long obsessed by Stalin and Caucasia, Montefiore's initial foray into Staliniana was a comic novel, *My Affair With Stalin*, in which a malevolent eleven-year-old adopts Stalin's tactics to dominate his schoolmates. Reborn as a popular historian, Montefiore was the author of a well-regarded biography of Prince Grigorii Potemkin, Catherine the Great's advisor and lover (two positions that often went together). A prodigious researcher, he mined Russian and Georgian archives, assisted by historians in Russia and Georgia with the required language skills, traveled to Stalin's birthplace, Georgia, to his various homes and hideaways as far away as war-torn Abkhazia, dug up unpublished memoirs, and carried on numerous interviews with anyone who knew Stalin and would talk to him (including most of his living descendants, with the notable exception of the reclusive Svetlana Allilueva, Stalin's daughter).

His study *Young Stalin* begins in the "Wild East," an exoticized Georgia where for many foreigners the locals were savage and noble, the terrain majestic and wild, and the rivers always turbulent.[78] Even what

---

77   See the study by S. J. Taylor, *Stalin's Apologist: Walter Duranty: The New York Times's Man in Moscow* (New York: Oxford University Press, 1990). Taylor credits Duranty with coining the term "Stalinism," which he distinguished from both socialism and Leninism and characterized as "a collectivist system … which actually is not far removed from state capitalism" (p. 167).

78   Simon Sebag Montefiore, *Young Stalin* (New York: Alfred A. Knopf, 2007).

is familiar in Montefiore's story is told in a vivid narrative rich with new details and sensational revelations. Born in the provincial town of Gori to a shoemaker, Beso Jughashvili, and his stern, religious wife, Keke, young "Soso" was the mother's boy who obediently attended seminaries in order to become a priest as she desired. The precocious boy displayed a talent for singing and poetry and shared the romantic Georgian nationalism of his compatriots. But, as a teenager embittered by the draconian regime of teacher-priests, Soso abandoned both church and nationalism and joined the fledgling Marxist movement. Adopting the nickname "Koba" from a fictional Georgian outlaw, young Jughashvili soon became a militant activist, leading workers into a bloody confrontation with the police and organizing an armed terrorist band that knocked off enemies and staged daring robberies to finance the party. Stalin was repeatedly arrested and exiled to Siberia, only to escape and resume his work in the revolutionary underground. Rumors spread that he had ties with the tsarist police, but such speculations testify more to his Machiavellian intrigues than to any role as an agent of the *Okhrana*.

Leading us through these obscure years of Stalin's revolutionary evolution, Montefiore focuses almost exclusively on his personal rather than political side. Young Stalin is already a "gangster godfather, audacious bank robber, killer, pirate and arsonist," a Marxist fanatic with a need to command and dominate.[79] The savage Caucasus was the essential environment in which this "murderous egomaniac" was nurtured.[80] The violence of the Russian Empire's southern periphery, both that of rebellious workers and peasants, anarchists and Marxists, as well as the state's brutal reprisals shaped Stalin's conviction that bloodshed and terror were necessary means to his desired ends. "Only in Georgia," writes Montefiore, "could Stalin the poet enable Stalin the gangster."[81] Even his human side, such as it was, was perverse. He neglected his devout and devoted mother, subordinated his first wife to his revolutionary work, which led to her death, and took up with whatever woman, regardless of age, who could satisfy his appetites. Stalin as womanizer is a new angle on the man of steel, but the evidence for his sexual exploits, while tantalizing, is extremely thin.

Montefiore's portrait is often overwrought, and though this does not fall into the category of psychohistory, as an explanation of Koba's path to power it fails like many in that genre to deal adequately with his politics

---

79   Ibid., p. 15.
80   Ibid., p. 16.
81   Ibid., p. 11.

and thought. There is almost nothing on his intense involvement in the Bolshevik versus Menshevik factional squabbles or his role as a theorist of nationalism. Geography is insufficient as context for a historian. Growing up in autocratic Russia where suppression of open political dissent convinced thousands of people that the only way out of backwardness and oppression was by taking up arms, Stalin was in one sense not very unusual. But in another he was unique. His particular talents and lack of scruples enabled him to climb rapidly up the ladder of party politics, impressing Lenin and those taken by his dark charisma. Far from the action in February 1917, exiled in the bitter cold of eastern Siberia, Stalin at thirty-eight was an impotent outlaw when the fall of the tsar thrust him unexpectedly into the maelstrom of revolutionary politics.

In his massive volume treating Stalin in power, Montefiore takes the reader inside to delve deeply into Stalin's family and friendships, to give us the personal side of Stalin the man, the husband, the suspicious comrade, the stern father, as well as the public actor.[82] He has recorded every rumor and whisper, each bit of gossip, late night table talk, each personal slight or suspicious sideway glance, and through them given us a portrait of the tyrant. Montefiore's Stalin will not surprise most readers. The brute is familiar to us. But, in the relentless detail, the mood-setting descriptions of the leader's surroundings, the sketches of the people around him, and Stalin's own words, pranks, and tempers, Montefiore provides not only a most intimate view of the General Secretary but a rounded and complex portrait of a man who could be both charming and lethal in the space of a few seconds.

Montefiore's Stalin is, first of all, a Bolshevik, which, for the author, means a disciplined, ruthless person ready to use violence whenever necessary. "War was the natural state of the Bolsheviks and they were good at it."[83] Given that in this book as well as in his other there is almost no discussion of Marxism or the history of the Social Democratic movement in Russia, no serious engagement with the complexities of inner party disputes about doctrine and practice, Montefiore offers an overly simplified view of Bolshevism as being what it became under Stalin. The man himself had the requisite qualities to succeed almost unimpeded in the competitive world of party politics. He possessed both an indomitable will and supersensitive antennae attuned to the political airways. Emotionally stunted, incapable of true empathy, indifferent to

---

82 Simon Sebag Montefiore, *Stalin: The Court of the Red Tsar* (New York: Alfred A. Knopf, 2004).

83 Ibid., p. 439.

the suffering that he caused, he was, nevertheless, occasionally able to extend a kind and generous gesture to a victim. Though he had been damaged as a boy by the violence in his family, and remained insecure and suspicious to the end of his life, he was a "people person," a "master of friendships," and ruled as much through personal charm as through raw fear.[84] He was abnormal like most politicians, Montefiore says, with a totally obsessive character that fitted Marxism. Like other members of the Bolshevik elite, he suffered from inferiority complexes, had chips on his shoulders, and exploded in irrational tempers. Yet he inspired trust, and even deep love, from those around him—even from those whom he had imprisoned and tortured. His simplicity, personal asceticism, feigned modesty, and mocking humor attracted people, especially women, to him. But throughout his life, especially after the suicide of his second wife, Nadezhda Allilueva, in 1932, and increasingly toward the end, he was lonely. He desperately required people around him and forced his courtiers to indulge in long nocturnal banquets that stretched into morning and ended up with the drunken Kremlin denizens staggering into their limousines.[85]

Montefiore gestures toward the contribution of "vast political, economic and diplomatic forces," like those that led to the Great Terror of the late 1930s, but he is far less concerned with those forces than with more mundane, quotidian matters and personal relations. It can certainly be argued that, when a politician accumulates the degree of power that Stalin did, in a system without institutional restraints on that power, his personal whims and preferences take on a power comparable to great economic and social forces. At the same time, however, even absolute monarchs or totalitarian dictators are constrained by forces beyond their control. The level of development of the country or the strength of other states confronting the ruler's state make certain moves possible and others not. Moreover, once certain choices are made, certain paths chosen, others are precluded.

The large historiographical questions that have puzzled professional historians—for example, whether Stalinism is simply a continuation of Leninism or a decisive, bloody break with it—are not addressed. Was the revolution doomed from its onset, as conservative scholars have argued, or were there choices that might have led to a different outcome? Stalin had various options at decisive moments, but they were limited.

---

84   Ibid., p. 48.
85   For an exemplary account of the court politics of the Stalin years, see Fitzpatrick, *On Stalin's Team*.

The Soviet Union was in his time a relatively poor country, backward by European standards, with the overwhelming majority of its people impoverished, uneducated peasants living in isolated villages. And it was faced with powerful adversaries—imperial Britain in its first decade, Nazi Germany in the 1930s and early 1940s, and the United States after 1945—that limited his options. But at the same time Stalin's own actions— declaring war on his own peasantry in the collectivization campaigns of the early thirties, employing massive terror against his own party, the intelligentsia, and, most disastrously for the security of the state, the military—determined what in that new environment the dictator could do and how others would react. Poignantly, at certain moments Stalin turned to one or another of his policemen and asked about a certain comrade that he wanted for a certain job only to be told that that person had been executed.

The picture drawn by Montefiore is a dark one of court intrigues, debauched satraps vying for the emperor's ear. Alcohol was the drug of choice among the Soviet elite, and many died of alcoholism. Stalin's henchman Lavrentii Beria had a well-known proclivity for young women, who either satisfied his needs or ended up in prison; yet the level of sexual promiscuity that Montefiore reports will be new to most readers. Bolsheviks have conventionally been renowned for their Puritanism (Stalin did not like kissing in films), and the most durable of Communists, like Molotov and Mikoyan, were dedicated family men. But Montefiore, whose most frequently used word appears to be "womanizer," documents the sexual adventures of other magnates. Stalin himself, the object of attention of many women, appears to have been moderate in his sexual appetites. ("Stalin was no womanizer: he was married to Bolshevism and emotionally committed to his own drama in the cause of Revolution."[86]) Montefiore holds that Stalin's greatest personal suffering came with the loss of his beautiful Nadia. He grieved alone for days, wept bitterly at her funeral, and threatened to resign from his high office. His greatest affection was directed to his daughter, Svetlana, though even she could be brusquely excluded from his company. When the young girl found affection from an older man, the film writer Alexei Kapler, Stalin flew into a rage, had Kapler sentenced to five years in the notorious Vorkuta camp, and banished Svetlana for months.

Stalin's rage in this case was not simply that of a patriarchal Georgian upset at his daughter's relationship with a married man. Kapler was

---

86 Montefiore, *Stalin: The Court of the Red Tsar*, p. 15.

Jewish, and Stalin shared the general views of his countrymen that ethnicity (Jews were a nationality in the USSR) based in culture and social
environment determined character. Such ideas were difficult to reconcile
with a Marxism that proposes social determination as prior to cultural
and sees the nation as a product of a definite stage of history and ethnicity as situational and malleable. The Soviet state had been from its earliest
days a place where many Jews had flourished. Although Zionists and
religious Jews were persecuted, the pre–World War II USSR legislated
against expressions of anti-Semitism and sponsored mass demonstrations against Hitler's persecutions of Jews. The Soviet Union was among
the first states to grant *de jure* recognition to the state of Israel, even before
the United States. Yet, whether positive or negative, stereotypic views of
Jews and other nationalities were part of Soviet discourse. By the late
1940s Stalin was convinced that the "rootless" Jews were a global danger
to the Soviet Union, and he turned on Soviet Jews with a vengeance. In
his last years he was preoccupied with purges of Jewish intellectuals,
personally ordering the murder of the Yiddish actor Solomon Mikhoels,
engineering the blatantly anti-Semitic "Anti-Cosmopolitan" campaign,
and prodding his torturers to obtain confessions from the victims in the
completely fabricated "Doctors' Plot."

When it came to state terror, Stalin was at the center. Here, the
strengths and weaknesses of Montefiore's approach to history are most
evident. Like Robert Conquest before him, Montefiore sees Stalin as
indispensable to the Terror, though he maintains that the killing began
with Lenin and "reflected the village hatreds of the incestuous Bolshevik sect where jealousies had seethed from the years of exile and war."[87]
Terror is part of Bolshevism for Montefiore. He makes no effort to distinguish the scale and purpose of the Great Terror from the far less
murderous Red Terror of the Civil War days, when White killings far
outstripped Red ones in the context of a fratricidal war. In the 1930s,
the regime turned on its own for reasons that remain unfathomable for
many historians. Montefiore piles on possible explanations in addition
to the nature of Bolshevism: Stalin was replicating Ivan the Terrible's
campaign against his boyars, strengthening and centralizing his state as
his admired predecessor had done; he was dealing with the corruption
of the old elite and making way for a new Soviet-trained elite; he was
curbing regional lords, removing the threat to his power from the generals, and eliminating the last remnants of political opposition, while

87   Ibid., p. 230.

creating scapegoats for economic and social disruptions caused by the regime's own policies. Too many explanations are almost as bad as none. What does emerge is what most historians have always proposed, that Stalin ordered, directed, propelled forward, and ultimately called a halt to the Terror largely from a Machiavellian fear of actual and potential opposition to his consolidation of autocratic power. In the great blood-letting of the late 1930s, three-quarters of a million people were executed and countless hundreds of thousands tortured, imprisoned, or exiled. Just days after Stalin died, the imprisoned doctors, at least those who had survived, were released, and, within months, an amnesty freed both criminal and political prisoners. Terror was replaced by a more familiar police state in which arbitrary arrest on trumped up charges was no longer systemic.

With Montefiore's bedroom revelations, one would think that we have reached the bottom of the barrel. Where to go next? Into the bath-room? Indeed, he has a scene of Stalin defecating by a railroad track with his traveling companions looking on! Still, there are moments in both books where the grandeur of the decisions made by petty and vicious men elevate the story. The drama of the war years when Stalin managed to pull himself together and act on the world stage as genera-lissimo and statesman is brilliantly told as a tale of small men reaching beyond themselves against the backdrop of heroic sacrifice on the part of millions. For Montefiore, however, great ideas or grand visions are less what the Red Tsar was about than insecurity and intrigue. Deadly intraparty politics had been Stalin's training ground, and it contributed both to his unsentimental, realist appreciation of international power politics and to his overly suspicious attitude that foreclosed certain opportunities. Montefiore's two books together give us a picture of a stunted brute's improbable rise to power and, once that power was secured, the banality of politics at his court. Whether a son of a cobbler, the son of a president, or a clueless real estate developer leads the court, politics up close looks far less like the pomp of costume pictures and more like a mafia council. However finely they dress in public, emperors really have no clothes.

Once he accumulated power, Stalin not only dominated the Soviet Union but through his control of foreign Communist parties extended his reach across the globe. One of the distinguished elder statesmen of Russian and Soviet history, Alfred J. Rieber, published an important study of Soviet foreign policy under Stalin that deals with many of the questions of biography examined in this chapter.[88] In a sequel to his earlier volume, *The Struggle for the Eurasian Borderlands*, Rieber argues that Russian foreign policy has largely been determined over centuries by four persistent factors: "a multinational social structure; porous or permeable frontiers; cultural alienation; and relative economic backwardness."[89] To these characteristics he adds two more particular "powerful existential and intellectual influences" for the period under study, 1918–45, derived from Stalin himself. The great dictator's own *Weltanschauung* was shaped by "his early life experiences growing up in the Georgian cultural milieu precariously surviving under the pressure of Russification within the shatter zone of the South Caucasus" and "his evolution as a professional Marxist revolutionary also shaped by the socio-economic peculiarities of an underdeveloped borderland."[90] The first chapter embeds the young Stalin in the Caucasian context, which, for Rieber, is a fraught and fought-over borderland from which the future ruler would extract lessons that had profound effects on international affairs a few decades later.

As portrayed by Rieber, Stalin learned from experience and circumstances more than from Marxism as an abstracted and fixed doctrine. His position as People's Commissar of Nationalities during the Civil War years (1918–21) convinced him that Soviet security depended on the tight integration of the non-Russian borderlands with the more developed Russian center. The unique focus of this book is to link internal nationality policy, the formulation to which Stalin was key, and foreign policy, which over time moved from the margins of his attention until it became his exclusive domain into which few of his collaborators were allowed entry. While Stalin defended Lenin's notion of national self-determination, he interpreted and revised its meaning to enable the forging of a unitary state in the guise of a federation based on national territorial units. Both men sought to "domesticate" foreign policy by stabilizing and controlling the internal Soviet borderlands and, most assiduously with Stalin, transforming the Communist International into an instrument of Soviet state policy.

---

88   Alfred J. Rieber, *Stalin and the Struggle for Supremacy in Eurasia* (Cambridge: Cambridge University Press, 2015).

89   Ibid., p. 3.

90   Ibid., p. 8. For the influences of Georgia, the frontier, and his early years on Stalin, see Alfred J. Rieber, "Stalin, Man of the Borderlands," *American Historical Review* CVI, 5 (2001), pp. 1651–91; and "Stalin as Georgian: The Formative Years," in Sarah Davies and James R. Harris (eds.), *Stalin: A New History* (Cambridge: Cambridge University Press; 2005), pp. 18–44.

In line with the portraits of Stalin by most scholars, Rieber's Stalin is shrewd, devious, manipulative, and often cynical. "In the witches' brew of Stalin's personality," he writes, "there were the now all-too-familiar ingredients of pathological suspicion, vengefulness, cunning, and cruelty."[91] Pragmatism and an understanding of how to use power were laced with a willingness to use the most brutal means to achieve his ends. Less clearly presented throughout the book is Rieber's idea that Stalin worked from a "borderland thesis." By this the author seems to mean that Stalin was consistent in his drive to territorialize the revolution, that is, to prioritize the defense of the Soviet Union, vulnerable as it was at its borders because of the uneven power relationship with hostile European and Asian states. Not simply *Realpolitik*, the borderland thesis involved the cultural and ideological preferences that Stalin had imbibed as well.

The borderlands within the USSR had to be fully integrated, ethnically cleansed of "foreign" elements, and securely tied into the Soviet project. In foreign policy, this meant at times diplomatic arrangements with neighboring states; at other times extension of Soviet power and influence across the ostensible border, as in Iran, Mongolia, Manchuria, and Xinjiang; at still other times, full annexation of others' territory, as in the Baltic region at the outset of World War II. The Nazi–Soviet Pact and the Treaty of Neutrality with Japan are best understood, Rieber tells us, as pragmatic manifestations of the borderland thesis: first secure your frontiers, no matter what the costs might be, and keep your most dangerous opponents involved in conflicts far from your borders. For Stalin, who in the interim between the Pact and the German invasion annexed the Baltic republics and parts of Finland, Poland, and Rumania, "subjugating and integrating the borderlands was for him the best guarantee of state security. The opinion of the outside world counted for very little."[92]

For the World War II period, Rieber uses the concept of "civil wars," by which he means to include the partisan wars, anti-Communist resistance movements, collaboration with the Germans, as well as the ethnic cleaning and genocidal mass killing that took place in the Western borderlands. He distinguishes his own account from the more familiar story of Timothy Snyder in *Bloodlands*, pointing to the differences between the aims of Hitler, who intended to exterminate millions of Jews and Slavs and colonize the region with ethnic Germans, and Stalin, whose

---

91   Rieber, *Stalin and the Struggle for Supremacy in Eurasia*, p. 92.
92   Ibid., p. 200.

considerably more moderate aims were designed to integrate the lands between Germany and the USSR into a Soviet-dominated buffer zone.[93]

Rieber concludes the book with a moderately revisionist account of the origins of the Cold War. Stalin hoped to maintain the Grand Alliance with his Western allies but at the same time was determined to reshape the demographic complexion of and to establish friendly governments in the lands close to the USSR.[94] Rather than revolutionary transformation, he was primarily concerned with strategic depth, the securing of territory, expansion of the Soviet sphere of influence, and cooperative allies. Stalin repeatedly held back zealous Communists—in Greece, Finland, Yugoslavia, Germany, and elsewhere—who wanted Soviet military might to aid them to come power and move on to a socialist revolution. Once it became clear to Stalin that the West would not accept his territorial and political advances, the Soviet leader retreated to the most basic understanding of his borderland thesis: the USSR was a besieged fortress and had to rely on its own resources in a ferociously hostile world. While facile comparisons between Stalin and Vladimir Putin confuse more than enlighten, Rieber's "persistent factors" and Stalin's borderland thesis eerily force thinking about how this story provides insights about the current Russian president's strategic thinking. Putin continually brings up the past to illuminate the relative position of his country in relation to the more powerful West. History, after all, is the only database that we have to assess why we are where we are, how we got here, and where we might be going.

Reading through dozens of lives of Stalin, not all of which are reviewed here, it appears that there is a kind of justice when a great despot like Joseph Stalin, who made millions suffer during his lifetime, suffers at the hands of his biographers. Approaches differ, as we have seen, and yet without exception the biographers we have surveyed, from Trotsky to Montefiore, have drawn dark and sanguinary pictures of a worthy successor to Ivan the Terrible. In the first volume of a planned trilogy, Princeton historian Stephen Kotkin aims to give a less tendentious and more balanced interpretation of the dictator and his times, without

---

93   Timothy Snyder, *Bloodlands: Europe Between Hitler and Stalin* (New York: Basic Books, 2010).

94   For a complementary account of Soviet policy in Europe during the Cold War that demonstrates Stalin's flexibility and opportunism, see Norman M. Naimark, *Stalin and the Fate of Europe: The Political Struggle for Sovereignty* (Cambridge, MA: Harvard University Press, 2019).

excusing or avoiding the viciousness of his rise to power and rule.[95] Already known for his "biography" of the Soviet steel-producing city, Magnitogorsk, during the turbulent 1930s, Kotkin surrounds the young and middle-aged Stalin with the events and major figures that accompanied the rise of the poor son of an alcoholic cobbler to prominence within an outlawed revolutionary party, ultimately to become the all-powerful ruler of the largest country on the globe.

Historians are great advocates of context—temporal and spatial, cultural and social—along with the other four "cons" of historical writing: contingency, conjuncture, contradiction, and, yes, confusion. Accidents and chance play influential roles in the processes that in the past have determined the failure of empires and the victories of seemingly marginal men and parties. But those successes and defeats occur in time and space and are complexly determined by prior events and human choices, the consequences of which cannot be predicted. Context, structures, institutions, and environments do not determine human choices in an unmediated one-directionality. Consider the improbability of Ioseb Jughashvili, a small wiry child whose affections circled around singing, wrestling, poetry, and Georgian Orthodoxy and nationalism, who could have died from typhus or Siberian frost or a well-aimed bullet, but who was lifted through adversities and reversals to the pinnacle of political power in a faltering revolutionary state. Kotkin reminds his readers repeatedly how slight shifts of fortune could have thwarted the fortuitous fate of Lenin and Stalin. But great historical forces and geopolitical setting have to be meaningfully joined to the momentary twists of fate and the choices people make. Their emotional makeup and intellectual passions, along with their ideological formation, must be taken seriously.

Kotkin skillfully officiates over the elusive marriage of personality, context, and historical conjuncture. Stalin's bitter rivalry with Trotsky is shown to be an uneven struggle between a deeply embedded Bolshevik with the political chops of a ward boss and a flamboyant militant, often his own worst enemy. Kotkin focuses on the context in which Stalin took advantage of the chances he was given and avoided the pitfalls of years as an underground revolutionary, repeated Siberian exiles, and the violent clashes of the Russian Revolution and Civil War. Stalin's considerable talents as politician, organizer, and infighter are highlighted here in contrast to earlier portrayals of Stalin as a "mediocrity" or a "grey blur."

95   Stephen Kotkin, *Stalin, Volume I: Paradoxes of Power, 1878–1928* (New York: Penguin Press, 2014).

Yet the wide-angle lens of the author sometimes loses sight of his protagonist, a secretive political operator who left no diary and few personal
letters to flesh out his personal and more intimate moments.

The prerevolutionary Stalin is only lightly sketched in Kotkin's
breezy run through his first thirty years. Abjuring Freudian analysis
(fair enough) and explicitly avoiding relating the mature Stalin to his
upbringing, the author leaves the reader with a richness of context but a
thinness of explanation of how Jughashvili grew into Stalin. He deprives
the reader of any sense of how Stalin's early experience as a writer and an
outlaw influenced what the former seminarian became. Only once he is
elevated to People's Commissar of Nationality Affairs in 1917 and General
Secretary of the Communist Party in 1922 does the central character
emerge from the whirling background. The authoritarian preferences of
Stalin's mentor and superior, Vladimir Lenin, paved the way for a dictatorship by a person whom few suspected would be the likely successor.
Lenin recognized the strengths of Stalin's character—his toughness, even
ruthlessness—and his talents—organization, the ability to knock heads
and get things done—and had him appointed to the key position in the
party apparatus. Reversing Trotsky's famous conclusion—"Stalin did not
create the apparatus. The apparatus created him"—Kotkin shows convincingly that "Stalin created the apparatus, and it was a colossal feat."[96]
His "power flowed from attention to detail but also to people—and not
just any people, but often to the new people."[97] In contrast to Trotsky,
but like most successful politicians, Stalin was skilled in attracting supporters, loyalists whose ascendency was accelerated by their closeness
and fidelity to their potent patron. With the mammoth amount of new
archival material available, this hefty volume of nearly a thousand pages
details better than any previous account the viciousness of the personal
conflicts that brought down, one after another, the opponents of Stalin
and in a real sense buried the original aims of the revolution.

"The fundamental fact about him," writes Kotkin, "was that he viewed
the world through Marxism."[98] He was "marinated in Communist ideology."[99] Yet here again, as in many of the earlier biographies, there is
little discussion of Soso Jughashvili's gravitation from romantic Georgian
nationalist to "Russian" Marxist, passionately, doggedly concerned with
intricacies of party organization and the nuances of Marx's historical

96   Ibid., p. 362.
97   Ibid., p. 386.
98   Ibid., p. 394.
99   Ibid., p. 400.

analysis of social change. Marxism is a collection of diverse and often contradictory understandings of history and the present, a sociology of capitalism with little prescription of what would follow. Marxist movements are fraught with disputes and conflicts that have at times led to the physical elimination of opponents. Here, however, the intensity of the differences and debates within the party are reduced to personality, and the author treats Stalin's philosophical universe with hostility tempered by condescension.

As in other biographies, Stalin is seen as an ambitious and talented intriguer, a man who combined pathological suspiciousness with overweening self-confidence (perhaps stemming from underlying insecurity). More intelligent than usually given credit, he posed as a proletarian and expressed pride in his rudeness. Above all, he was a survivor. In what undoubtedly will be the most controversial assertion in the book, Kotkin argues that the sensational "Political Testament" of the dying Lenin, a dictation bitterly critical of Stalin and calling for his removal as General Secretary, was not authored by Lenin but by a cabal of his secretaries and his wife, possibly assisted by Trotsky. Few other scholars doubt the actual authorship of the document, which accurately reflected Lenin's views, nor was it questioned at the time it was written and debated in high party circles. Kotkin's reading, fascinating as it is, relies on speculation and conjecture rather than on any evidence. Forgery or not, the letter seriously threatened Stalin, who obsessively feared it might undermine his authority. Ultimately, his comrades did not heed Lenin's warning and remove Stalin, thereby missing the best (and last) real chance to demote Stalin and change history, a mistake that would prove fatal to most of them.

This is a big and ambitious book, replete with witty aphorisms, vividly told anecdotes, and sweeping conclusions about power and politics. Contingencies that favored Stalin's rise, like the untimely death of Lenin in January 1924, are set against the conjunctures of larger global forces that constrained the fledgling Soviet state. The Stalin that Kotkin presents was a strategic thinker, both realistic to the point of cynicism and ideological to a fault. The Communists' "paranoid class politics," reflected in their mistrust of others and their unrelieved push for international revolution, created an environment in which enemies were everywhere—within the party, among the peasants and intellectuals, and in the capitalist states that sought to contain or destroy the USSR.[100] Kotkin radically simplifies

---

100   Ibid., p. 489.

"socialism" to mean anti-capitalism as practiced in Stalin's Soviet Union and sees Marxist-Leninist ideology as the straightjacket within which the Communists chose to destroy a society and build a new order. Even Mussolini's fascism, he argues, was preferable; at least *Il Duce* did not eliminate the most productive economic players. Once Stalin became dictator, already while Lenin was still alive, the road to collectivization and the bloodletting of the 1930s was foreordained. Kotkin concludes that only another lucky accident, perhaps Stalin's death, could have saved the world from those catastrophes.

A frenzy of hunting for spies and subversives shook the Soviet Union in the late 1930s as Stalin propelled his police to unmask "Trotskyite-fascists," Rightist and Leftist deviationists, wreckers, and hidden enemies with party cards. Yet if we apply the perverse logic of Stalinism, the greatest subversive agent to undermine the promise of the revolution of 1917 and transform the aspirations of millions into a bloody despotism—*objectively*, as Stalinists would have said—was the dictator Joseph Stalin himself. Stalin actually killed more Communists and undermined the international Communist movement more than did Adolf Hitler. Rather than Lenin's comrades Kamenev, Zinoviev, Bukharin, and Trotsky allying with Hitler, as they were falsely accused of doing in the great show trials of 1936–38, it was Stalin who in 1939, as Trotsky explained, advanced "his candidacy for the role ... of Hitler's main agent."[101]

In the second volume of his trilogy, Kotkin centers on the 1930s, the decade of the "revolution from above" that dispossessed the peasants and converted them into agricultural suppliers to the state, the city, and the army, the time when the state unleashed mass terror against elites and ordinary people that decimated the Soviet Communist Party itself, decapitated the Red Army, disciplined the intelligentsia into straight-jacketed conformity, and drove millions of people into exile, prison camps, and emigration, if they managed to survive. Stalin proclaimed that collectivization, the end of market relations, and the descent into despotism was in fact the building of socialism—and Kotkin agrees—but to Stalin's critics on the Left (Trotskyists, Social Democrats, and independent Marxist intellectuals) it was the "revolution betrayed," a sanguinary counterrevolution.

Kotkin focuses on the figure of the despot himself and relates who entered and left his office, what documents (many of them denunciations

---

101   Stephen Kotkin, *Stalin, Volume II: Waiting for Hitler, 1929–1941* (New York: Penguin Press, 2017), p. 670.

and thousands of torture-induced confessions) landed on his desk, and who was in favor and who had fallen out. The police supplied him with stories of spies and saboteurs. The steady stream of intelligence reports possessed Stalin, feeding the dictator's own predilection for uncovering conspiracies and plots, many of them deliberately fabricated. Kotkin's story moves from Stalin's Little Corner beyond the Kremlin, ranging widely through the swirling events in Europe and Asia that Stalin believed presented existential dangers to his regime and his "socialist" project.

The Soviet Union was profoundly isolated, as was Stalin himself, particularly after the suicide of his wife in 1932 and the murder of his friend, Sergei Kirov, in 1934. Hitler was visible on the horizon; Spain was riven by a civil war that was seen by many as the first round of the future battle between fascism and communism; and enemies plotted against the USSR on the Soviets' far-flung borders, from Poland in the West to Japan in the East. A constant source of anxiety was Great Britain, the country that Stalin consistently imagined as the greatest danger. Stalin's own "worldview and governing style," his imagining of enemies within the country, his sensitivity at any personal slight or perceived, potential opposition, and his ruthlessness at destroying those whom he believed might pose a future threat gravely weakened his state and society on the eve of invasion and war.[102]

A central mystery lurks at the heart of this book: why did Stalin launch the Great Terror, which damaged so profoundly the very system he painstakingly built? Kotkin moves beyond some of the more familiar explanations—Stalin's unwillingness to settle for a spot at the top of the bureaucracy; a search for unity within the country inspired by the negative example of divisions on the Left in Spain; or Stalin's personal paranoia. Rather, he contends that the cause lies in a particular mentality that originated in Marxism and lethally meshed with Stalin's peculiar psychology. "The combination of Communist ways of thinking and political practice," he argues, "with Stalin's demonic mind and political skill allowed for astonishing bloodletting."[103] "Perceived security imperatives and a need for absolute unity once again turned the quest in Russia to build a strong state into personal rule…. Tyranny has a circular logic: once a dictator has achieved supreme power, he becomes keener still to hold it, driving him to weed his own ranks of even potential challengers."[104] As damaging as the purges were, Stalin was not irrational, Kotkin

102   Ibid., p. 429.
103   Ibid., p. 378.
104   Ibid., p. 430.

contends, but calculating and strategic. The dictator believed that the replacement of a contentious, competitive elite of old Communists with younger, Soviet-trained, presumably more loyal cadres, as well as mobilizing people through fear, were effective ways to preserve the Soviet system and his own power. Stalin emerges as a murderous pedagogue, using violence to teach his people how to behave. He told subordinates to check their underlings by punching them in the face. Ultimately, he would do far worse, making fateful, fatal decisions based on the documents he read and on his own intuition.

Interspersed with domestic disasters, the narrative veers into the thickets of foreign policy, and Kotkin presents the story of the unthinkable alliance of Hitler and Stalin in the August 1939 Molotov–Ribbentrop Pact as Stalin's triumph. While the British and French frittered away the possibility of an agreement with the Soviets, Hitler seized the bait offered by Stalin in order to launch his war of destruction against Poland without fear of a two-front confrontation. Not only did Stalin gain time to prepare for the eventual war with Germany that he anticipated but wished to avoid, he also was handed carte blanche in the Baltic republics, Finland, and Bessarabia. His destructive policies within the Soviet Union that can hardly be described as fully rational are contrasted with his ruthless, unsentimental *realpolitik* in foreign policy.

Kotkin builds on the mountain of previous scholarship on Stalin and Stalinism but has his own sometimes idiosyncratic (but always intriguing) take on major issues. "Hitler," he states categorically (as he is wont to do), "was at least as great a threat as Stalin." Really? Well, maybe not, because, in the next paragraph, he qualifies this assertion: "Despite Stalin's domestic house of horrors, as well as the Comintern's unscrupulous, albeit often pitiful, machinations abroad, the main armed, expansionist power seeking domination in Europe was Nazi Germany …. Hitler's Versailles revisionism was unlimited; Stalin's was limited to opportunities others might present."[105]

An engaging writer, Kotkin for some reason decided in this volume to adopt a rigidly chronological organization of his history with almost day-by-day recounting of events. Such an approach gives readers a sense of the kaleidoscope in which Stalin was forced to work, but at the same time it leads to a kind of mental whiplash. The strict chronicling of events might jerk from one paragraph on the conflicts in China between Communists and Nationalists, to another taking us into the tyrant's family

105   Ibid., p. 675.

circle, to the next inside the mind of Hitler. The book has a hurried quality about it, so one appreciates those sections when, after masses of information and shocking stories of callous brutality, the author occasionally pauses and takes some time for synthesis, interpretation, and explanation. But no biography or history is definitive, no matter what publishers' publicists proclaim, and anyone with the time and upper arm strength to prop up the book, which weighs in at about three pounds, will experience an exhausting, exhilarating journey.

It is no accident that biographies are among the best-selling books dealing with history. Personalities, especially of celebrated figures, offer readers apparently easy access to dense and difficult questions about politics. But the emphasis on personality, so essential in a biography, can lead to an overemphasis on the determining effect of the person and a neglect of context and social forces. Remembering Philip Abrams's suggestion at the beginning of this chapter that life history must be meshed with social history "in a singular fate," biographers of Stalin have increasingly located the life of this exceptional individual "in a particular historically organised milieu and the interactional patterning of the series of experiences through which individuation is then achieved." Some Stalin biographers, like Trotsky, Deutscher, Tucker, and Ulam, have come closest to achieving that meshing; others, like the psychohistorians in particular, discount context too radically; and still others, like Kotkin, do not take the emotional and intellectual evolution of their subject as seriously as they might. Reading the biographers together brings out a fuller picture, but few readers have either the time or inclination to do what scholars of Stalin are required to do. Puzzles and underexplored aspects of the Stalin story remain: the ethnographic culture of Georgia, the complex history of Russian Social Democracy, and the inner workings of the Soviet political system. Open-endedness, admission of ignorance, irony, and paradox must be admitted into the study of Stalin and Stalinism. Great historical conjunctures, like revolutions or wars, or major historical actors require complexly conceived questions and explanations that avoid the neat and deceptive harmonies of organic narratives.

The problem of Stalin will be with us as long as anyone is concerned with the history of Russia and revolutions. Russia has often been seen as a country fatally doomed to violence and authoritarianism. Biography should lead us in a different direction, toward the examination of motivation and choice. The contingencies and contradictions of human experience allow us to come away with a sense that while people cannot choose the circumstances in which they live, the choices they make matter enormously. Rather than Russia's repeated fatal fall into despotism—a powerful trope that the Stalin story may convince us is true—other paths might have been taken.

Thanks to the biographies here discussed, as well as the more general treatments of the Terror and the specific dissections of other acts of mass murder, there is no longer any reason not to understand the full perversion of socialism associated with Stalin's regime. So powerfully embedded in the Soviet experience was the autocracy and the Terror that in attempting to disentangle Stalinism from the Soviet system, that system itself fell apart.

The Soviet past has never just been about one country at one time but about the hopes, rightly or wrongly placed, about alternatives in human history. For the Right, and for many liberals, the collapse of actually existing socialism indicts socialism in all its forms and sanctions capitalism as the only possible modern organization of human life. The utopia of the market is imagined as the resolution of the social problems that state "socialism" could not solve. But, rather than replacing one archaic ideology with a refurbished belief in the invisible hand, historians might do what they do best and introduce complexity, skepticism, and uncertainty into their stories about Stalin and the Soviet experiment.

2

Stalin and His Stalinism: Power and Authority in the Soviet Union, 1930–53

This chapter answers a deceptively simple question: How did Stalin rule? How did he maintain his authority while establishing a personal autocracy?[1] His extraordinary and brutal political achievement was to act in the name of the Communist Party and its Central Committee against that party and Central Committee, while remaining the unchallenged head of party and state and, evidently, a vastly popular leader. At the end of the process, his absolute grip on power allowed him to declare black white and completely reverse the foreign policy of the Soviet Union and the line of the Comintern by embracing Nazi Germany in a nonaggression pact. The colossal and costly destruction he brought upon the country on the eve and in the early days of World War II gave rise to no organized opposition, and the centralized apparatus of control that he had created was not only able to weather the Nazi invasion but to organize a victory that would preserve the essence of the system he forged for another half century.

The simplest, though inadequate, answer to the question would be that Stalin's power was maintained through the exercise of terror and monopolistic control of the means of communication throughout society. Though certainly an important part of the answer, an exclusive focus on terror and propaganda does not explain how Stalin won his authority within the party in the 1920s and maintained it among

1   This chapter was originally prepared for the conference Twentieth-Century Russia–Germany in Comparative Perspective, September 19–22, 1991, University of Pennsylvania; after several revisions it was published in Ian Kershaw and Moshe Lewin (eds.), *Stalinism and Nazism: Dictatorships in Comparison* (Cambridge: Cambridge University Press, 1997). I wish to express my gratitude to Lewis Siegelbaum and Moshe Lewin for their careful and critical readings of earlier drafts.

his own supporters even before the advent of the Great Terror. Once initiated, terror operated through collaboration, and Stalin's associates almost never attempted to free themselves from the source of their fears. Many within and outside the party supported the terror, convinced that extraordinary measures against vicious and hidden enemies were required. Tens of millions regarded Stalin as the indispensable leader of the "socialist" camp, perhaps someone to be feared as was Ivan Groznyi, a leader who filled the hearts of enemies with awe.[2]

Power and Persuasion in the 1920s

The paradox of the October Revolution was that the Bolsheviks possessed the physical power to overthrow the Provisional Government and disband the Constituent Assembly but did not yet have either a popular mandate to rule all of Russia (let alone the non-Russian peripheries) or an unassailable legitimizing myth to sanction their claim to govern. Even as they successfully built a new state during the years of Civil War, the Bolsheviks were (as Lenin usually admitted) a minority party that needed to justify its hold on power. The Bolsheviks required more than passive acquiescence in the new order; they wanted active support that could be mobilized toward heroic goals. One of the central dilemmas of the Communists in the first two decades of their rule was to move from an exercise of power through force toward creating a base of support through the construction of a widely accepted, hegemonic understanding of the historical moment, a passage from coercive to discursive power, from naked power to authority and legitimacy.

Although military victory, the practice of state terror, or the repression of opposition might bring short-term benefits to a regime, "authority-building is necessary to protect and expand one's base of political support."[3] As George Breslauer has written about a later period in Soviet history, "Authority is legitimized power," and Soviet leaders had to legitimize their power and policies by demonstrating their competence or indispensability as rulers.[4] In their own search for legal authority in the 1920s, the Bolsheviks could rely neither on tradition (associated with the *ancien régime*), nationalism, or religious faith. They sought—in Weber's

---

2   Michael Cherniavsky, "Ivan the Terrible as Renaissance Prince," *Slavic Review* XXVII, 2 (June 1968), pp. 195–211.

3   George W. Breslauer, *Khrushchev and Brezhnev as Leaders: Building Authority in Soviet Politics* (London: George Allen Unwin, 1982), p. 10.

4   Ibid., p. 4.

terms—a "value-rational" "belief in the absolute validity of the order as the expression of ultimate values."[5] Over time, legal authority was supplemented (and compromised) in Stalin's USSR by charismatic authority in which the "charismatically qualified leader ... is obeyed by virtue of personal trust in his revelation, his heroism or his exemplary qualities so far as they fall within the scope of the individual's belief in his charisma."[6]

Yet even as they attempted to construct a legitimizing cultural and political hegemony, the Communists steadily narrowed the political field, centralizing power and eliminating dissent. One of the most "democratic" (in the sense of grassroots popular participation) polities in the world (in the revolutionary years 1917–18) rapidly turned step-by-step into a dictatorship of a single party. In the very first days of the October seizure of power, the rival socialist parties, the Mensheviks and Right Socialist Revolutionaries, walked out of the Congress of Soviets and left the field of play to the Bolsheviks and their last allies, the Left Socialist Revolutionaries. In the next weeks and months, the establishment of Soviet power and the dissolution of *zemstva* (local assemblies), dumas, and the Constituent Assembly eliminated the upper and middle classes, the clergy, and the moderate socialists from the *pays legal* (legal country). When, in the months before the Civil War began, the coalition partners of the Bolsheviks, the Left Socialist Revolutionaries, resigned from the Sovnarkom (Council of People's Commissars), the Bolsheviks ruled alone in a one-party government. During the Civil War, the vitality and autonomy of local soviets declined, as the working class of 1917 itself fragmented and dissolved.[7] Agents of the central government, along with Red Army officers and soldiers, the police, and the party officials increased their power at the expense of local committees and soviets. Manipulation of elections, coercive practices, indifference and apathy of voters, all in the context of the vicious fratricidal warfare of 1918–21, steadily weakened the power and legitimacy of the local soviets and eroded the rival political parties.[8] A new state power emerged from the

5   Max Weber, *Economy and Society: An Outline of Interpretive Sociology*, edited by Guenther Roth and Claus Wittich (Berkeley: University of California Press, 1968), p. 33. "In the case of legal authority, obedience is owed to the legally established impersonal order. It extends to the persons exercising the authority of office under it by virtue of the formal legality of their commands and only within the scope of authority of the office" (pp. 215–6).

6   Ibid., p. 216.

7   William G. Rosenberg, "Russian Labor and Bolshevik Power After October," *Slavic Review* XLIV, 2 (Summer 1985), pp. 212–38; and the discussion with Moshe Lewin and Vladimir Brovkin, pp. 239–56.

8   Vladimir Brovkin, *The Mensheviks After October: Socialist Opposition and the*

war, under the control of Communists imbued with habits of command and ready to use violence to maintain their political monopoly.[9]

Both Lenin and Stalin had imbibed the bitter lesson that politics was a kind of warfare, the aim of which was to render your enemy impotent. By 1922, interparty politics were a historical memory, and the only arena for political discussion and infighting was within the Communist Party. Fear of the peasantry and armed resistance to their government led Lenin to issue the ban on factions in 1921 and the party leaders to sanction the progressive elimination of political oppositions through the 1920s. The steady accumulation of power by a single faction reduced the political arena even further, until a handful of influential figures decided the course for the rest of the party.[10] Within the party political manipulation, Machiavellian intrigues, and a willingness to resort to ruthlessness were certainly part of Stalin's repertoire, but he also managed to position himself in the immediate post-Lenin years as a pragmatic centrist supportive of the compromises and concessions of the New Economic Policy and unwilling to risk Soviet power in efforts to promote elusive revolutions abroad.

In the post-October scramble to hold on to the reins of government, Lenin and the Bolsheviks had justified their actions by reference to a variety of historic claims—that they represented the vanguard of the proletariat organized in the soviets; that they were the only party able to bring peace and order to the country and willing to give the land to the peasants; that the transition to socialism was at hand and the weakest link in the capitalist chain had been broken. Russia's October Revolution would receive its ultimate sanction in the rising of the European working class, and all talk of the prematurity of the Bolshevik seizure of power would cease. The Civil War provided a new justification for

Rise of the Bolshevik Dictatorship (Ithaca, NY: Cornell University Press, 1987).

9   Leonard Schapiro, The Origin of the Communist Autocracy: Political Opposition in the Soviet State: First Phase, 1917–1922 (Cambridge, MA: Harvard University Press, 1955); Robert Service, The Bolshevik Party in Revolution: A Study in Organizational Change, 1917–1923 (New York: Macmillan, 1979); T. H. Rigby, Lenin's Government: Sovnarkom 1917–1922 (Cambridge: Cambridge University Press, 1979); Orlando Figes, Peasant Russia, Civil War: The Volga Countryside in Revolution, 1917–1921 (Oxford: Oxford University Press, 1989); Mark von Hagen, Soldiers in the Proletarian Dictatorship: The Red Army and the Soviet Socialist State, 1917–1930 (Ithaca, NY: Cornell University Press, 1990); Alexander Rabinowitch, The Bolsheviks in Power: The First Year of Soviet Rule in Petrograd (Bloomington: Indiana University Press, 2008); and Lara Douds, Inside Lenin's Government: Ideology, Power and Practice in the Early Soviet State (London: Bloomsbury Academic, 2018).

10   Robert Vincent Daniels, The Conscience of the Revolution: Communist Opposition in Soviet Russia (Cambridge, MA: Harvard University Press, 1960).

holding power—the fight against enemies domestic and foreign, the preservation of the victories of 1917, and the prevention of a restoration of the old order. As unpopular as the Communists were in many parts of the country, they were accepted as the lesser of evils, and acquiescence to, if not positive acceptance of, Lenin's government spread through different social strata and groups—workers, many peasants, intellectuals, and certain nationalities, like the Jews, who were the targets of White anti-Semitism. "As long as the peasants feared the Whites, they would go along, feet dragging, with the demands of the Soviet regime.... Thus the Bolshevik dictatorship climbed up on the back of the peasant revolution."[11] Without a proletarian victory in the West (without which, according to Lenin and Trotsky, socialism was impossible in Russia), millenarian rhetoric was supplemented with a hard-nosed reliance on force, terror, armed might, organization, and new kinds of propaganda.[12]

Particularly effective were Lenin's concessions to the non-Russian peoples. Originally opposed to a federal structure for the postrevolutionary state, Lenin quickly readjusted his views after the October seizure of power. For both Lenin and Stalin, who soon emerged as the key players in the formation of the multinational Soviet Union, nationality policy was a temporary tactical adjustment, not unlike the party's agrarian policy and New Economic Policy, to deal with problems that would be resolved once the international proletarian revolution occurred. But far more than most other party members, Lenin promoted the concept of national self-determination, even to the point of separation from Russia. In 1922 Lenin and Stalin fought over the relationship between the Russian republic and the other fledgling socialist states of the periphery. Stalin favored a much more centralized arrangement, with the formally independent states reduced to autonomies within the Russian Soviet Federative Socialist Republic (RSFSR), whereas Lenin proposed that the republics remain powerful members of a new federation, the USSR. As his own power increased, Stalin consistently shifted the emphasis in Lenin's nationality policy until it became an ideology for a new, disguised form of empire in which the center and the Russian Communist Party

11 Figes, *Peasant Russia, Civil War*, p. 354.
12 The standard interpretation is that Lenin and Trotsky believed that building socialism (or at least completing the building of socialism in peasant Russia) required aid from a revolution in more advanced industrial capitalist countries. Dutch historian Erik Van Ree, however, argues that in the last pre-revolutionary years, Lenin worked out a conception of a socialist economy in Russia that would be superior to those in the West and would aid the revolution in the West. See his "Lenin's Conception of Socialism in One Country, 1915–17," *Russian Review* XXIII, 2 (December 2010), pp. 159–81.

emerged superordinate and sovereign and the non-Russian peripheries fell into a state of tutelage.

Building the Apparat

In his prerevolutionary career, Stalin had been primarily a *komitetchik* (committee man), a party operative rather than an intellectual theorist or hands-on activist among the workers.[13] Never gifted in theoretical analysis and synthesis, so prized by party intellectuals, Stalin was a *praktik*, a man who got things done, a skillful political infighter able to sense when he needed to retreat or keep silent and when he could act with impunity. Whatever his personal predilections for unchallenged power, his inability to accept frustration or criticism, and his visceral suspiciousness directed even at those close to him, Stalin was also the product of the particular political culture and internal party practices of Bolshevism. Disputes were fierce and often personal; subordination to higher authorities within the movement was required; force and repression could be used in the service of socialism, which was eventually defined in Stalin's mind as identical to his own policies and preservation of his personal position. Once he had reached his exalted position as chief oligarch, he spoke in the name of the party and the Central Committee without consulting anyone else. And he molded his own version of Leninism as an effective weapon against those whom he considered pretenders.

In the early months of Soviet rule, Stalin worked at the very center of power, in Smolny, close to Lenin, constantly in contact with party members and state officials by telegraph.[14] Over time, and like other high party leaders, Stalin took on a wide range of assignments—from People's Commissar of Nationalities (Narkomnats, 1917–23), People's Commissar of State Control (from 1919) and Worker-Peasant Inspection (Rabkrin, 1920–22), to membership in the Military-Revolutionary Soviet of the Republic, the Politburo, and the Organizational Bureau (Orgburo, from their creation in March 1919) to political commissar on various fronts in the Civil War and participant in a variety of commissions set up to solve specific problems.[15] In what, at the time, seemed to many to be a

---

13   For Stalin's prerevolutionary career, see Ronald Grigor Suny, *Stalin: Passage to Revolution* (Princeton, NJ: Princeton University Press, 2020).

14   This is clear from working through Stalin's personal archive in the Rossiiskii Gosudarstvennyi Arkhiv, Sotsial'noi i Politicheskoi Istorii, f. 558, op. 1 (hereinafter RGASPI).

15   The Central Committee worked through a system of commissions, among the most important of which was the Instructional Commission, which prepared the text

trivial appointment, the Eleventh Party Congress in the spring of 1922 elected Stalin a member of the party Secretariat with the title "general secretary."[16]

By the time of Lenin's incapacitation in 1923, Stalin was fast becoming indispensable to many powerful figures. He worked with his political allies, Grigorii Zinoviev and Lev Kamenev, to prevent Trotsky's growing influence. On the eve of Politburo meetings, this troika would meet, at first in Zinoviev's apartment, later in Stalin's Central Committee office, ostensibly to approve the agenda. In fact, they decided what positions they would take on specific issues and what roles each would play in the meeting.[17] In 1924–25, the group was expanded to seven (the *semerka*) and included Stalin, Zinoviev, Kamenev, Nikolai Bukharin, Aleksei Rykov, Mikhail Tomskii, and Valerian Kuibyshev.[18]

The Secretariat was supposedly subordinate to the Orgburo, which, in turn, was subordinate to the Politburo, but by statute any decision of the Secretariat that was not challenged by the Orgburo became automatically the decision of the Orgburo. Likewise, any decision of the Orgburo unchallenged by a member of the Politburo became the decision of the Politburo. A decision by the Politburo might be challenged by a member of the Central Committee, but, unless a plenum of the Central Committee annulled that decision, it remained in force. No strict division was maintained between political and organizational questions.[19]

In general, the Politburo was to decide on policy, and the Orgburo was to allocate forces—under the authority and guidance of the Central Committee. But both of these small committees met more frequently and proved more effective in day-to-day decision-making than the larger, more unwieldy Central Committee. From the earliest years of the Soviet

of directives to be sent to local party organizations. In the early 1920s, Molotov or Kaganovich presided over this commission. Boris Bazhanov, *Bazhanov and the Damnation of Stalin*, trans. and commentary by David W. Doyle (Athens, OH: Ohio University Press, 1990), p. 17.

16 Stalin was overburdened to the point that his health suffered. In the summer of 1922, the Politburo ordered Stalin to spend three days a week out of the city at his dacha. *Izvestiia TsK KPSS*, no. 4 (1989), pp. 185–6.

17 Bazhanov, *Bazhanov and the Damnation of Stalin*, pp. 34–5.

18 "Pis'ma I. V. Stalina V. M. Molotovu (1925–1936 gg.)," *Izvestiia TsK KPSS*, no. 9 (1990), p. 185.

19 As Lenin had told the Eleventh Party Congress, "It is impossible to differentiate a political question from an organizational one. Any political question might be organizational, and vice versa. And only the established practice that any question can be transferred from the Orgburo to the Politburo has made it possible to get the work of the Central Committee going correctly." *Odinnadtsatyi s'ezd RKP (b). Mart-Aprel' 1922 goda: Stenograficheskii otchet* (Moscow: Gosudarstvennoe izdatel'stvo politicheskoi literatury, 1961), p. 143.

government, small overlapping groups of high officials made the most important and wide-reaching decisions, and Stalin was the only person who was a member of all of these groups. Even more important, with his complete dominance over the Orgburo, Stalin was able to use this institution to make appointments throughout the party and to work out his own policies. For example, many of the documents concerning Stalin's "autonomization" plan for the new Soviet federation initially emerged from discussions in a special commission of the Orgburo.[20]

Each of the top party institutions had its own secretariat—for example, *Sekretariat Politbiuro, Sekretariat Orgbiuro,* and *Sekretariat Tsentral'nogo komiteta.* The Secretariat of the Central Committee in turn had a Bureau, established on September 12, 1921, which was replaced by the so-called *Sekretnyi otdel* [Secret Department] in March 1926.[21] All the while, Stalin, as the leading member both of the Orgburo and the Central Committee Secretariat, built up his own staff, which soon amounted to a personal chancellery. Despite his suspicious nature and his intellectual limitations (certainly exaggerated by political rivals and opponents), Stalin was able to attract a number of loyal subordinates, whose fortunes would rise with him. Most important among them were Viacheslav Molotov, with whom he worked from 1917; his comrades from the Caucasus, Anastas Mikoyan and "Sergo" Orjonikidze; and his Civil War associate, Kliment Voroshilov.[22] Stalin's assistants within the apparatus of the Central Committee included Amaiak Nazaretian, his secretary in 1923; Boris Bazhanov, secretary of the Politburo and assistant to Stalin for Politburo affairs; Ivan Tovstukha, who would remain Stalin's secretary almost until his death in 1935; Lev Mekhlis, Stalin's personal secretary; Grigorii Kanner, secretary for matters dealing with the police; Georgii Malenkov, who replaced Bazhanov as secretary of the Politburo; and, eventually, Aleksandr Poskrebyshev, who rose from clerk in the Central Committee

20   *Izvestiia TsK KPSS*, no. 9 (1989), pp. 191–218.
21   RGASPI, f. 17 (Central Committee), op. 84; documents from the *Biuro Sekretariata* and the *Sekretnyi otdel* can also be found in op. 85 and 86.
22   A later witness to the relationship of Stalin and Molotov noted that "Molotov was the only member of the Politburo whom Stalin addressed with the familiar pronoun *ty* ... Molotov, though impotent without Stalin's leadership, was indispensable to Stalin in many ways. Though both were unscrupulous in their methods, it seems to me that Stalin selected these methods carefully and fitted them to circumstances, while Molotov regarded them in advance as being incidental and unimportant. I maintain that he not only incited Stalin into doing many things, but that he also sustained him and dispelled his doubts ... it would be wrong to underestimate Molotov's role, especially as the practical executive." Milovan Djilas, *Conversations with Stalin* (New York: Harcourt, Brace & World, 1962), pp. 62, 70–1.

mailroom to replace Tovstukha as Stalin's principal secretary.[23] In 1928, Poskrebyshev became the head of the *Osobyi sektor Secretariata TsK*, a "special section" of the Central Committee's secretariat in charge of security matters and secret communications within the party apparatus. Receiving information from the state security service, the *Osobyi sektor* oversaw a hierarchy of "special sections" at the regional and local level.[24] Eventually, by 1934, the *Osobyi sektor* replaced the *Sekretnyi otdel*, and Poskrebyshev moved into the position held formerly by Tovstukha.[25] Stalin's relationship with all of them was never one of partnership or equality but of subordination. He usually addressed them with the formal *vy*, with exceptions made for Nazaretian, Orjonikidze, Voroshilov (who in turn called him "Koba"), and later Molotov.[26]

Before 1926, no voting member of the Politburo owed his position to Stalin, and Stalin did not use his influence in the Central Committee to force changes in the Politburo. T. H. Rigby argues that Stalin employed the Central Committee to keep his shifting majority in the Politburo in power.[27] But James Harris has shown that Stalin's secretariat did not fully control the appointments process and that local party committees could refuse to accept cadres or negotiate with the center. Stalin's greatest influence came from guaranteeing officials tenure and resolving the many disputes within party circles over local power.[28] Stalin worked to strengthen the party secretaries and considered democracy in the absence of developed political culture inappropriate.[29] "Many Party secretaries voted for Stalin at Party Congresses. They helped him defeat his rivals in the Politburo because they had a common interest in it, not because they felt personally beholden to Stalin."[30] Only after the routing of the Zinoviev-led Opposition in December 1925 did close supporters of

---

23   Bazhanov, *Bazhanov and the Damnation of Stalin*, pp. 34–40.

24   Niels Erik Rosenfeldt, *Knowledge and Power: The Role of Stalin's Secret Chancellery in the Soviet System of Government* (Copenhagen: Rosenkilde and Bagger, 1978), pp. 86–92.

25   Ibid., p. 177.

26   Bazhanov, *Bazhanov and the Damnation of Stalin*, p. 37; Djilas, *Conversations with Stalin*, p. 62.

27   T. H. Rigby, *Communist Party Membership in the U.S.S.R., 1917–1967* (Princeton, NJ: Princeton University Press, 1968), p. 113.

28   James Harris, "Stalin as General Secretary: The Appointments Process and the Nature of Stalin's Power," in Sarah Davies and James Harris (eds.), *Stalin: A New History* (Cambridge: Cambridge University Press, 2006), p. 82. See also J. Arch Getty, "Stalin as 'Prime Minister': Power and the Politburo," in Davies and Harris (eds.), *Stalin*, pp. 83–107, for the change in the 1930s.

29   Harris, "Stalin as General Secretary," p. 75.

30   Ibid., p. 65.

Stalin join the Politburo. Kamenev was demoted to candidate member, and Molotov, Voroshilov, and Kalinin were elevated to the highest party body. In July 1926, Rudzutak replaced Zinoviev, and in October, Trotsky and Kamenev both lost their seats. In the next month, Orjonikidze joined the Politburo. By December 1927, Lenin's major lieutenants had been eliminated from the Politburo, with the exception of Nikolai Bukharin, and Stalin had an absolute majority. As the crisis over grain collection strained Stalin's alliance with Bukharin, Stalin changed "from being the soul of caution and moderation" to becoming "intransigence itself."[31] By 1930, he removed the so-called "Right," those unwilling to follow him unreservedly through collectivization, and revamped the apparatus of the Central Committee. With the fall of Bukharin, Rykov, and Tomskii, Stalin had established an unchallenged oligarchy with himself as chief oligarch.

Stalin insisted that all important decisions be made at the highest level. In 1925 he was concerned about the loss of direct control over economic matters by the Politburo, as he indicated in a letter to Molotov:

> The business with the STO [the Council of Labor and Defense] is, of course, not very good.... The Politburo itself is in an uncomfortable position, as it is cut off from economic matters. Look at *Ekonomicheskaia zhizn'* [Economic Life, an economics journal] and you will understand that our funds are being distributed by Smilga and Strumilin plus Groman [all of whom were working in Gosplan, the principal planning agency], and the Politburo ... has been turned from the leading organ into a court of appeals, something like a "council of elders." Sometimes it is even worse—Gosplan is not leading, but the "sections" of [bourgeois] specialists of Gosplan.... Business can only suffer from this, of course. I see no way out except a restructuring [*perestroika*] of STO with members of the Politburo there in person.[32]

Early in the 1930s, Stalin pushed hard for the end of any duality between party and state, urging Molotov in a series of private letters to end Prime Minister Rykov's tenure and take the job himself.

> The top (*verkhushka*) of our central soviet [apparatus] (STO, SNK [Council of People's Commissars], the conference of deputy commissars) is sick with a fatal disease. STO has turned from a business-like

31   Ibid.
32   "Pis'ma I. V. Stalina V. M. Molotovu (1925–1936 gg.)," *Izvestiia TsK KPSS*, no. 9 (1990), p. 187.

and fighting organ into an empty parliament. SNK is paralyzed by the wishy-washy and, essentially, anti-party speeches of Rykov. The conference of deputy commissars, which was earlier the staff of Rykov, As, and Sheiman, now has the tendency to turn into the staff of Rykov, Piatakov, Kviring or Bogolepov (I see no great difference between the latter and the former), setting itself up against the Central Committee of the party. It is clear that this can continue no further. Fundamental measures are needed. I will discuss what kind when I return to Moscow.[33]

A week later, he urged the dismissal of Rykov and Shmidt and the dissolution of "their entire bureaucratic consultative, secretarial apparatus." By securing the premiership for Molotov, one of the few people he seems to have trusted through the 1930s, Stalin sought to prevent the development of a state apparatus that could rival the party. Any *razryv* (schism) between party and state was unacceptable, and discussion in the Sovnarkom that delayed the carrying out of his policies had to end. All decision-making was to be concentrated within a loyal Politburo. "With this combination we will have full unity of the soviet and party summits (*verkhuski*) that will undoubtedly double our strength."[34]

Overall, Stalin's organizational project was aimed at monopolization of decision-making at the highest possible levels. Yet his drive for centralization and the reduction of local power, in fact, often had the opposite effect, fostering local centers of power, "family circles" *atamanshchina* [warlordism], and low-level disorganization. "Little Stalins" were created throughout the country, and in the national republics ethnopolitical machines threatened the reach of the central government.[35]

Building Hegemony in the 1930s

Though the relative peace, stability, and economic improvement of the New Economic Policy years, in contrast to the preceding seven years

33 The correspondence on the top government officials to be removed can be found in "Pis'ma Stalina Molotovu," *Kommunist*, no. 11 (1990), pp. 102–5 and in Lars T. Lih, Oleg V. Naumov, and Oleg CV. Khlevniuk (eds.), *Stalin's Letters to Molotov* (New Haven, CT: Yale University Press, 1995), pp. 213–18. The translations from Russian here are my own.

34 *Kommunist*, no. 11 (1990), p. 105.

35 Merle Fainsod, *Smolensk Under Soviet Rule* (Cambridge, MA: Harvard University Press, 1958), pp. 48–61; Ronald Grigor Suny, *The Making of the Georgian Nation* (Bloomington and Stanford: Indiana University Press and Hoover Institution Press, 1988), pp. 260–91.

of war, revolution, and civil war, had given the Leninist state a degree of acceptance and authority in the eyes of many, that acceptance was fragile and based on the compromises and limits of what the Communists almost invariably saw as a transitional period, a temporary retreat from socialism. The launching of the Stalin revolution, first in the countryside and then in industry, destroyed the basis of the regime's fragile relationship with the great majority of the population and created a new crisis of legitimacy and authority. The alliance of workers and peasants (the *smychka*), symbolized by the sickle and hammer, dissolved in a war by the city on the village.

By ending New Economic Policy and almost all private production and trade, Stalin created the first modern non-market, state-run economy, one that simultaneously eliminated rival sources of power and resistance to the will of the central authorities. "Industrialists" no longer held property in the means of production. Workers could no longer effectively organize in order to raise the price of labor. Farmers were unable any longer to withhold grain to affect market prices. Yet all of these groups devised ways within the command economy to exercise limited degrees of power, autonomy, and resistance. To take one example: workers were able to undermine harsh factory regimes by taking their skills, so desired by managers, to another workplace. Bosses, caught between demands from above for higher productivity, had to satisfy, however inadequately, some of the needs and demands of their workers and even permit a degree of worker autonomy on the shop floor.[36] Much of the time and effort of Soviet officials was concerned with raising output and productivity, and successive state strategies required accommodations and concessions as often as additional pressure and repression.[37] Thus, while Stalin was actively concentrating power at the top, it was being diffused downward and outward throughout the economic and political systems by thousands of *vintiki* (little screws) who had their own requirements for survival and "making out." The state grew; in Moshe Lewin's sense, it "swallowed" society; but, at the same time, it was unable to realize

---

36   Hiroaki Kuromiya, *Stalin's Industrial Revolution: Politics and Workers, 1928–1932* (Cambridge: Cambridge University Press, 1988).

37   Karen Petrone, *Life Has Become More Joyous, Comrades: Celebrations in the Time of Stalin* (Bloomington: Indiana University Press, 2000). Much of the work of Lewis Siegelbaum has explored the various strategies by which the regime attempted to raise productivity. See, for example, his "Soviet Norm Determination in Theory and Practice, 1917–1941," *Soviet Studies* XXXVI (1984), pp. 48–67; and *Stakhanovism and the Politics of Productivity in the USSR, 1935–1941* (Cambridge: Cambridge University Press, 1988).

the vision presented by a totalitarian theory of complete atomization of society. The limits of state power were met when people refused to work efficiently, migrated from place to place by the millions, or informally worked out ways to resist pressure from above. Totalitarian control may have been an ambition of Stalinism, but the dark aim of atomization of an impotent, obedient, terrified people was never achieved.

Stalin came to power in the absence of a broad consensus on the legitimacy and necessity of his personal rule. Using the instruments of state power to mobilize people in a grand program of social transformation, the regime confidently conceived of itself as possessing a popular and historically sanctioned mandate and worked assiduously to increase support for itself through education and propaganda, leadership cults, election campaigns, broad national discussions (on the constitution and other topics), public celebrations (like the Pushkin centennial of 1937), the creation of celebrity heroes (aviators, arctic explorers, and exemplary workers), show trials, and political rituals.[38] Most important, the party/ state made real concessions to the populace and satisfied the ambitions and aspirations of many (though certainly not all) for social mobility and an improved living standard. Peasants who became workers and workers who became managers and party bosses were moving up, while many of their envied social "betters" of the past were experiencing an enforced downward mobility.[39]

In the Stalinist formulation, the "revolution from above" of the 1930s, though initiated by the state, was supported from below by millions of peasants and workers struggling to create a new society based on collective farms and socialist industry. The state-initiated industrialization of the 1930s mobilized millions of men and women into the most mammoth building project in modern times, and a romance of dams and power stations, new cities on the steppe and in Siberia, created enthusiasts among the new workers and managers. The enormous difficulties that the breakthrough into "socialism" entailed—resistance from farmers, famine, economic bottlenecks and breakdowns—were seen as the work

38 Christel Lane, *The Rites of Rulers: Ritual in Industrial Society—the Soviet Case* (Cambridge: Cambridge University Press, 1981).

39 Social mobility has been a frequent theme in the work of Sheila Fitzpatrick. See, for example, *Education and Social Mobility in the Soviet Union, 1921–1934* (Cambridge: Cambridge University Press, 1979); "Stalin and the Making of a New Elite, 1928–1939," *Slavic Review* XXXVIII, 3 (September 1979), pp. 377–402; and for a darker picture of ordinary Soviets coping with material and political difficulties, *Everyday Stalinism: Ordinary Life in Extraordinary Times: Soviet Russia in the 1930s* (New York: Oxford University Press, 1999).

of enemies and saboteurs, rather than inherent in the party's policies or a by-product of popular recalcitrance and massive coercion. Though the disjuncture between these forced images of imagined harmony and purpose and the hardships and dislocations of actual worksites created unease among many who attempted to govern a vast country, the sheer scale of the transformation and its construction as a human epic engendered the broad social support that the regime had sought for two decades.[40] Collectivization of peasant lands was fiercely resisted, but industrialization, for all its hardships, was enthusiastically embraced.[41]

The naked exercise of unrestrained power was key to Stalin's victory, but his regime simultaneously worked to create authority and acceptance, borrowing from and supplementing the repertoire of justifications from Lenin's day. While appropriating the mantle of Lenin and much of the rhetoric of Bolshevism, Stalin revised, suppressed, and even reversed much of the legacy of Lenin. Internationalism turned into nationalism; the *smychka* between the workers and the peasants was buried in the ferocity of collectivization; radical transformation of the family and the place of women ended with reassertion of the most conservative "family values." And, in the process, almost all of Lenin's closest associates fell victim to the self-proclaimed keeper of the Leninist flame.

Within ten years of his dispute with Lenin, Stalin transformed nationality policy from a series of concessions to non-Russians into a powerful weapon of imperial state-building. He reversed Lenin's focus on "Great Russian chauvinism" as the principal danger in nationality relations and emphasized instead the dangers from the nationalism of non-Russians.[42] In 1923, he turned on Mirsaid Sultan-Galiev, a former associate in Narkomnats and a spokesman for the aspirations of Muslim Communists, accused him of *national-uklonizm* (national deviationism),

40   As the Harvard Project interviews in the early 1950s demonstrated and Donna Bahry has emphasized, "one of the cardinal values defining the Soviet system's claim to legitimacy was industrial transformation .... Rapid industrialization appeared to have near-universal backing." Donna Bahry, "Society Transformed?: Rethinking the Social Roots of Perestroika," *Slavic Review* LII, 3 (Fall 1993), p. 524.

41   Two first-person accounts of the period are illustrative: Maurice Hindus, *Red Bread* (Bloomington: Indiana University Press, 1988); and John Scott, *Behind the Urals: An American Worker in Russia's City of Steel* (Boston: Houghton Mifflin, 1942). An enlarged edition was prepared by Stephen Kotkin (Bloomington: Indiana University Press, 1989); see also Kotkin's *Magnetic Mountain: Stalinism as a Civilization* (Berkeley: University of California Press, 1995).

42   The fullest treatment of this shift from what he calls "the Affirmative Action Empire" to the policy of "Friendship of the Peoples" is by Terry Martin, *The Affirmative Action Empire: Nations and Nationalism in the Soviet Union, 1923–1939* (Ithaca, NY: Cornell University Press, 2001).

had him "tried" before a party conference, arrested, and expelled from the party.[43] Five years later, the state police "discovered" a new plot, the "Sultan-Galiev counter-revolutionary organization," and in the next decade the *Ob'edinennoe gosudarstvennoe politicheskoe upravlenie* (OGPU, United State Political Administration) and its successor, the *Narodnyi komissariat vnutrennykh del* (People's Commissariat of Internal Affairs) "unmasked" dozens of conspiratorial groups promoting nationalism from Ukraine to Central Asia.[44] In a letter to Levon Mirzoian, first secretary of the Kazakh *kraikom* (territorial party committee), in 1933, Stalin called for intensifying the struggle against local Kazakh nationalism "in order to create the conditions for the sowing of Leninist internationalism."[45] Five years later, after having carried out purges against Kazakh intellectuals and "deviationist" party members, Mirzoian himself was arrested and executed.[46]

Stalinism was both a revolutionizing system, unwilling to accept backward Russia as it was (and here it differs from many traditionally authoritarian dictatorships), and a conservative, restorative one, anxious to re-establish hierarchies, affirm certain traditional values like patriotism and patriarchy, and create political legitimacy based on more than victorious revolution.[47] The revolution and the restoration were both

43   *Tainy natsional'noi politiki TsK RKP: "Chetvertoe soveshchanie TsK RKP s otvetstvennymi rabotnikami natsional'nykh respublik i oblastei v g. Moskve 9–12 iiunia 1923 g.": Stenograficheskii otchet* (Moscow: Insan, 1992); N. Tagirov, "Sultan-Galiev: Pravda i domysly," *Kommunist Tatarii*, no. 9 (September 1989), pp. 68–76; "Schitaem svoim revoliutsionnym dolgom," ibid., no. 6 (June 1990), pp. 51–5; Alexandre A. Bennigsen and S. Enders Wimbush, *Muslim National Communism in the Soviet Union: A Revolutionary Strategy for the Colonial World* (Chicago: University of Chicago Press, 1979); Stephen Blank, "Stalin's First Victim: The Trial of Sultangaliev," *Russian History/Histoire Russe* XVII, 2 (Summer 1990), pp. 155–78; Douglas Taylor Northrop, "Reconsidering Sultan-Galiev," in Gail Lapidus and Corbin Lydey (eds.), *Selected Topics in Soviet Ethnopolitics* (Berkeley: University of California Press, 1992), pp. 1–44.

44   "V komissii Politbiuro TsK KPSS po dopolnitel'nomu izucheniiu materialov, sviazannykh s repressiiami, imevshimi mesto v period 30-40-kh i nachala 50-kh godov," *Izvestiia TsK KPSS*, no. 9 (1990), pp. 71–6; "O tak nazyvaemom 'national-uklonizme,'" in ibid., pp. 76–84.

45   Ibid., p. 79.

46   Boris Levytsky (comp.), *The Stalinist Terror in the Thirties: Documentation from the Soviet Press* (Stanford, CA: Hoover Institution Press, 1974), pp. 176–9; Martha Brill Olcott, *The Kazakhs* (Stanford, CA: Hoover Institution Press, 1987), pp. 218–19.

47   Nowhere was this more evident than in the state's shifting strategies toward women and the family. See Wendy Z. Goldman, "Women, Abortion and the State, 1917–36," in Barbara Evans Clements, Barbara Alpern Engel, and Christine D. Worobec (eds.), *Russia's Women: Accommodation, Resistance, Transformation* (Berkeley: University of California Press, 1991); and her *Women, the State and Revolution: Soviet Family Policy and Social Life, 1917–1936* (Cambridge: Cambridge University Press, 1993).

evident in the 1930s, with the former powerfully present in the First Five-Year Plan period and the latter dominating in the mid-1930s. The contradictions between those aspects of Stalinism that extended the revolutionary egalitarian and participatory impulses of 1917 and those that resurrected stratification and authoritarianism remained in irresolvable tension with one another.

The ultimate "man of the machine," Stalin was one of the least likely candidates for charismatic hero. Short in stature, reticent in meetings and on public occasions, neither a talented orator like Trotsky or Zinoviev, nor an attractive and engaging personality like Lenin or Bukharin, Stalin did not himself project an image of a leader—until it was created for him (and by him) through the cult. First the promotion of a cult of Lenin, which Stalin actively encouraged, then his identification as a loyal Leninist, and eventually his merger with and substitution for the image of Lenin were important props for Stalin's authority both within the party and in society.[48] All this was accomplished in a political culture based on the prerevolutionary Bolshevik traditions in which emphasis on personality, the exaggerated importance of the leader, and the attendant sacral notions of infallibility were all alien. In his revealing study, historian Jan Plamper illustrates how the Stalin cult embodied the "five characteristics that typify a modern personality cult: the secularism and the new basis on popular sovereignty; the patricentrism; the targeting at the masses; the use of mass media and uniform, mass-produced cult products; and the limitation to closed societies."[49] The first appearance of a Stalin cult was on his purported fiftieth birthday on December 21, 1929, but the cult was kept modest for some years afterwards. By 1935 Stalin had taken control of how he would be presented to the public, and close comrades like Kliment Voroshilov worked with him to refine and define his image.[50] Manipulation of photographs and films, the elimination of disgraced figures, left Stalin as the principal personification of the achievements of Soviet socialism.

48   Robert C. Tucker, "The Rise of Stalin's Personality Cult," *American Historical Review* LXXXIV, 2 (April 1979), pp. 347–66. A key role in the effort to link Stalin with the legacy of Lenin was played by Stalin's assistant, Tovstukha, who worked in the Lenin Institute from 1924 to 1926, helped edit the first two volumes of Lenin's collected works, edited the first nine editions of Stalin's collection of articles *Problemy leninizma*, and wrote the first official Soviet biography of Stalin (1927). Rosenfeldt, *Knowledge and Power*, pp. 170–74; *Pravda*, August 10, 1935, pp. 1, 3; I. B. Rusanova, "I. P. Tovstukha. K 80-letiiu so dnia rozhdeniia," *Voprosy istorii KPSS*, no. 4 (1969), pp. 128–30.

49   Jan Plamper, *The Stalin Cult: A Study in the Alchemy of Power* (New Haven, CT: Yale University Press, 2012), p. 5.

50   Ibid., pp. 119–64.

The ideological props of the Stalin dictatorship were both a radically revised Marxism and a pro-Russian nationalism and étatism. Class warfare was seen as inevitable and intensifying rather than diminishing as the country approached socialism. As long as the country was surrounded by hostile capitalist states, it was claimed, state power had to be built up. When the Soviet Union was declared to be socialist by Stalin in 1936, the positive achievement of reaching a stage of history higher than the rest of the world was tempered by the constant reminders that the enemies of socialism exist within the country and are deceptive and concealed and must be "unmasked," and powerfully threaten the USSR from outside ("capitalist encirclement"). Repeated references to dangers and insecurity and to the need for "vigilance" justified the enormous reliance on the "steel gauntlets of Ezhov," a reference to the People's Commissar of Internal Affairs (1936–38), Nikolai Ezhov, who orchestrated the major purges of the late 1930s.

Inventing Opposition

The enthusiasm for industrialization was tempered by much less support for Stalin's agrarian revolution. The peasants' open and often violent resistance to collectivization was reflected in less dramatic form by quiet forms of opposition within the party. The oligarchy that carried out the Stalin revolution was a very narrow political elite but not one that had effectively closed the party to debate and consideration of alternatives. Between the fall of Bukharin in 1928–29 and the murder of Sergei Kirov in December 1934, Stalin-faction rule produced and reproduced actual and potential oppositions. The evident failures and costs of rapid industrialization and full collectivization and dekulakization fueled real disagreements with Stalin's General Line. In his own statements Stalin refused to accept any blame for the economic chaos or the resultant famines in Ukraine, the Volga region, and Kazakhstan. In his words, "the last remnants of moribund classes," some of which had "even managed to worm their way into the party," were actively sabotaging the building of socialism. Therefore, more repression was needed: "The abolition of classes is not achieved by the extinction of the class struggle, but its intensification.... We must bear in mind that the growth of the power of the Soviet state will intensify the resistance of the last remnants of the dying classes."[51] In a letter replying to the Cossack writer Mikhail Sholokhov's

---

51   Originally this was an idea put forth by Trotsky. I. V. Stalin, "Itogi pervoi

protests against the systematic brutality of the grain collection, Stalin sneered at his sympathy for the villagers:

> One must take into account ... the other side. And that other side amounts to the fact that the respected corn-growers of your region (and not only your region) have gone on a sit-down strike (sabotage!) and shown no concern about leaving the workers, the Red Army, without grain. The fact that the sabotage was peaceful and outwardly bloodless in no way alters the realities—that the respected grain-growers have in essence carried out a "peaceful" war with Soviet power. A war by starvation [*voina na izmor*], dear Comrade Sholokhov.[52]

The growing gap between the public statements and images put forth by the state, on the one hand, and the real destruction in the countryside, on the other, prompted prominent party members to resist the cover-up of the failures. Already in late 1930, some in the leadership of the RSFSR and the Transcaucasian Federation expressed misgivings, which, in turn, were interpreted by the Stalin center as a widespread and united oppositional tendency (the Syrtsov-Lominadze Right-Left Bloc).[53] Swift retribution (demotion in these cases) did not deter a number of other critical foci to emerge, notably the Riutin Platform and Appeal (1932) and the Smirnov, Tolmachev, and Eismont opposition (1932). Within the Central Committee and the Politburo, more moderate elements opposed

---

piatiletki: Doklad 7 ianvaria 1933 g.," *Sochineniia* (Moscow: Gosudarstvennoe izdatel'-stvo politicheskoi literatury, 1951), XII, pp. 211–12.

52   Quoted by Khrushchev, *Pravda*, March 8, 1963; *Pravda*, March 10, 1963; Jonathan Haslam, "Political Opposition to Stalin and the Origins of the Terror in Russia, 1932–1936," *The Historical Journal* XXIX, 2 (1986), p. 403.

53   R. W. Davies, "The Syrtsov–Lominadze Affair, *Soviet Studies* XXXIII, 1 (January 1981), pp. 29–50. Indicative of the mood in the party is a conversation with Lominadze reported by a friend: "When I saw him, with another of his friends, in 1931, he was boldly critical of Stalin's leadership. Now that opposition from both Left and Right had been suppressed, he thought the next logical step was a radical reform of the Party and its personnel.

'What about the General Secretary?' asked his friend. 'If there is a spring cleaning, every piece of furniture has to be removed, including the biggest one.'

'But who could replace him?'

'That's up to the Congress.' It was time for younger men to take a share of the responsibility—men who had some practical experience but had been less involved in the struggle between the factions.

Needless to say, this was extremely risky talk. It even occurred to me that Lominadze saw himself as a suitable successor to Stalin." Joseph Berger, *Shipwreck of a Generation: The Memoirs of Joseph Berger* (London: Harvill Press, 1971); American edition: *Nothing But the Truth* (New York: John Day, 1971), p. 166.

the rapid tempos in industry and proposed a more conciliatory attitude toward society, particularly the peasantry.

The short-lived attempt to organize opposition to Stalin by Martem'ian Ivanovich Riutin never went further than a few meetings of like-minded party members, the formation of an organization (the Union of Marxist-Leninists), the discussion of Riutin's report "Stalin and the Crisis of the Proletarian Dictatorship," and an appeal to party members to join their efforts. Riutin condemned Stalin's emerging dictatorship as the negation of the collective leadership of the Central Committee and the principal cause of the growing disillusionment of the people with socialism. He believed that the only way to save Bolshevism was to remove Stalin and his clique by force. If Riutin was right that "the faith of the masses in socialism has been broken, its readiness to defend selflessly the proletarian revolution from all enemies weakens each year," then the regime had either to move immediately toward conciliation and the rebuilding of confidence or turn to even more radical and repressive measures.[54]

Riutin's circle was an unusual instance of coherence and organization among those who opposed Stalin.[55] Much more evident was a broad, inchoate discontent with Stalin's rule that permeated political and intellectual circles. Several loyal Stalinists, like G. N. Kaminskii, Stanislav Kosior, Iosif Vareikis, and K. Ia. Bauman, harbored serious doubts about Stalin's agricultural policies. Others, like Mykola Skrypnyk, a co-founder of the Ukrainian Communist Party who had sided with Stalin in the 1920s

---

54   On Riutin, see "Stalin i krizis proletarskoi diktatury" [Platform of the Union of Marxist–Leninists (the Riutin Group)], *Izvestiia TsK KPSS*, no. 8 (1990), pp. 200–7; no. 9, pp. 165–83; no. 10, pp. 191–206; no. 11, pp. 161–86; no. 12, pp. 180–99, with commentary, pp. 200–2; M. Riutin, "Ko vsem chlenam VKP(b)" [the Appeal], reprinted in Kh. Kobo (ed.), *Osmyslit' kult Stalina* (Moscow: Progress, 1989), pp. 618–23; "O dele tak nazyvaemogo 'Soiuza Marksistov–Lenintsev'," *Izvestiia TsK KPSS*, no. 6 (1989), pp. 103–15. See also the biography of Riutin by B. A. Starkov in *Izvestiia TsK KPSS*, no. 3 (1990), pp. 150–63, followed by Riutin's letters, pp. 163–78.

55   The members of the Riutin group were arrested a few weeks after their first meeting. Riutin had been expelled from the party in 1930, and his seventeen associates were expelled by the Central Control Commission on October 9, 1932, for "having attempted to set up a bourgeois, kulak organization to re-establish capitalism and, in particular, the kulak system in the USSR by means of underground activity under the fraudulent banner of 'Marxism–Leninism.'" A number of accounts hold that Stalin demanded the death penalty for Riutin but was thwarted by Kirov and other moderates. Boris I. Nicolaevsky, *Power and the Soviet Elite: "The Letter of an Old Bolshevik" and Other Essays* (New York: Frederick A. Praeger, 1965), pp. 3–65; Arkadii Vaksberg, "Kak zhivoi s zhivymi," *Literaturnaia gazeta*, June 29, 1988; Lev Razgon, "Nakonets!" *Moskovskie novosti*, June 26, 1988; Dmitrii Volkogonov, *Triumf i tragediia: Politicheskii portret I. V. Stalina*, I, part 2 (Moscow: Novosti, 1989), pp. 85–6. Riutin was sentenced to ten years solitary confinement. On January 10, 1937, he was secretly tried and shot.

and early 1930s, were critical of the growing ethnocentrism in the party and state and the evident pro-Russianness of Stalin's nationality policies.[56] Perhaps most ominously, tensions arose between the Red Army commander, Mikhail Tukhachevskii, who called in 1930 for expansion of the armed forces, particularly aviation and tank armies, and Stalin and Voroshilov, who opposed what they called "Red militarism."[57] During the famine in Ukraine high military officers, like Iona Iakir, angered Stalin by reporting their upset at peasant resistance, which, they felt, could spread to the troops, and demanding that more grain be kept in the region.[58]

Even among Stalin's closest supporters, there were fractures, though their precise nature remains mysterious. The open disagreement at the Seventeenth Party Congress (January–February 1934) between Orjonikidze and Molotov over industrial targets was a rare public sign of a deeper split between moderates and radicals.[59] The popular Sergei Kirov, the only real rival left to Stalin by 1932, was, in all his public and political appearances, completely loyal to the General Secretary, though he often emphasized the need for "revolutionary legality," which was understood to be a lessening of repressive measures.[60] Stalin still represented for the majority of party members the militant turn toward socialism—collectivization, rapid industrialization, the destruction of organized political opposition. However, his personal proclivity toward the use of force seemed to some to have gone beyond the broad bounds of Bolshevik practice.

The private letters from the vacationing Stalin to his closest comrade Molotov (from 1930 and 1933) reveal in a striking way the less public characteristics of the dictator and his methods of rule. He wrote short, terse memoranda to Molotov on the important matters that were before the Politburo and did the same with Voroshilov, Lazar Kaganovich, Orjonikidze, and others. "From the boss (*khoziain*) we are receiving

---

56   Skrypnyk committed suicide in 1933, as Ukrainian national communists were systematically being purged.

57   R. W. Davies, *The Industrialisation of Soviet Russia, 3: The Soviet Economy in Turmoil, 1929–1930* (Cambridge, MA: Harvard University Press, 1989), pp. 446–7. In May 1932 Stalin apologized to Tukhachevskii and endorsed some of his proposed reforms.

58   Eventually some grain was sent to Ukraine in January 1933 along with the new party boss, Pavl Postyshev.

59   Kendall E. Bailes, *Technology and Society under Lenin and Stalin: Origins of the Soviet Technical Intelligentsia, 1917–1941* (Princeton, NJ: Princeton University Press, 1978), pp. 275–80; J. Arch Getty, *Origins of the Great Purges: The Soviet Communist Party Reconsidered, 1933–1938* (Cambridge: Cambridge University Press, 1985), pp. 13–17.

60   S. Kirov, *Stati i rechi, 1934* (Moscow, 1934).

regular and frequent directives," Kaganovich wrote Orjonikidze in 1932.[61] While he preferred to work through his own narrow circle of friends— Molotov, who was his principal executor, Voroshilov, Mikoyan, Orjonikidze, Kaganovich—Stalin was quick to turn on any of them if he felt challenged. In 1933, he severely criticized Orjonikidze for objecting to remarks by Andrei Vyshinskii that attacked those working in the industrial and agricultural ministries: "The behavior of Sergo (and Iakovlev) in the story of the 'completeness of production' is impossible to call anything else but anti-party, because it has as its objective goal the defense of reactionary elements of the party *against* the CC VKP(b)."[62] Because Kaganovich had sided with Orjonikidze, he too fell under Stalin's wrath. Nothing came of this dispute at the time, nor of the more serious accusations made against Mikhail Kalinin.

The OGPU was carrying out investigations in 1930 into a series of anti-Soviet "parties" made up of former Mensheviks, industrial specialists, and Ukrainian activists.[63] Stalin received regular reports from Genrikh Iagoda and insisted that Molotov circulate them among the members of the Central Committee and the Central Control Commission, as well as among "the more active of our *khoziaistvenniki* (economic managers)." He told Molotov that he was convinced that these conspiratorial elements were linked with the Rightists within the party: "It is absolutely essential to shoot Kondrat'ev, Groman and a pair of the other bastards (*merzavtsy*).... It is absolutely essential to shoot the whole group of wreckers in meat production and to publish this information in the press."[64] He personally demanded the arrests of the former Menshevik Nikolai Sukhanov, his Communist wife (who, he says, must have known what was going on in their home), Bazarov, Ramzin, and others.[65] The concocted stories of anti-Soviet conspiracies were fed throughout the top bureaucracy and created an atmosphere of suspicion that justified the use of precisely the kinds of harsh measures that Stalin advocated. The head of the party had developed a mentality that was fed by reports

---

61 "Pis'ma Stalina Molotovu," p. 94.
62 Ibid.
63 Ibid., p. 103.
64 Ibid.
65 The irony is extraordinary. Sukhanov was a principal chronicler of the Russian Revolution, a Menshevik-Internationalist opposed to the Bolsheviks. His wife, on the other hand, was on the other side. On the eve of the October Revolution she made sure that her husband was out of their apartment and invited the Bolshevik Central Committee to meet there as they plotted the move against the Provisional Government, that is, the October Revolution.

from the police and intelligence agencies and confirmed what he already suspected—that there were enemies abroad, principally Britain, Poland, and Romania, preparing to attack the USSR, and that they were aided by domestic enemies, principally elements from tsarist society, White Army officers, political oppositionists, and even party members who resisted the new General Line of the Central Committee.

Fear and the need for vigilance, which were created both by the police findings and the real and imagined weaknesses and insecurities of the Soviet Union, made up an affective disposition—a mental universe of feelings and understandings—that exaggerated threats, envisioned conspiracies, and bound many leading Communists together around the leader who projected an image of Bolshevik toughness. At the same time the Stalinist settlement involved the creation of a highly hierarchical system of rewards and privileges, of access to information and influence, that effectively disenfranchised the great mass of the population and privileged a small number of party and state officials, intellectuals, and managers. The end of rationing in 1934–35 forced everyone below the privileged upper levels of society to forage in government stores and peasant markets for what they could afford. Social inequalities grew in an economy of permanent shortages where money talked less effectively than one's position and personal connections. A "ruling class without tenure," in Moshe Lewin's phrase, grew increasingly dependent on being in favor with those even higher up.[66] They were under a constant threat of demotion, expulsion from the party, arrest, and even death. Their success required absolute and unquestioning obedience, enforcement of the decisions from the top with determination, even ruthlessness, on those below, and a willingness to acquiesce and participate in what can only be considered criminal activity (denunciations of the innocent, approval of lawlessness, collaboration with a regime based on deception).[67] Their dilemma was that it was dangerous for them to be anything but responsive to the top, and yet their position and requirements to increase production and satisfy the demands of the top and the center pulled them toward making arrangements with the bottom and the periphery.

---

66   Moshe Lewin, "The Social Background of Stalinism," in Robert C. Tucker (ed.), *Stalinism: Essays in Historical Interpretation* (New York: W. W. Norton, 1977), p. 130.

67   Roi Medvedev, *Oni okruzhali Stalina* (Moscow, 1990); English translation: *All Stalin's Men* (Garden City, NY: Doubleday, 1984); Sheila Fitzpatrick, *On Stalin's Team: The Years of Living Dangerously in Soviet Politics* (Princeton, NJ: Princeton University Press, 2015).

Conservative Revolutionary

Neither a consistent moderate nor radical, Stalin himself shifted from center-right (during his alliance with Bukharin in the mid-1920s) to left (during the so-called Cultural Revolution, 1928–1931) and then back to a more moderate position around 1931–32. Responding to a growing mood among party leaders concerned with industry, Stalin announced in June 1931 a major change in the party's wage policy (the end of *uravnilovka*, leveling of wages, and the introduction of greater differentials between skilled and unskilled workers in order to end labor migration) and a much more tolerant and supportive policy toward the technical intelligentsia.[68] Whether or not this policy shift was imposed on Stalin or corresponded to a genuine re-evaluation of his position, during the next half decade he steadily began to reverse the more radical policies of the end of the 1920s and the early 1930s (collectivization and recklessly rapid industrialization) and pull back from egalitarianism and collectivism toward a promotion of hierarchy, cultural traditionalism, and social conservatism that has come to be known as the Great Retreat.[69]

On a variety of fronts, the Stalinists retreated from their forward positions of just a few years earlier. Though the collective farms remained firmly under the tutelage of the state and continued to operate essentially as grain-collection apparatuses, a series of decisions allowed the collective-farm peasants to possess some livestock, to sell their surpluses on the market, and to own their houses and work household plots.[70] While workers were increasingly restricted in their movements through the 1930s, an essentially "bourgeois" system of remuneration was created: "from each according to his ability, to each according to his work." Workers were encouraged to compete with one another not only to maximize output but also to win material rewards, and various collective

---

68   I. V. Stalin, "Novaia obstanovka—novye zadachi khoziaistvennogo stroitel'stva," *Sochineniia*, XIII, pp. 51–80. Bailes shows how this conciliatory move was initiated by Orjonikidze and others involved in industrial production: *Technology and Society*, pp. 144–55.

69   Nicholas Timasheff, *The Great Retreat: The Growth and Decline of Communism in Russia* (New York: E. P. Dutton & Co., 1946).

70   Moshe Lewin, "'Taking Grain': Soviet Policies of Agricultural Procurements Before the War," *The Making of the Soviet System: Essays in the Social History of Interwar Russia* (New York: Pantheon, 1985), pp. 142–77. "Peasants in Stalin's times were indeed legally bound to their place of work, submitted to a special legal regimen, and—through the kolkhoz—to a form of collective responsibility with regard to state duties. They were transformed, not unlike as in pre-emancipation times, into an estate placed at the very bottom of the social ladder" (p. 176).

forms of organizing work and payment were eliminated.[71] Progressive piecework was introduced in the spring of 1934, and while real wages fell for most workers a significant number of *udarniki* (shock workers) and *stakhanovtsy* participated in the more "joyous" life that Stalin had promised.[72] Worker power declined and that of managers and technicians increased.[73] "The Party wanted the bosses to be efficient, powerful, harsh, impetuous, and capable of exerting pressure crudely and ruthlessly and getting results 'whatever the cost'.... The formation of the despotic manager was actually a process in which not leaders but *rulers* were made."[74] In the words of Mikhail Kaganovich, Lazar's brother, "The ground must shake when the factory director enters the plant."

The severe economic crisis of the winter of 1932–33, as well as the coming to power of Hitler in Germany, helped accelerate the swing toward state policies that favored the educated and ambitious and eased the pressure on others. By the middle of 1933 arrests and deportations declined; production targets for the Second Five-Year Plan were reduced; and consumer goods were given higher priority. As one historian sums it up:

> In the mid-1930s Soviet society struck a balance that would carry it through the turmoil of the purges, the Great War and reconstruction. The coercive policies of the Cultural Revolution [1928–31] were replaced or supplemented by the use of inducements. Benefits were quickly apparent: education opened professional opportunities; a stable countryside improved dietary standards; increased production and income encouraged consumerism. A lightened mood swept the nation. Women wore make-up; young people revived ballroom dancing. Life, as Stalin said, and Lebedev-Kumach's popular song repeated, had become better and happier.[75]

71   Lewis H. Siegelbaum, "Production Collectives and Communes and the 'Imperatives' of Soviet Industrialization, 1929–1931," *Slavic Review* XLV, 1 (Spring 1986), pp. 65–84.

72   Siegelbaum, *Stakhanovism and the Politics of Productivity in the USSR, 1935–1941*, particularly Chapter 6, "Stakhanovites in the Cultural Mythology of the 1930s."

73   Kuromiya, *Stalin's Industrial Revolution*, pp. 50–77.

74   Moshe Lewin, "Society, State, and Ideology during the First Five-Year Plan," in Sheila Fitzpatrick (ed.), *Cultural Revolution in Russia, 1928–1931* (Bloomington: Indiana University Press, 1978), p. 74.

75   James van Geldern, "The Centre and the Periphery: Cultural and Social Geography in the Mass Culture of the 1930s," in Stephen White (ed.), *New Directions in Soviet History* (Cambridge: Cambridge University Press, 1992), p. 62.

A new Soviet middle class developed with its own form of "bourgeois values." More attention was paid to private life. From Stakhanovite workers, with their newly acquired bicycles and wristwatches, to factory managers and their wives, who were on the receiving end of Stalin's "Big Deal," a certain level of security and material improvement, "a sense of pride and participation," wedded them to the order created by Stalin.[76]

James van Geldern emphasizes how Soviet citizens were turned into spectators in the 1930s, rather than active participants. Formal, meaningless voting, viewing the leaders atop Lenin's mausoleum, were "rituals of participation," public observations of political spectacles.[77] The promotion of new heroes, from aviators to polar explorers, and extended public dramas—like the rescue of downed female fliers and ice-bound sailors—riveted public attention and reinforced the values of the modernizing party/state.[78] An empire was created disguised as a voluntary federation of free peoples, with a reconstructed Moscow at its center, and festivals of reaffirmation, like the Moscow Olympiad of Folk Music, periodically reminding people of the unbreakable unity of a diverse, continent-size country. Ideas of progress—the conquest of recalcitrant nature, the overcoming of peasant "darkness" and the isolation of remote villages, the building of the Moscow Metro—enhanced the heroic nature of Soviet leaders and the efforts of the Soviet people. Sacrifice and vigilance went along with pride in *nashi dostizheniia* (our achievements). The image of the motherland (*rodina*) was revived, gradually displacing that of the international community of proletarians, until, in 1943, Stalin cavalierly dissolved Lenin's Third International. In 1939, he had proposed, as a joke to German Foreign Minister Ribbentrop: "Let's drink to the new anti-Cominternist—Stalin!"[79]

In his public rhetoric of these years, Stalin maintained his severity and toughness, qualities that had long been part of Bolshevik culture, but showed that, under pressure, he could be more flexible and accommodating. He seemed to be not only a competent commander to many

76   Ibid.; Siegelbaum, *Stakhanovism and the Politics of Productivity in the USSR, 1935–1941*, pp. 210–46. The idea of the "Big Deal," Stalin's exchange of material goods and security for loyalty, is the theme of Vera Dunham, *In Stalin's Time: Middleclass Values in Soviet Fiction* (Cambridge: Cambridge University Press, 1976).

77   Van Geldern, "The Centre and the Periphery," p. 71.

78   For a textured treatment of life in Moscow at the height of Stalinism, see Karl Schlögel, *Moscow 1937*, trans. Rodney Livingstone (Cambridge, UK and Malden, MA: Polity Press, 2012).

79   *Sto sorok besed s Molotovym: Iz dnevnika F. Chueva* (Moscow: Terra, 1991), p. 19; *Molotov Remembers: Inside Kremlin Politics: Conversations with Felix Chuev*, edited by Albert Resis (Chicago: Ivan R. Dee, 1993), p. 12.

but indeed an indispensable leader in a time of political stress and economic crisis. A high party official, Barmin, wrote about this period (1932): "Loyalty to Stalin was based principally on the conviction that there was no one to take his place, that any change of leadership would be extremely dangerous, and that the country must continue in its present course, since to stop now or attempt a retreat would mean the loss of everything."[80] Rumors that Stalin had suggested that he resign (probably after the suicide of his second wife, Nadezhda Allilueva, in November 1932) were embellished by reports of his associates rallying around him.[81]

The years of upheaval and uncertainty of the early 1930s were clearly coming to an end by the opening of the Seventeenth Party Congress in late January 1934. Though the full story has yet to be told, there appears to have been a movement at the Congress to replace Stalin with Kirov, but Kirov's differences with Stalin were not great enough for the Leningrad leader to repudiate the General Secretary as many others wished. Oppositions had been rendered impotent, and a new emphasis on "revolutionary legality" seemed to promise a more orderly, procedural, less disruptive mode of governance. The oligarchic bureaucratic system appeared more secure than ever, though many still feared the trend toward personal autocracy by Stalin. As Lewin notes:

> Stalin was not ready to accept the role of just a cog, however powerful, in his own machine. A top bureaucrat is a chief executive, in the framework of a constraining committee.... But Stalin had had the power, and the taste for it—for ever more of it—since he had led the early stage of the shattering breakthrough and gotten full control over the state in the process. At this point, the traits of his gloomy personality, with clear paranoid tendencies become crucial. Once at the top and in full control, he

---

80   A. Barmine, *One Who Survived* (New York: G. P. Putnam's Sons, 1945), pp. 200–1. When the Menshevik Fedor Dan asked Bukharin in 1936 why he and other Communists had so blindly trusted Stalin, Bukharin answered, "You don't understand this; it is completely different. It is not he who is trusted but a man whom the party trusts; it happened that he became a kind of symbol of the party, [and] the lower ranks, the workers, the people believe in him; maybe this is our fault but that is how it happened, that is why we all climb into his mouth ... knowing for sure that he will eat us. And he knows this and only chooses the right moment." "On pozhret nas," from the archive of L. O. Dan in the Institute of Social History, Amsterdam, published in Kh. Kobo (ed.), *Osmyslit' kul't Stalina: perestroika—glasnost', demokrati´ia, so´t'sializm* (Moscow: Progress, 1989), p. 610.

81   On Stalin's relationship with his second wife, see "'Nadezhde Sergeevne Allil-uevoi, lichno ot Stalina' (Perepiska 1928–1931 godov)," *Istochnik: Dokumenty russkoi istorii*, no. 0 (1993), pp. 9–22.

was not a man to accept changes in the pattern of his personal power....
He therefore took the road of shaking up, of destabilizing the machinery
and its upper layers, in order to block the process fatally working against
his personal predilection for autocracy.[82]

Terror and Autocracy

The half-dozen years before the murder of Kirov (December 1934) might
be seen as the prehistory of Stalinism, the period of formation of the
political structures and social conditions that created the possibility for
a regime of extreme centralization of power, overwhelming dominance
of a weakened society, and particular ferocity. The unlimited despotism
of Stalinism was the product of the Great Purges, which simultaneously
eliminated all possible resistance and created a new and more loyal elite
with which the tyrant could rule.

Dissatisfaction with Stalin's rule and with the harsh material conditions was palpable in the mid-1930s, and the regime faced the difficulties
of controlling the family circles and local feudatories (particularly in
the union republics). One of the effects of the purges was the replacement of an older political and economic elite with a younger, potentially
more loyal one,[83] consisting primarily of promoted workers, party rank-
and-file, and young technicians, who would make up the Soviet elite
through the post-Stalin period until the early 1980s.[84] "Stalin—and, for
that matter, the majority of Soviet citizens" writes Sheila Fitzpatrick,

saw the cadres of the mid 1930s less in their old role as revolutionaries
than in the current role as bosses. There is even some evidence that Stalin
saw them as Soviet boyars (feudal lords) and himself as a latter-day Ivan
the Terrible, who had to destroy the boyars to build a modern nation
state and a new service nobility.[85]

---

82   Lewin, "The Social Background of Stalinism," pp. 130–1.

83   A. L. Unger, "Stalin's Renewal of the Leading Stratum: A Note on the Great
Purge," *Soviet Studies* XX, 3 (January 1969), pp. 321–30; Bailes, *Technology and Society
under Lenin and Stalin*, pp. 268–71, 412–3; Sheila Fitzpatrick, "Stalin and the Making
of a New Elite, 1928–1939," *Slavic Review* XXXVIII, 3 (September 1979), pp. 377–402.

84   Bailes criticizes Fitzpatrick for not distinguishing between those who rose into
the intelligentsia through formal education, many of whom were workers (the *vydvizhentsy*), and the *praktiki*, who were elevated through their work experience. "Stalin
and the Making of a New Elite: A Comment," *Slavic Review* XXXIX, 2 (June 1980),
pp. 286–9.

85   Sheila Fitzpatrick, *The Russian Revolution* (Oxford: Oxford University Press,
1982), p. 159. Comparisons to the Russian past—autocracy, the service nobility, the

There is no consensus among scholars as to the motivations behind the purges. Interpretations range from the idea that purging was a permanent and necessary component of totalitarianism in lieu of elections (Zbigniew Brzezinski) to seeing the Great Terror as an extreme form of political infighting (J. Arch Getty).[86] Yet neither arguments from social context nor functionalist deductions from effects to causes have successfully eliminated the principal catalyst to the Terror, the will and ambition of the dictator himself.[87] The Great Purges have been seen traditionally as an effort "to achieve an unrestricted personal dictatorship with a totality of power that [Stalin] did not yet possess in 1934."[88] Stalin guided and prodded the arrests, show trials, and executions forward, aided by the closest members of his entourage: Molotov, Kaganovich, Andrei Zhdanov, Malenkov, Mikoyan, and Ezhov.[89] Stalin's personal involvement in the details of the Terror have been indisputably demonstrated by archival documents released in the late 1980s and early 1990s. One such note to Ezhov will suffice to illustrate the type of intervention the *vozhd'* exercised. In May 1937, he wrote: "One might think that prison for Beloborodov is a podium for reading speeches, statements which refer to the activities of all sorts of people but not to himself. Isn't it time to squeeze this gentleman and make him tell about his dirty deeds? Where is he, in prison or in a hotel?"[90] Here, personality and politics merged, and the degree of excess repression was dictated by the peculiar demands of Stalin himself, who could not tolerate limits on his will set by the very ruling elite that he had brought to power.

---

collective-farm peasantry as serfs—are used metaphorically by Moshe Lewin and are central to the analysis of Robert C. Tucker in *Stalin in Power: The Revolution from Above, 1928–1941* (New York: W. W. Norton, 1973).

86   Getty, *Origins of the Great Purges*, p. 206; and his *Practicing Stalinism: Bolsheviks, Boyars, and the Persistence of Tradition* (New Haven, CT: Yale University Press, 2013). For a range of views on the purges, particularly of the so-called "revisionists," see J. Arch Getty and Roberta T. Manning (eds.), *Stalinist Terror: New Perspectives* (Cambridge: Cambridge University Press, 1993).

87   See the excellent review article by Oleg Khlevniuk, "Top Down Vs. Bottom Up: Regarding the Potential of Contemporary 'Revisionism'," *Cahier du monde russe* LIV, 4 (2015), pp. 837–57.

88   Robert C. Tucker, "Introduction," in Robert C. Tucker and Stephen F. Cohen (eds.), *The Great Purge Trial* (New York: Grosset & Dunlap, 1965), p. xxix. This is essentially the argument of the second volume of his Stalin biography, as well as the view of Robert Conquest in *The Great Terror: Stalin's Purge of the Thirties* (New York: Macmillan, 1968); *The Great Terror: A Reassessment* (New York: Oxford University Press, 1990).

89   Boris A. Starkov, "Narkom Ezhov," in Getty and Manning (eds.), *Stalinist Terror*, pp. 21–39.

90   *Dialog* (Leningrad), no. 4 (1990), p. 21; cited in Starkov, "Narkom Ezhov," in ibid., p. 29.

Whatever his authentic political aspirations, Stalin was marked by his deep suspiciousness and insecurity. Bukharin told the old Mensheviks Fedor and Lydia Dan that Stalin

> is even unhappy because he cannot convince everyone, and even himself, that he is greater than everyone, and this is his unhappiness, perhaps the most human feature in him, perhaps the only human feature in him, but already not human. Here is something diabolical: because of his great "unhappiness" he cannot but avenge himself on people, on all people, but especially on those who are somehow higher, better than he.[91]

His affective disposition, which sensed and exaggerated threats to himself and the Soviet political system, was reinforced by his perception that real dangers to Soviet power were intensifying from both outside the USSR and within. He grew increasingly anxious about the potential catastrophe presented by the Spanish Civil War and divisions within the Left.[92] Historian Oleg Khlevniuk points out:

> On 29 September 1936, the same day that the Politburo passed its resolution to intervene in Spain, Ezhov was named the new head of the People's Commissariat of Internal Affairs. Repression received a renewed impetus. Stalin was extraordinarily active in following the situation in Spain as it escalated in 1937–1938. He issued a great many orders to the Soviet representatives in that country. He concluded that the headquarters of the Republican forces contained many spies and hidden enemies, and ordered their unmasking and elimination. Explaining the key to the "conspiracy" in the leadership of the Red Army to the members of the War Council of the USSR People's Commissar of Defense on 2 June 1937, Stalin declared, "They wanted to make a second Spain in the USSR." The expansion of the army and of war industries began to accelerate in

---

91   "On pozhret nas," p. 610.

92   In the memoirs of Pavl Sudoplatov, the spymaster recalls in dubious detail his conversation with Stalin and Beria when he was assigned to organize the assassination of Trotsky in Mexico. He quotes Stalin as saying, "Trotsky should be eliminated within a year, before war inevitably breaks out. Without the elimination of Trotsky, as the Spanish experience shows, when the imperialists attack the Soviet Union we cannot rely on our allies in the international Communist movement. They will face great difficulties in fulfilling their international duty to destabilize the rear of our enemies by sabotage operations and guerrilla warfare if they have to deal with treacherous infiltrations by Trotskyites in their ranks." Pavel Sudoplatov and Anatoli Sudoplatov, with Jerrold L. and Leona P. Schecter, *Special Tasks: The Memoirs of an Unwanted Witness—A Soviet Spymaster* (Boston: Little, Brown and Company, 1994), p. 67.

1936. The list of related facts might continue. All of this bears witness to the fact that Stalin considered the world situation threatening. The very idea of a "fifth column" first appeared during the Spanish Civil, which he considered a possible scenario for the USSR.[93]

In his study of Stalin's purge of the military, Peter Whitewood focuses on the fabrication of conspiracies by Ezhov and argues, "Stalin attacked the Red Army because he seriously misperceived a serious security threat."[94] Rather than a pragmatic effort to achieve unity and conformity as preparation for war, Whitewood contends, "Stalin seems to have genuinely believed that foreign-backed enemies had infiltrated the ranks and managed to organize a conspiracy at the very heart of the Red Army."[95] The particular Marxist lens through which Stalin and leading Communists understood the world distorted the level of threat both foreign and domestic, and the Red Army in particular was perceived "as an obvious target of foreign agents and domestic counterrevolutionaries throughout the 1920s and 1930s."[96] Whitewood believes that Stalin, acting from vulnerability and misperception rather than strength and confidence, took these threats seriously and responded with the devastating execution of his leading officers and the arrests of thousands of others. Convinced that another war lay not far in the future and that an anti-Soviet "Fifth Column" existed in the army, there was no alternative—so Whitewood argues—to the purging of the military and the subsequent "mass operations" that targeted former kulaks, criminals, and national minorities.

Suspicion of the army was not new in the late 1930s. Already during the Civil War (1918–21), the principal secret police agency, the Cheka, and its successors considered the army to be riddled with spies. Bolsheviks were deeply suspicious of the so-called "military specialists," those who had served in the tsarist army and now made up a large part of the officer corps of the Red Army. The "political police's particular conception of army vulnerability ... eventually achieved dominance in 1937."[97]

---

93   Khlevniuk, "Top Down Vs. Bottom Up," p. 845. See also Oleg Khlevniuk, "The Reasons for the 'Great Terror': The Foreign-Political Aspect," in S. Pons and A. Romano (eds.), *Russia in the Age of Wars, 1914–1945* (Milan: Giangiacomo Feltrinelli, 2000), pp. 159–69; and Hiroaki Kuromiya, "Accounting for the 'Great Terror,'" *Jahrbücher für Geschichte Osteuropas* LIII, 1 (January 2005), pp. 86–101.

94   Peter Whitewood, *The Red Army and the Great Terror: Stalin's Purge of the Soviet Military* (Lawrence: University Press of Kansas, 2015), p. 12.

95   Ibid., p. 276.

96   Ibid., p. 13.

97   Ibid., p. 42.

Within this siege mentality people like Stalin imagined and exaggerated dangers to the weak and beleaguered Soviet state. Yet, through the 1920s, the People's Commissar of the Military and Navy, Voroshilov, managed to shield the army from suspicions that foreign agents or Trotskyists had made the state's military arm vulnerable. The old doubts lingered, but no purges took place until many rank-and-file soldiers supported those who resisted the drive to collectivize the peasants in 1928. Two years later, the police rounded up and arrested military specialists, fabricating a scenario that they had conspired to overthrow the Soviet state.

Already predisposed to see foreign agents worming their way into the Soviet system, Stalin was especially receptive to the conspiracies "uncovered" by his political police. He hesitated on several occasions when evidence was presented that his most talented officer, Mikhail Tukhachevskii, was unreliable, too close to the Germans, and cited by informers to be part of a plot against the regime. Tukhachevskii was despised by Stalin's close ally, Voroshilov, whom most historians consider to have been a military lightweight. The Marshal was far too aggressive in asserting his own views, even provoking Stalin, but his ultimate fall was the result of a carefully embroidered fabric of false confessions. One might doubt that Stalin sincerely believed that the accused officers were guilty. More convincingly, he simply calculated that unity and conformity were more important than innocence or guilt in the light of imminent war. Ultimately, Stalin was the principal wrecker of the Red Army, and millions of Soviet people would die because of his suspicious, conspiratorial frame of mind and ruthless will to rid the country of anyone whom he considered a potential threat.

The military purge was the first series of massive arrests and executions in the late 1930s that went beyond elimination of former political oppositionists. The mass operations that followed, in which well over a million people were arrested and more than 700,000 executed, marked the height of the mass killing. The purges not only destroyed those in power but members of border nationalities and diasporas, dekulakized peasants, and myriad random individuals and groups deemed to be threats to the regime. As Khlevniuk sums up the nature of the principal victims:

> the primary focus of the terror, regardless of its intensity, was directed at members of social strata who actively resisted Stalinist politics or who were considered potential threats to the regime. Their ranks included the so-called "kulaks," peasants who resisted collectivization. Persistent targets of repression included: the pre-revolutionary privileged classes;

those who had served in the White Army; and members of groups who had rivaled the Bolshevik Party (Socialist Revolutionaries, Mensheviks, etc.). Over time, the most prominent "risk groups" came to include the Old Bolsheviks, those who had formed various oppositions, as well as rank-and-file party members who at different times had voiced "qualms" or criticized Stalin and his course of action. For much of the 1930s, criminal offenders, especially repeat offenders who had been convicted several times, were considered apolitical but still "socially harmful elements."[98]

Though the greatest number of victims came with the mass operations of 1937–38, it was the bloodletting at the top of society—the executions of Lenin's closest associates, Old Bolsheviks, prominent poets—that the world noticed. "It is one of the mysteries of Stalinism," Lewin summarizes,

> that it turned much of the fury of its bloody purges against this very real mainstay of the regime. There were among the *apparaty*, probably, still too many former members of other parties or of the original Leninist party, too many participants and victors of the civil war who remembered who had done what during those days of glory. Too many thus could feel the right to be considered founders of the regime and base on it part of the claims to a say in decisions and to security in their positions. Probably, also letting the new and sprawling administration settle and get encrusted in their chairs and habits could also encourage them to try and curtail the power of the very top and the personalized ruling style of the chief of the state—and this was probably a real prospect the paranoid leader did not relish.[99]

Stalin's initiation and personal direction of the purges was the catalyst to thousands of smaller settlings of scores.[100] "The incarceration or physical liquidation of more than a million and a half human beings," writes Stephen Kotkin,

> apparently posed no moral dilemma for him. On the contrary, to pity class enemies would be to indulge sentiment over the laws of objective historical development. Ignorance of history could be fatal, Stalin

98   Khlevniuk, "Top Down Vs. Bottom Up," p. 840.
99   Moshe Lewin, "Grappling with Stalinism," *The Making of the Soviet System*, pp. 308–9.
100   Sheila Fitzpatrick, "How the Mice Buried the Cat: Scenes from the Great Purges of 1937 in the Russian Provinces," *Russian Review* LII, 3 (July 1993), pp. 299–320.

argued, and he spent a great deal of time during the terror midwifing an accessible history of the Russian state, from its origins to the present, as a tool of mass civic training. Stalin was a massacring pedagogue.[101]

In the context of deep and recurring social tensions, the state gave the green light to resentments against the privileged, the intelligentsia, other ethnicities, outsiders. The requirement to find enemies, to blame and punish worked together with self-protection and self-promotion (and plain sadism) to expand the purges into a political holocaust. Almost all of the first secretaries of the Communist Party, the top leaders in the republics, regional and territorial committees, were arrested and shot. At the end, the Soviet Union resembled a ruined landscape, seriously weakened economically, intellectually, and militarily, but, at the same time, dominated by a towering state apparatus made up of new loyal *apparatchiki*, disciplined by the police, and presided over by a single will.

Victory and Decline, Finale and Conclusion

By the outbreak of World War II, the central government, the military, the republics and local governments, the economic infrastructure had all been brutally disciplined. Obedience and conformity had eliminated most initiative and originality. Ruling through his like-minded lieutenants, Stalin relied on specialists whenever he needed expertise or greater competence. After decimating the high command of the armed forces, his control over his military was greater than Hitler's over his, at least at the beginning of the war. He intervened and interfered in both minute and major decisions and was often abrupt and threatening, yet he was more willing to rely on his generals than was Hitler, who became progressively more involved with operational command and more contemptuous of the military leaders. Hitler's generals, writes Severyn Bialer, "exercised less influence on the decisions of their High Command at the moment they were most able to act effectively; Stalin's generals exercised more."[102] Stalin stood at the center of all strategic, logistical, and political

---

101   Stephen Kotkin, *Stalin: Waiting for Hitler, 1929–1941* (New York: Penguin Press, 2017), p. 435.

102   Severyn Bialer, *Stalin and His Generals* (New York: Pegasus, 1969), p. 43. "As supreme head of army command, Hitler was centrally involved in the formulation of day-to-day tactics in a way which occupied no other head of state during the Second World War. For the German army, this was catastrophic. The command structure which he had devised placed him in charge of both the general management of

decisions. He was chairman of the State Defense Committee, which included the highest party officials (Molotov, Lavrenti Beria, Malenkov, Voroshilov, Kaganovich, and later Nikolai Voznesenskii and Mikoyan); the chairman of Stavka, the supreme military headquarters; General Secretary of the party and chairman of the Politburo; chairman of the Council of Ministers and People's Commissar of Defense. Real business often took place in late night meetings at Stalin's apartment or dacha, and the exigencies of total war reinforced and accelerated the centralization of power.[103]

As willful and despotic as Stalin could be, his conduct during the war demonstrated flexibility and adaptability over time as well as the cruelty and stubbornness he exhibited earlier in the war. His refusal to react quickly to warnings of a German invasion, combined with his rejection of calls for retreat as the Germans rapidly advanced, caused hundreds of thousands to lose their lives or to be captured by the invaders. Later, however, his resoluteness about withdrawal from Stalingrad helped fortify his troops, save the city, and turn the war to the Soviets' advantage.[104] The infamous Order no. 270, issued by Stalin in August 1941, demanded that Soviet commanders fight to the death; those who deserted or were taken prisoner were to be considered traitors. The "indiscriminate violence" promoted in that order was moderated in Order no. 227 the following year: "the bulk of those soldiers who would have been summarily shot under Order no. 270 were sent to penal units instead."[105] Hardly a full reprieve, though now soldiers had a possibility of rehabilitation, tens of thousands of Soviet soldiers were still sentenced to death and executed by their own officers, sometimes summarily—as were several commanders and political commissars by General Vasilii Chuikov when he took over in Stalingrad. Stalin's own methods of enforcing obedience seeped down into the ranks of those who commanded others.

Official propaganda convincingly identified the victory over Nazism with the superiority of the Soviet system, its organic link with *rodina* (the motherland), and the personal genius of Stalin. The triumph over fascism provided the Communists with another source of legitimation

military campaigns and its detailed tactics." Ian Kershaw, *Hitler* (London and New York: Longman, 1991), p. 175.

103   Djilas, *Conversations with Stalin*, passim; A. I. Mikoyan, "V pervye mesiatsy Velikoi Otechestvennoi Voiny," *Novaia i noveishaia istoriia*, no. 6 (1985), pp. 93–104.

104   For revealing insights into the Soviet victory, see Jochen Hellbeck, *Stalingrad: The City That Defeated the Third Reich*, trans. Christopher Tauchen and Dominic Bonfiglio (New York: Public Affairs, 2015).

105   Ibid., p. 59.

and authority. Now Russia and the Soviet Union were melded into a single image. Patriotism and accommodation with established religious and national traditions, along with the toning down of revolutionary radicalism, contributed to a powerful ideological amalgam that outlasted Stalin himself. In the postwar decades, the war became the central moment of Soviet history, eclipsing the revolution and the *velikii perelom* [Great Turnover] of the early 1930s.[106] And though there would be sporadic uses of repression and terror against individuals or groups (the "Leningrad Affair" of 1947, the "Doctors' Plot" of 1953), as well as a series of ethnic deportations of repatriated Armenians, Kurds, Meskhetian Turks, and others, no massive terror on the scale of 1937 was employed after the war.

The Stalinist system was restored and consolidated after the devastation of the war years. Stalin used the enormous advantages that victory brought the Soviet Union to reassert party and his personal control over Soviet society and to consolidate the USSR's postwar position in Europe and Asia. He restrained the revolutionary impulses of Communists and leftist activists abroad in order to achieve two principal foreign policy goals: the establishment of spheres of influence in East Central Europe and the northern Pacific; and the continuation of the Grand Alliance into the postwar period to secure loans and reparations to rebuild the devastated USSR. The goals proved to be contradictory once the United States rejected Soviet hegemony in the countries along its Western borders. Like a revivified Bismarck, Stalin opted for a conventional sphere of influence policy and clamped down hard on Eastern Europe. Europe was divided, and the Marshall Plan and NATO isolated the Soviets from much of the developed world. Stalin essentially lost the Cold War almost as soon as it began.

As a single political cultural synthesis became hegemonic within the Soviet Union and the more disruptive violence of the prewar period receded, pervasive fear, which disciplined people into obedient silence, coexisted with genuine acceptance of the system. The figure of Stalin stood symbolically for ideal behavior in an ideal society. Enemies were still omnipresent; a single simplified reading of historical reality was at hand in the Kratkii *kurs* (the official "short" history of the Communist Party) and the official biography of Stalin; and the USSR was still the future in the present. Isolation in a hostile world, autarchy in economics

---

106   Nina Tumarkin, "The Great Patriotic War as Myth and Memory," *Atlantic Monthly* CCLXVII, 6 (June 1991), pp. 26, 28, 37, 40, 42, 44.

and politics, inaccessibility to the outside world, and a pervasive siege mentality powerfully bound the overwhelming majority of the Soviet people to the beleaguered state and party.

Whatever benefits accrued to the Soviet system from the unity of decision-making at the top must be weighed against the costs of over-centralization and the resultant paralysis lower down in the apparatus. In the years of the Cold War, as Stalin deteriorated physically and mentally, the entire country—its foreign policy, internal politics, cultural life, and economic slowdown—reflected the moods of its leader and was affected by his growing arbitrariness, seclusion, and inactivity. No one could feel secure. The ruling elite was concerned with plots, intrigues, the rivalries within Stalin's closest associates, the rise and fall of clients and patrons.[107] "All of us around Stalin," writes Khrushchev, "were temporary people. As long as he trusted us to a certain degree, we were allowed to go on living and working. But the moment he stopped trusting you, Stalin would start to scrutinize you until the cup of his distrust overflowed."[108] In his last years, Stalin turned against Molotov and Mikoyan, grew suspicious of Beria, Voroshilov, Kaganovich, and Malenkov. Khrushchev overheard him say, "I'm finished. I trust no one, not even myself."[109]

Ironically, it was Stalin's closest comrades who not only succeeded him but would dismantle his public legacy and untarnished image. Excising Stalin from Soviet history, however—or, indeed, Stalinism from post-Stalin and post-Soviet society and politics—proved to be beyond the capacity of political leaders, historians and other intellectuals, or ordinary people. No clean break was possible, for Stalin had left an indelible mark on Russia and the Soviet successor states. His statues could be moved to parks memorializing the Soviet experiment, but his most durable monu-ments—the destruction of the peasantry, the forced industrialization, the catastrophic destruction of the intelligentsia, the devastation of countless individuals and families, the victory over fascism, and the transformation of peoples into nations with all the accouterments of statehood (except real sovereignty)—persisted as both achievements of an incontrovertible past and burdens for an unpredictable future.

107   Yoram Gorlizki and Oleg Khlevniuk, *Cold Peace: Stalin and the Soviet Ruling Circle, 1945–1953* (Oxford: Oxford University Press, 2004).
108   *Khrushchev Remembers*, trans. and ed. by Strobe Talbott (Boston: Little, Brown and Co., 1970), p. 307.
109   Ibid.

3

Rethinking Soviet Studies: Bringing the Non-Russians Back In

The series of crises in the late 1980s and early 1990s that led to the collapse of the Soviet Union and the evaporation of the "socialist choice" were matched by a parallel crisis in the field of Soviet studies.[1] Enjoying a new celebrity, pundits flourished in the fertile fields between predictions and postmortems, while scholars observed the creative chaos of the post-Soviet Union with concern about the fate of Sovietology. What had been an established discipline was soon moribund, and its evident limitations were discussed and dissected: overemphasis on stability and stagnation of the old regime and the resultant failure to predict the kinds of reforms initiated by Gorbachev; obsession with the political and a lack of attention to the social and cultural; excessive focus on the Russian center with consequent neglect of the non-Russian peoples.[2] One might also

1   This chapter was originally prepared for the Soviet Studies Workshop: Session One: Nationalities, sponsored by the Ford Foundation at the Woodrow Wilson Center, Kennan Institute for Advanced Russian Studies, July 24, 1992. I extend my gratitude to the members of the seminar at the Kennan Institute who read and criticized the original draft of this paper and give special thanks to Teresa Rakowska-Harmstone and Aram Yengoyan, who were kind enough to provide me with extensive written comments. It was first published in Daniel Orlovsky (ed.), *Beyond Soviet Studies* (Washington, DC: The Woodrow Wilson Center Press, 1995), pp. 105–34.
2   For two assessments in the early post-Soviet years of the death of Communism and the crisis of Sovietology, see Theodore Draper, "Who Killed Soviet Communism?" *The New York Review of Books* XXXIX, 11 (June 11, 1992), pp. 7–8, 10, 12–14; and Stephen R. Gaubard (ed.), "The Exit from Communism," a special edition of *Daedalus*, Spring 1992. A highly influential earlier discussion of the profession and its problems was Stephen F. Cohen, *Rethinking the Soviet Experience: Politics and History Since 1917*

mention the over-hasty leap to model-building without adequate empirical underpinning (a practice only in part and only in the early years of the profession necessitated by inaccessibility and lack of sources); the shaping of the field by the Cold War division of East from West, Left from Center and Right; the conditioning of research by sources of funding and policy needs of sponsors; and the generational differences between the field's founders and those who came after and sought to "revise" their mentors' orthodoxies.[3]

Yet too often the urge to overthrow and rebuild (here I am showing my age) led to a dismissive, even derisive, attitude toward the real achievements of fifty years of academic writing on the USSR. That record is varied and uneven, but even in the polarized years of the Cold War serious engagement with the difficulties of an unknown world produced studies of great power. For all the limitations of the totalitarian model —its rush to assimilate Stalinism into fascism; its narrow focus on the leader and politics at the top; its inability to deal with change within the system; its blindness on the national question—fundamental aspects of the Stalinist regime were illuminated by scholars, like Merle Fainsod and Zbigniew Brzezinski, writing in this tradition. Though one might legitimately take issue with the fatalism of the totalitarian approach and its original reading of Stalinism as the culminating point of the Soviet revolution, one should at least acknowledge that some of its proponents, like Brzezinski or Alex Inkeles and Raymond A. Bauer, did attempt to adjust the model to fit ever-shifting realities and were able to produce extremely suggestive works, like *The Soviet Bloc* and *The Soviet Citizen*, that provided both analyses of change and a range of prospective

(New York: Oxford University Press, 1985); and for later ones, see David C. Engerman, *Modernization from the Other Shore: American Intellectuals and the Romance of Russian Development* (Cambridge, MA: Harvard University Press, 2003); and David C. Engerman, *Know Your Enemy: The Rise and Fall of America's Soviet Experts* (New York: Oxford University Press, 2009).

3   A recent treatment of the connection of intelligence agencies and the Russian studies community can be found in Sigmund Diamond, *Compromised Campus: The Collaboration of Universities with the Intelligence Community, 1945–1955* (Oxford: Oxford University Press, 1992); see especially the two chapters on the Russian Research Center of Harvard University (pp. 50–110), where he discusses the regular reporting by university officials to the FBI and the quiet removal of H. Stuart Hughes from the administration of the center because of his connections with the Henry Wallace presidential campaign of 1948. In an interview one of the early members of the center, sociologist Talcott Parsons, remembered that "there was an avoidance of getting what you might call political fireballs onto the staff, either pro- or anti-Soviet. I remember, for one year, as a visitor, they had Isaac Deutscher here, but, of course, he is an old Trotskyite and therefore was very anti-Stalin" (p. 76).

evolutions.[4] In its various incarnations, the totalitarian approach was tied to the restructuring of political alliances and loyalties after World War II and may have had a pernicious influence that reached far beyond scholarship. But it never totally dominated scholarship itself, even in the most frigid years of the Cold War, and within the totalitarian school there were those, like Inkeles and Bauer, who focused on society as much as on the state and wrote, however briefly, on the nationality problem.[5] Finally, as pretentious as the totalitarian model's claims to explanatory completeness may have been, one can agree with Alexander J. Motyl that "the radical rejection of totalitarianism as a conceptual mode pushed Sovietology away from theory; to a certain degree it may be argued that, in ridding themselves of the bath water, Sovietologists also threw out the baby."[6]

Whatever the ultimate failure to predict indicates about social science in general and Sovietology in particular, for several decades the major empirical historical and sociological work on the USSR was carried out in a foreign community of scholars, working under difficult circumstances of limited access to primary sources. The quite extraordinary monographic literature of the 1970s and 1980s, particularly in Russian history, testifies to the ability of the "children" and "grandchildren" of the founders to develop their own scholarly agenda; reconceptualize Western thinking of such contested issues as the revolution of 1917 and the viability of New Economic Policy; and deepen understanding of the imperial state and nobility, the revolutionary movement, the costs of collectivization and the purges. Even though government and many scholars were deeply invested in an unmodulated condemnation of all Soviet policies and practices, no intellectual consensus or single discourse was ever imposed on Russian/Soviet studies, and after the 1950s, a healthy and relatively tolerant exchange characterized the field. Against those who collapsed the whole Soviet experience into Stalinism or saw an unbroken continuity between Lenin and Stalin, the work of Isaac Deutscher, Moshe Lewin, Robert C. Tucker, and Stephen F. Cohen offered an alternative picture of the varieties of Bolshevism and possible trajectories. In

4   Zbigniew Brzezinski, *The Soviet Bloc: Unity and Conflict* (Cambridge, MA: Harvard University Press, 1960); Alex Inkeles and Raymond A. Bauer, *The Soviet Citizen: Daily Life in a Totalitarian Society* (Cambridge, MA: Harvard University Press, 1961).

5   Raymond A. Bauer, Alex Inkeles and Clyde Kluckhohn, *How the Soviet System Works: Cultural, Psychological and Social Themes* (Cambridge, MA: Harvard University Press, 1956; New York: Vintage Books, 1961).

6   Alexander J. Motyl, *Sovietology, Rationality, Nationality: Coming to Grips with Nationalism in the USSR* (New York: Columbia University Press, 1990), p. 5.

my own experience a teacher like Alexander Dallin provided a welcome skepticism about the harder line visions of the Cold War world. And for all the criticism directed at them, revisionists of various types remained a vital part of a professional dialogue—so much so that many conservative critics of Sovietology in their post-Soviet reassessment saw "revisionism" as the hegemonic reading of Soviet history among Western scholars by the mid-1970s.[7]

Soviet Nationality Studies: From Cold War to Hot Wars

Besides the chasm that, for most of the forty-five years since World War II, separated Soviet scholars from Western scholars, another hard-to-bridge gap divided those Western scholars studying non-Russians from those doing Russian history and Soviet politics. Just as it had been acceptable until recently for historians to treat all humankind as if it were male, so the study of imperial Russia and the Soviet Union could be treated unapologetically as if these empires were homogeneously Russian. For the first several decades, the central concerns of mainstream Sovietology had to do with politics, economic growth, and foreign policy, and sociologists, applied anthropologists, and social psychologists played the most important roles in the founding moments of postwar studies of the USSR. Along with political scientists and political historians, they focused almost exclusively on the party and regime studies. The non-Russian nationalities were left to *émigrés* with strong emotional and political affiliations with nationalist movements, whose personal experiences with the brutalities of Stalinism indelibly colored their writing. Studies of non-Russians, so often pungently partisan and viscerally anti-Communist, were relegated to a peripheral, second-rank ghetto within Soviet studies and associated with the right-wing politics of the "captive nations."

Until the turn toward social history in the late 1960s and 1970s, concentration on the state left society relatively, though not entirely, ignored, and the legacy of the totalitarian approach encouraged seeing the non-Russians as objects of political manipulation and central direction, sometimes as victims of Russification, sometimes as pathetic, archaic resisters to the modernizing program of the central authorities.

---

7   See, for example, the essays by Richard Pipes, Martin Malia, and Robert Conquest on "Sins of the Scholars" in *The National Interest* XXXI (Spring 1993), pp. 68–98.

Nationalities were homogenized; distinctions between them and within them were underplayed; and political repression and economic development, with little attention to ethnocultural mediation, appeared adequate to explain the fate of non-Russian peoples within the Soviet system. Since studying many nationalities was prohibitively costly and linguistically unfeasible, one nationality (in the case of the Harvard Project on the Soviet Social System, the Ukrainians, "clearly the outstanding candidate for this purpose") was chosen to stand in for the rest.[8]

In the locus classicus of the totalitarian model—Carl Friedrich and Brzezinski's *Totalitarian Dictatorship and Autocracy*—nationalities were not mentioned as potential "islands of separateness," along with family, church, universities, writers, and artists; however, in time the non-Russian nationalities were conceived of as possible "sources of cleavage" in the Soviet system and, therefore, of significance.[9] As Inkeles and Bauer wrote in 1961:

> Much attention has been given to the nationality problem as perhaps the weakest link in the chain of Soviet armor. Interest in the question has been intensified because exiled representatives of the national minorities have been extremely vocal in calling attention to the nationality question and its potentialities as a focus for psychological warfare. Indeed some of those leaders have gone so far as to insist that they can, if given sufficient resources, foment internal revolutions and successful independence movements among those of their own nationality inside the Soviet Union.[10]

Though the thrust of their findings emphasized the salience of social class, Inkeles and Bauer noted, "National and ethnic membership constitutes a basis for loyalties and identifications which cut across the lines of class, political affiliation, and generation. Nationality could, therefore, easily be a major determinant of the attitudes and life experiences of the individual and consequently a central element in the functioning

---

8   Inkeles and Bauer, *The Soviet Citizen*, p. 339.

9   "To this day, one can read in the Soviet press virulent denunciations of 'bourgeois-nationalists' in the national republics, and periodic purges of such resisters are a common feature of the Soviet scene …. But after all is said and done, the most this sort of activity does is to maintain the self-respect of those participating because of the shared common danger." Carl Friedrich and Zbigniew Brzezinski, *Totalitarian Dictatorship and Autocracy* (Cambridge, MA: Harvard University Press, 1956; revised edition: New York: Frederick A. Praeger, 1965), p. 282.

10   Inkeles and Bauer, *The Soviet Citizen*, p. 339.

of Soviet society."[11] Here, the social was at least introduced, but social and ethnic were contrasted and seen as largely opposed to one another. Later studies would demonstrate how variety among nationalities in economic well-being and differential access to social resources could create complex patterns of class/ethnic complementarity in which the social and ethnic would combine to reinforce cleavages between rulers and ruled.[12]

When attention was turned to non-Russians in the early postwar years, the dominant Western conclusions stood in stark contrast to the Soviet claim to have solved the "national question." Émigré scholars from the Soviet Union, with their unique experience and linguistic endowments, were key in the generation of information and analysis of the non-Russian nationalities. The Institute for the Study of the USSR, founded in 1950 in Munich and secretly funded by the Central Intelligence Agency until it was closed in 1971, published a series of monographs, symposia, and periodicals, in which the brutalities and horrors of Bolshevik repression during the Civil War and the Stalinist period and the excesses of police rule were carefully documented.[13] But the polemical style and enflamed language of many of the texts compromised their value as scholarship. In a collection of essays entitled *Genocide in the USSR: Studies in Group Destruction*, Soviet nationality policy as a whole was treated exclusively as a series of cultural, demographic, and social genocides. Like the term "Red Fascism," the use of the neologism "genocide" linked Stalinism to the universally despised Nazism, and the accompanying imagery of inevitable expansionism generated by totalitarianism (with any negotiation with such an adversary considered appeasement) was applied to considerable effect to the major existing threat to the West. Genocide, it was argued, was "one of the inevitable concomitants" of Soviet totalitarianism. "Various forms of genocide may disappear and new ones may

---

11   Ibid.

12   See, for example, the revealing study by Nancy Lubin, *Labour and Nationality in Soviet Central Asia: An Uneasy Compromise* (Princeton, NJ: Princeton University Press, 1984), where she concluded that "economic strains are growing among a rapidly expanding and relatively immobile population. Labour surpluses are growing and affecting the Central Asians to a greater degree than the Europeans .... The combination of growing economic strains and relatively low native participation in the economy's most modern spheres would suggest that political unrest might follow, and be articulated in ethnic terms." (p. 225)

13   Among the institute's periodical publications were *Azat Vatan, Backauscyna, Bielaruski Zbornik, Caucasian Review, Der Christliche Orient, Dergi, The East Turkic Review, Kavkaz, Ob'edinennyi Kavkaz, Suchasna Ukraina, Türkeli, Ukrainsky Zbirnik,* and *Vestnik instituta.*

appear, but the practice itself must continue, irrespective of changes in the leadership of the Communist regime. It cannot be relinquished as a Soviet means to its goal until the Communist totalitarian system itself comes to an end."[14] Published after Stalin's death, well into the period of Khrushchev's reforms, similar works became part of the debate about the possibilities of change within the Soviet system and Western strategic responses to an unyielding Communist threat. Ironically, the efforts of Western political scientists, in particular, to improve the totalitarian model occurred as the very Stalinist system on which it was based was in the process of political reform.[15]

Whether expressed in the extremely charged language of the Munich Institute or the more modulated words of the influential Walter Kolarz or Richard Pipes, the Bolshevik revolution and the Soviet state were presented as a fundamentally imperial arrangement, a colonial relationship between Russia and the borderlands.[16] The revolution and Civil War were conceived as a series of conquests of ethnic peripheries by the Russian Communist center, with legitimacy and morality on one side and cynical manipulation of ideals in the interest of naked power on the other. In his remarkable survey of the revolution in the non-Russian regions, Pipes wrote with great sympathy for the nationalist perspective, though he often overestimated the degree of popular nationalism and political coherence of the non-Russian populations—particularly in his discussion of Central Asia. The activities and proclamations of nationalist leaders or writers were used as indicators of the attitudes of whole peoples, and the widespread support for socialist programs, particularly in the early

---

14 Institute for the Study of the USSR, *Genocide in the USSR: Studies in Group Destruction* (Munich: Institut zur Erforschung der UdSSR, 1958), p. 19.

15 Doubts about the efficacy of the totalitarian model in light of Khrushchev's reforms led to a scramble for alternatives, such as Allen Kassof's "administered society: totalitarianism without terror," and a move toward integrating the study of Soviet-type societies into a comparative politics approach. See, for example, Frederic J. Fleron, Jr., *Communist Studies and the Social Sciences: Essays on Methodology and Empirical Theory* (Chicago: Rand McNally, 1969) and Jerry F. Hough, *The Soviet Union and Social Science Theory* (Cambridge, MA: Harvard University Press, 1977).

16 Walter Kolarz, *Russia and Her Colonies* (New York: Frederick A. Praeger, 1952); Richard Pipes, *The Formation of the Soviet Union: Communism and Nationalism, 1917– 1923* (Cambridge, MA: Harvard University Press, 1954). For variations on the theme of empire, see also Olaf Caroe, *Soviet Empire: The Turks of Central Asia and Stalinism* (New York: Macmillan, 1953); Robert Conquest, *The Soviet Deportation of Nationalities* (London: Macmillan, 1960), reprinted and expanded as *The Nation Killers: The Soviet Deportation of Nationalities* (London: Macmillan, 1970); Hugh Seton-Watson, *The New Imperialism* (Chester Springs, PA: Dufour Editions, 1962); and outside of scholarship: US Congress, Senate Committee on the Judiciary, *The Soviet Empire* (Washington, DC: Government Printing Office, 1958; revised edition, 1965).

years of the revolution and Civil War, was played down. Moreover, by not treating the Baltic countries, where Bolshevik strength, particularly among Latvians, was considerable, the role of foreign intervention in the victory of the nationalists decisive, and the pragmatism of Lenin in recognizing the independence of Poland, Finland, Estonia, Latvia, and Lithuania notable, Pipes reduced the interconnected complexities of civil and ethnic warfare into a simple picture of military expansionism from Russian center to non-Russian periphery. Selection of cases, as any social scientist knows, can determine explanations and conclusions. By including Central Asia, Caucasia, Ukraine, and Belorussia and leaving out the peoples around the Baltic, Pipes told a partial story that confirmed the standard view of Soviet expansionism.[17]

Deservedly respected as a synthetic treatment of the histories of dozens of nationalities, Pipes's encyclopedic account dealt primarily with politics and parties. A more social historical approach would have led to different emphases. Much of the social history of the 1970s and 1980s depicted the revolution in the central Russian cities as a struggle between increasingly polarized social classes, or at least an intense pulling apart of the *verkhi* (top) and the *nizy* (bottom) of society, while historians of the borderlands traditionally emphasized ethnic rather than social struggles and did not illuminate the ways in which the two were interconnected. Yet in multinational regions, social conflicts were very often conceived in ethnic terms and given cultural meanings that obscured the sources of conflict.[18] The revolution and Civil War can be seen as a single experience that engulfed the millions of Russians and non-Russians in both a common maelstrom of imperial collapse and social revolution. Bolshevism was not everywhere the enemy of non-Russian actors but was seen by many as the preferred alternative to a national independence promoted by a small nationalist elite in the name of a peasant majority. The difficult choice for both Russians and non-Russians was whether to support the central Soviet government and the revolution as now defined by the Leninists or to accept a precarious existence in alliance with undependable allies from abroad with their own agendas. Ethnic considerations were always bound up with estimations of the relative

17   For a critical review of Richard Pipes's work and role in shaping US perceptions of the Soviet Union, see Sean Guillory, "Richard Pipes, the Historian as Essentialist," *Jacobin*, no. 29 (Spring 2018), https://jacobinmag.com/2018/07/richard-pipes-anticommunism-soviet-union-obituary.

18   Ronald Grigor Suny, *The Revenge of the Past: Nationalism, Revolution, and the Collapse of the Soviet Union* (Stanford, CA: Stanford University Press, 1993).

advantages to be gained from the options available, which, in turn, were influenced by the cultural determinants of interest calculations.

The conception of the Soviet Union as an empire certainly makes comparative sense, but the nature of this peculiar empire requires more detailed investigation. The product of migration as much as conquest and ideological as well as economic linkages, both the tsarist and Soviet empires were remarkable in the ways they contributed to the formation of nations within them. Like Pipes, most scholars writing on the Soviet peoples before the collapse of the USSR treated nationality as an unproblematic category and national consciousness and nationalism as natural reflections and expressions of a national essence that needed little historical explanation. Though Pipes demonstrated that the full mobilization of many peoples was accomplished only with great difficulty, if at all, the assumption seemed to be that it was only a matter of time before nationalism spread beyond the intelligentsia, that its absence may be explained by political immaturity or the effectiveness of Bolshevik propaganda. The authenticity and legitimacy of the nationalists' formulations were never in doubt, and they were opposed to the artificiality of the Communists' claims. Though his story goes up to 1923 and the foundation of the Soviet Union, Pipes included no discussion of Soviet policies directed at preservation and development of national cultures within the USSR. Indeed, in the decade following Pipes, few discussions of Soviet nationality policy dealt with the *korenizatsiia* (nativization or indigenization) policies of the Soviet party/state in the 1920s, with the notable exception of the work of Mary Matossian on Armenia.[19]

A discordant note in the chorus of voices of 1950s and early 1960s that echoed the nationalist vision of the Communist world was the work of Inkeles and Bauer, whose

> most important and striking findings on the nationality problem cast serious doubt upon the assertions most often made by emigre nationality leaders concerning the central role of nationality status in determining the attitudes of Soviet minorities. The basic social and political values of our respondents, their attitudes toward the Soviet regime, and their life experiences were on the whole strikingly little determined by their nationality as compared with their social origins or their class position in the Soviet system. On most questions a Ukrainian or Georgian lawyer's or doctor's responses are more like a Russian lawyer's or doctor's

---

19   Mary Matossian, *The Impact of Soviet Policies in Armenia* (Leiden: Brill, 1962).

than like a Ukrainian or Georgian peasant's. And the same goes for the Russian member of the intelligentsia as against the Russian peasant. ... Thus, we may conclude that basically a man's nationality is not a good predictor of his general social and political attitudes in the Soviet system, but rather that these attitudes are better predicted by knowledge of his occupation or social class.[20]

The major conclusion of the Harvard Project—"that ethnic identity is of comparatively minor importance relative to social class member-ship as a predictor of the individual's life chances, his attitude toward the regime, and many of his general socio-political values"[21]—was not taken to mean that nationality was irrelevant in all matters. Though there was "little evidence of gross discrimination in life chances which the Soviet regime provides to youths of Ukrainian as against Russian origin when the background [of] the two was otherwise comparable," there were differences between occupational achievements "with more restricted opportunity and lesser rewards being the apparent lot of the Ukrainians."[22] The salience of nationality was felt more by Ukrainians than Russians when it came to marriage and family life. Ukrainians were also about twice as likely as Russians to recommend dropping an atom bomb on Moscow.[23] One third of Ukrainians interviewed were very pro-Ukrainian and more anti-Russian than anti-Soviet; another third showed some nationality consciousness on some issues but not on others; and a final third exhibited no visible anti-Russian feeling, did not experience discrimination on the basis of nationality, and were unconcerned about the national question.

> Our data indicate that it is primarily the older people who are knowl-edgeable about and identified with Ukrainian culture and folklore, which indicates some success for the regime's effort to suppress knowledge of certain historical figures and events. Even more important, however, is the fact that the younger, well-educated respondents are least likely to charge the regime with mistreatment of the Ukrainian people.[24]

In retrospect, two other aspects of the Harvard Project are noteworthy. First, there was not a wholly negative evaluation of Soviet nationality

---

20   Bauer et al., *How the Soviet System Works*, pp. 238–9.
21   Inkeles and Bauer, *The Soviet Citizen*, p. 351.
22   Ibid., p. 347.
23   Ibid., p. 353.
24   Bauer et al., *How the Soviet System Works*, pp. 239–40.

policy on the part of the refugees interviewed. "Refugees from the less well-developed areas point to the positive achievements in the direction of racial equality, increased educational opportunities, and technological and industrial advance. The regime has claimed and received credit in the eyes of many non-Russians for improved medical facilities, the increased literacy rate, the growth of the theater and cinema, and other developments."[25] Muslims, however, more than any other large minorities,

> feel deprived of their cultural heritage. Furthermore, the relative isolation from the center of many Moslem groups and the wide gulf between their culture and that of the European Russian probably facilitate the relative endurance of a Moslem subsociety in the villages which is both an actual and a potential source of passive resistance to Soviet and Russian penetration. However, resistance groups within the USSR are atomized.... Russification and diminishing of strong nationality feeling have proceeded rapidly during and since World War II, owing to the movements of peoples, liquidation of dissident leaders, industrialization, and increased literacy in Russian.[26]

A second conclusion was that the USSR was a relatively stable society and that the nationality issue was not one that threatened that stability.

> Time is mainly on the side of the regime as far as the nationality issue goes, particularly because of the trend among the youth noted above. Population transfers and purges of the national, political, and cultural leaderships, while increasing the resentments of articulate elements in the national populations, have even further reduced the possibility of their raising an effective opposition against the regime. Most of the various minority borderlands are increasingly dependent on Moscow because of more and more economic specialization. Local situations in some cases (e.g., Armenian fears of the Turks and jealousy of a strong Georgia) also reinforce ties to the center. Most of all, the drift through time is enhanced by larger processes which tend to destroy folkways and nationality feelings, such as urbanization, industrialization, and increasing Union-wide literacy in Russian. Project data show rather dramatically the extent to which, even a decade ago, attitudes had become homogenized along social class rather than nationality lines. However,

25   Ibid., p. 243.
26   Ibid., p. 236.

the very process of minimizing national differences in the USSR pro-
duces resentments, especially in the trouble spots of the moment.[27]

The work of Inkeles, Bauer, and Kluckhohn was a model of applied
social science—coolly detached, mildly critical of existing paradigms,
and cautious in its predictions. Much of the Manichaean moralism of
the totalitarian school had been left behind.[28] Yet *The Soviet Citizen* was
decidedly a product of a particular moment in Western social science.
Already marked in its conclusions by modernization theory—the idea
that industrialization and urbanization were fundamental in shaping the
life experience and psychology of the Soviet peoples—it also flirted with
convergence theory, the assumption that industrial societies, both democratic and totalitarian, had common features:

> The distinctive features of Soviet totalitarianism have for so long com-
> manded our attention that we have lost our awareness of an equally basic
> fact. The substratum on which the distinctive Soviet features are built
> is after all a large-scale industrial order which shares many features in
> common with the large-scale industrial order in other national states of
> Europe and indeed Asia. ... Many of the general features of the modern
> industrial order are remarkably close to the special features of the Soviet
> system.[29]

But Inkeles and Bauer saw neither an incompatibility between totalitarianism and industrialism nor the likelihood of a "managerial-revolution."
And on the nationality front there was little prospect of the national
republics becoming "that tinder box, which so many have asserted them
to be."[30]

---

27   Ibid., p. 243.
28   Some writers find the loss of the "solid moral ground" of the totalitarian model
regrettable; see, for example, Motyl, *Sovietology, Rationality, Nationality*, p. 8. Others
are convinced that in divided, violence-prone pluralistic societies where a woman's
reproductive choice is seen by some as murder of a child, moral vacuums may be more
salutary than solid moral grounds.
29   Inkeles and Bauer, *The Soviet Citizen*, pp. 383–4.
30   Ibid., pp. 372–3; see also Alex Inkeles, "Soviet Nationality Policy in Perspective,"
in Abraham Brumberg (ed.), *Russia Under Khrushchev: An Anthology from Problems of
Communism* (New York: Frederick A. Praeger, 1962), pp. 300–21.

Out from under the T-Model

Toward the end of the 1960s Western Sovietology became less one-sided and provided a more balanced picture of successes and failures—to be sure, "on balance," still negative in its judgments. The post-Sputnik appreciation of Soviet economic and technical achievements, and the notion of a society, however alien, that seemed in some ways to be becoming more like ours, contributed to a reading of the Soviet experience as an alternative model for development. New possibilities for research in the USSR—and eventually outside of Moscow and Leningrad—and the availability of a wider range of contact and information, most notably the results of the 1959 census, affirmed the sense of a society in transition. "The verdict of the objective student," wrote Erich Goldhagen in his introduction to *Ethnic Minorities in the Soviet Union* in 1968,

> on the historical performance of the Soviet Government in the treatment of ethnic minorities under its rule cannot be rendered in clear-cut and unicolored terms.... Among the minorities material achievements, impressive as they are in many cases, have been attended by intellectual and cultural constrictions and the tailoring of their identities, and all have been exposed to the pressures of Russification. Yet all we know about the Soviet minorities suggests that their ethnic personalities are alive and that their muteness is a tribute to the efficiency of the totalitarian Leviathan rather than a sign of the absence of collective aspirations. If the incipient, feeble, and struggling trend toward pluralism in Soviet society increases, then these aspirations may assert themselves and profoundly affect the shape of Soviet society.[31]

The tension between the new interest in change and pluralistic aspects within the Soviet system, on the one hand, and older assumptions of the universalism of central command and domination, on the other, was evident in an influential article by John Armstrong.[32] Adopting a modified functionalist approach, Armstrong began with assertions that the Soviet elite was committed "to maintain control of the decision-making process in the present Soviet Union and to expand the power of the U.S.S.R. as

---

31   Erich Goldhagen (ed.), *Ethnic Minorities in the Soviet Union* (New York: Frederick A. Praeger, 1968), p. xiv.

32   John Armstrong, "The Ethnic Scene in the Soviet Union: The View of the Dictatorship," in ibid., pp. 3–49.

widely as possible" (not an unreasonable assumption for almost any state) and that this commitment in turn required "a unified national culture" that must be Russian.[33] Given those aims, much of nationality policy and effects on non-Russians was understood to be central manipulation calculated to realize the goals of the regime. Armstrong went beyond the customary treatment of "Soviet nationality policy, and, indeed, the entire ethnic problem in the U.S.S.R., as a single, homogeneous phenomenon" and outlined a number of "functional types of ethnic groups."[34] One of the "great accomplishments of the Soviet system is the absence of an "internal proletariat" made up of ethnic migrants. More characteristic are the "mobilized diasporas," educated, mobile ethnicities, like Jews and Armenians, that help in the modernization project. They are contrasted to "younger brothers," nationalities close to the dominant ethnic group culturally but low in social mobilization, like Belorussians and Ukrainians. "State nations," those like the Baltic peoples and the Georgians with "strong traditions of national identity," are distinguished from the "colonials" just entering the transition to modernity (for example, Soviet Muslims). Armstrong's schema was instructive, but his "view from the dictatorship" did not include consideration of ethnic elites within republics with their own agenda, not to mention the variety of cultural and social evolutions taking place among ordinary non-Russians that diverged from the stated goals of the central regime.

Reflecting the Sixties' interest in problems of "development," Alec Nove and J. A. Newth collaborated on a provocative study of *The Soviet Middle East* to test Soviet economic and social achievements against those of its neighbors to the south. On the question of industrialization, Nove and Newth argued that association with Russia had been a net benefit for the southern republics.

> Given that capital was relatively very scarce, given also the much richer untapped resources in Siberia and parts of European Russia and the Ukraine, it followed that, if economic rationality alone were adopted as a guide, there would be very little industry in [the Central Asian and Transcaucasian] republics. In a free-enterprise setting, in a huge free trade area within the USSR's present borders, it is very doubtful if there would be rapid industrial growth in these regions. They have benefited, therefore, not only from being part of a much larger whole, but also, or

33   Ibid., p. 5.
34   Ibid., p. 3.

even particularly, from the fact that the Government of the USSR had an industrializing ideology, equated social progress with industry, and paid special attention to the development in formerly backward areas.[35]

In the areas of education and other social services, the southern republics also benefitted from Soviet policies. In the area of finance, "by and large, with the possible exception of Azerbaijan, the republics contributed a less than average amount, per capita, to the revenue of the Soviet Union" and "were permitted to retain a more than average proportion of all-Union revenues raised in their territories, to finance economic and social development.... The Russian connection, membership of a large and more developed polity, greatly facilitated such social and economic progress as was achieved in these areas."[36] Soviet-style development was distinct from Western-style imperialism.

> Far from there being any economic exploitation, it is reasonable on the evidence to assert that industrialization, especially in Central Asia, has been financed with money raised in Russia proper. In other words, capital has tended to move to those outlying under-developed areas and there has been virtually no counterbalancing move of remittances of profit or interest, because in the Soviet Union capital grants are not repayable and do not bear interest. ... This may be contrasted with the very substantial remittances of profits to capitalist companies from Latin-America. No reasonable person can doubt that industrial growth would have been less rapid without Russian capital and Russian skills.[37]

The Soviet Union may have been an empire but a very peculiar one indeed, one in which the metropole operated at a disadvantage with respect to much of the periphery. Reluctant to call the relationship between center and periphery "colonial" in the sense of economically exploitative, Nove and Newth, nevertheless, pointed out that all real decision-making power

---

35   Alec Nove and J. A. Newth, *The Soviet Middle East: A Model for Development?* (London: George Allen & Unwin, 1967), p. 45. For an interesting contrast, these conclusions might be compared to those of Vsevolod Holubnychy, who argued that "wholly inexplicable gaps" in economic development existed among Soviet republics, with the RSFSR faring better than the rest, and that this confirmed the image of a colonial relationship between Russia and the non–Russian republics. See "Some Economic Aspects of Relations Among the Soviet Republics," in Goldhagen (ed.), *Ethnic Minorities in the Soviet Union*, pp. 50–120.

36   Nove and Newth, *The Soviet Middle East*, p. 97.

37   Ibid., p. 114.

rested with Moscow. "Therefore, if we do not call the present relation-ship colonialism, we ought to invent a new name to describe something which represents subordination and yet is genuinely different from the imperialism of the past."[38] However distinctive Soviet imperialism was, sovereignty remained with the center, and the developmental programs, the Soviet *mission civilisatrice*, were decided almost exclusively in the center, with the needs of the empire paramount and those of the indige-nous peoples secondary.

The post-Stalin opening of the Sovietological discussion occurred simultaneously with the arrival of a new generation of younger scholars, most born in the United States, the greater academic professionalization of Soviet studies, and a lessening of the conformist ideological pressures of early years. The work and career patterns of this generation soon rou-tinized into three or four years of graduate study at university, followed by a research year in the Soviet Union and a year or two of writing up the dissertation. However one's research interests might be connected with non-Russians, teaching appointments were defined as Russian or Soviet (read Russian), and almost all nationality specialists had to teach more broadly. In many ways, they carried a double burden: maintaining their field specialization and keeping up with the central interests of Soviet studies, which provided employability, an audience for their work, and a certain legitimacy.

The monographic literature of the 1970s and 1980s was part of a larger academic discourse that, in the wake of the dismantling of the totalitar-ian model, sought new paradigms for understanding the Soviet Union. The emphasis on Kremlinology and model building of political science of earlier years was supplemented by more empirical and historical studies, while historians turned from high politics and institutions to an obsessive interest in social history. While there was no guarantee that the social historical turn would lead to attention to non-Russians—consider the groundbreaking work of Moshe Lewin and Sheila Fitzpatrick, which assiduously left out non-Russians—a number of political scientists and sociologists turned toward non-Russians to deal with problems gener-ated from disciplinary concerns.[39] Zvi Y. Gitelman's discussion of the

38   Ibid., p. 122.
39   Among them: Ronald Grigor Suny, *The Baku Commune, 1917–1918: Class and Nationality in the Russian Revolution* (Princeton, NJ: Princeton University Press, 1972); Zvi Y. Gitelman, *Jewish Nationality and Soviet Politics: The Jewish Sections of the CPSU, 1917–1930* (Princeton, NJ: Princeton University Press, 1972); and Gregory J. Massell, *The Surrogate Proletariat: Moslem Women and Revolutionary Strategies in Soviet Central Asia, 1919–1929* (Princeton, NJ: Princeton University Press, 1974).

Evsektsiia [Jewish Section] of the party, for example, was both grounded in modernization theory and sensitive to the different models of development used in different periods of Soviet history.

> Without denying the usefulness of the totalitarian model in explaining much of Soviet history, we might find it more enlightening to view the first decade of Soviet power as a period in which an authoritarian regime attempted to mobilize social and economic resources for the purpose of rapid modernization, political integration, and political development … . The modernization strategy of the Bolsheviks in the 1920s differed substantially from the Stalinist pattern of modernization and in many ways resembled the "nationalist revolutionary" pattern as seen, for example, in Mexico and Turkey.[40]

Gitelman's story, like that of Gregory J. Massell, who explored the same period in Central Asia, was one of Communist failure "to combine modernization and ethnic maintenance," largely because of the poor fit between the developmental plans of the party and the reservoir of traditions and interests of the ethnic population. *Evkom* [Commissariat for Jewish National Affairs] and *Evsektsiia* had set out to destroy the old order among the Jews, Bolshevize the Jewish workers, and reconstruct Jewish life on a "socialist" basis, that is, "establishing the dictatorship of the proletariat on the Jewish street."[41] Jewish Communists were relatively successful in eliminating Zionism and Hebrew culture, "new and tender growths on Russian soil" and encouraging Yiddish culture, but they failed to "eradicate religion, so firmly rooted in Jewish life."[42] Bolshevism also failed to understand nationalism, and by the 1930s the party subordinated all ethnic concerns to the overall program of rapid state-dictated industrialization. In Central Asia, as Massell demonstrated, the failure to mobilize women as a "surrogate proletariat" with which to overturn the patriarchal social regime led to a curious accommodation with traditional society.

> A revolution in social relations and cultural patterns evidently could not be managed concurrently with large-scale political, organizational, and economic change…. Political institutionalization and stability as well

40 Gitelman, *Jewish Nationality and Soviet Politics*, pp. 3–4, 6–7.
41 Ibid., p. 491.
42 Ibid., p. 492.

as a modicum of economic growth had to be purchased at the price of revolutionary and ideological purity and of a lower rate of social transformation. This implied a willingness, on the part of the regime, to tolerate distinctly uneven development in political, economic, and socio-cultural spheres—indeed, a willingness to leave pockets of antecedent life-styles relatively undisturbed, if necessary, for an indefinite period of time.[43]

The best work in nationality studies through the 1970s and 1980s introduced a greater appreciation of the need for attention to chronology, periodization, and change and an increased awareness of contradictions and improvisations in Soviet policies, rather than the steady working out of an a priori Marxist blueprint. Exemplary in telling a story far messier and contradictory than had been told during the Cold War was a widely read article by Teresa Rakowska-Harmstone.[44] Using a "dialectical" approach to explain the "increasingly assertive ethnic nationalism among the non-Russian minorities," she illustrated how "powerful integrative forces ... released through the process of industrialization and the accompanying expansion of mass education and intensive socialization" were countered by "the retention of a federal administrative framework" that "safeguarded the territorial loci and formal ethnocultural institutions of most minorities, thereby preserving the bases for potential manifestations of national attitudes."[45] Distinguishing between "orthodox" and "unorthodox" nationalism, the first permitted within the system, the second advocating secession, independence, and/or the rejection of the system's ideological mold, she demonstrated how indigenous ethnic elites in republics sought "sources of legitimacy in their own unique national heritage" and established ties with their own nationality through the skillful manipulation of permissible "nationalism." The consolidation of ethnic power and consciousness in many (though by no means all) of the non-Russian republics was challenged continually by "the continued political, economic, and cultural hegemony enjoyed by the Great Russian majority and the national chauvinism manifested

43   Massell, *The Surrogate Proletariat*, pp. 408–9.
44   Teresa Rakowska–Harmstone, "The Dialectics of Nationalism in the USSR," *Problems of Communism* XXIII, 3 (May–June 1974), pp. 1–22. This article was profoundly influential on my own work, which attempted to marry the theoretical turn toward constructivism as an approach to studying nations and nationalism with the constitutive aspects of Soviet nationality policy in forming and reforming nations, which hitherto had largely been neglected in Soviet studies.
45   Ibid., pp. 1–2.

by this group vis-à-vis the minority nationalities."[46] Whatever the policy goals of the regime (*sblizhenie* [rapprochement] and eventually *sliianie* [merging together]), whatever the expectations that social mobilization and economic growth would blunt the edge of minority nationalism, in actuality national cohesion and nationalist expression were growing and were "on a collision course with party policies."[47]

An explosion of empirical studies—by Barbara Anderson and Brian Silver, Hélène Carrère d'Encausse, Murray Feshbach, Rasma Karklins, Gerhard Simon, and Victor Zaslavsky, among others—benefitted from the greater availability of Soviet statistics and the work of Soviet colleagues, like Iurii Arutiunian, Sergei Arutiunov, and Iulii Bromlei.[48] A general rise in interest in ethnicity and ethnic studies in the 1970s and 1980s brought new scholars and new resources into the field of Soviet nationality studies. Armenian studies programs and endowed chairs were established at Harvard, UCLA, Columbia, Michigan, Fresno State, and other universities. Institutes of Ukrainian studies were founded at Harvard and Alberta. A chair in Estonian studies was funded at the University of Toronto. Along with the development in knowledge of the variety of ethnic processes in the Soviet Union, several scholars, like Gail W. Lapidus and Alexander J. Motyl, encouraged broader conceptual thinking about the problem of nationality in the USSR.[49] Through

---

46   Ibid., p. 10.

47   Ibid., p. 21.

48   Barbara A. Anderson and Brian D. Silver, "Estimating Russification of Ethnic Identity Among Non-Russians in the USSR," *Demography* XX, 4 (November 1983), pp. 461–89; Barbara A. Anderson and Brian D. Silver, "Equality, Efficiency, and Politics in Soviet Bilingual Education Policy, 1934–1980," *American Political Science Review* LXXVIII (1984), pp. 1019–39; Hélène Carrère d'Encausse, *L'empire éclaté* (Paris: Flammarion, 1978; published in English as *Decline of an Empire: The Soviet Socialist Republics in Revolt* [New York: Newsweek Books, 1979]); Hélène Carrère d'Encausse, *The Great Challenge: Nationalities and the Bolshevik State, 1917–1930* (New York: Holmes & Meier, 1991); Murray Feshbach, "The Soviet Union: Population Trends and Dilemmas," *Population Bulletin* XXXVII, 3 (August 1982), pp. 1–44; Rasma Karklins, *Ethnic Relations in the USSR: The Perspective From Below* (Boston: Allen & Unwin, 1986); Gerhard Simon, *Nationalismus und Nationalitatenpolitik in der Sowjetunion: Von der totalitaren Diktatur zur nachstalinschen Gesellschaft* (Baden-Baden: Nomos Verlagsgesellschaft, 1986); Victor Zaslavsky, *The Neo-Stalinist State: Class, Ethnicity and Consensus in Soviet Society* (Armonk, NY: Sharpe, 1982); Iurii Arutiunov, *Sotsial'noe i natsional'noe: Opyt etnosotsiologicheskikh issledovanii po materialam Tatarskoi ASSR* (Moscow: Nauka, 1973); Iulii V. Bromlei, *Sovremennye etnicheskie protsessy v SSSR* (Moscow: Nauka, 1975). See also Mark Beissinger and Lubko Hajda (eds.), *The Nationality Factor in Soviet Society and Politics: Current Trends and Future Prospects* (Boulder, CO: Westview, 1989).

49   Gail W. Lapidus, "Ethnonationalism and Political Stability: The Soviet Case," *World Politics* XXXVI, 4 (July 1984), pp. 355–80; "The Nationality Question and the Soviet System," in Erik P. Hoffmann (ed.), *The Soviet Union in the 1980s, Proceedings*

the 1980s a series of volumes, under the general editorship of Wayne Vucinich, appeared in the Hoover Institution Press's "Studies of Nationalities in the USSR."[50] Praised by reviewer David D. Laitin as "the best historical and contextual accounts of Soviet nationalities available in English," they nevertheless failed in his view to develop a shared theoretical conceptualization of the problems of nationality and nationalism.

> For Olcott, once national boundaries are historically constituted, they remain relatively fixed; that is, national identifications are eternal .... Meanwhile Allworth opens his study of the Uzbeks by asking: "How will the creation of a corporate, retrospective nationality where none existed before affect people when it is politically motivated and applied and executed by outsiders?" (p. 4). He answers that a politically imposed category can take on social meaning by virtue of state action (chap. 11) and of the strategic activity of intellectuals who found it useful to call themselves Uzbek (pp. 229–31)—this in combination with a fear of Tatar domination over Central Asia that pushed Uzbek intellectuals away from a broader identity (p. 180). National traditions, that is, are created out of struggle; they are not a primordial given. Finally, Suny looks for answers in social analysis: the various Georgian nationalist movements are seen as the design of particular classes or coalitions of classes, aimed at securing wealth or legitimate domination. In sum, nationalities are variously presented in the volumes as primordially real, historically reconstituted, or socially organized—without any synthesis to reconcile these distinct visions.[51]

For all their extraordinary achievements, Soviet nationality studies were not prepared for the "rise of nations" in the USSR and the collapse of

---

of the Academy of Political Science XXXV, 3 (New York: Academy of Political Science, 1984), pp. 98–112; Alexander J. Motyl, Will the Non-Russians Rebel?: State, Ethnicity, and Stability in the USSR (Ithaca, NY: Cornell University Press, 1987); Sovietology, Rationality, Nationality: Coming to Grips with Nationalism in the USSR (New York: Columbia University Press, 1990).

50   Alan Fisher, The Crimean Tatars (1978); Azade-Ayse Rorlich, The Volga Tatars: A Profile in National Resilience (1986); Martha Brill Olcott, The Kazakhs (1987); Toivo U. Raun, Estonia and the Estonians (1987); Ronald Grigor Suny, The Making of the Georgian Nation (Bloomington and Stanford: Indiana University Press and Hoover Institution Press, 1988); Edward A. Allworth, The Modern Uzbeks, From the Fourteenth Century to the Present: A Cultural History (1990); Audrey Altstadt, The Azerbaijani Turks (1992); Andrejs Plakans, The Latvians: A Short History (1995); Charles King, The Moldovans: Romania, Russia, and the Politics of Culture (2000).

51   David D. Laitin, "The National Uprisings in the Soviet Union," World Politics XLIV, 1 (October 1991), p. 141.

the union. Though some scholars, like Robert Conquest and Carrère d'Encausse, warned of the coming nationality crisis in the USSR, most others would have answered Alexander Motyl's question, *Will the Non-Russians Rebel?*, as he did.

> Structural grounds for opposition are there: latent conflict tendencies are inherent in the ethnic pattern of domination of the Soviet Russian state. In time, if economic decline and ideological erosion set in and outside interference continues, behavioral reasons for rebellion may accumulate. At some point, non-Russians may massively want to rebel. But will they? As long as the public sphere is occupied and, more important, as long as the KGB remains intact, the deprivatization of antistate attitudes will be problematic, antistate collectivities and elites will be unlikely to mobilize, alliances between workers and intellectuals will not materialize, and rebellion, revolt, and insurrection will be well-nigh impossible. Because they cannot rebel, non-Russians will not rebel.[52]

Motyl was both wrong and right. In fact, non-Russian peoples, beginning with the Armenians and the Baltic peoples, did rebel, and in that rebellion further weakened the central state's authority and legitimacy. In the end, the erosion of central power and the unwillingness of Gorbachev to use violence against the population made possible the massive ethnic oppositional movements that unraveled the Soviet system.

With the disintegration of the "unbreakable union," Soviet nationality studies rapidly if briefly come to the center of both professional and public political attention. The expansion of awareness of non-Russians in the late Soviet period and in the early post-Soviet period was accompanied by a variety of initiatives from government, universities, foundations, and exchange programs to expand the possibilities for research in the newly independent republics. The number of graduate studies from "non-ethnic" backgrounds interested in Central Asia, the Caucasus, Ukraine, and other non-Russian regions exploded, and students working on primarily Russian topics were sensitized to the need to look at multinational and ethnic factors in their work. Ethnicity joined class and gender as part of the grand triad of references of which historical and social scientific thinking was supposed to be aware.

52 Motyl, *Will the Non-Russians Rebel?*, p. 170. For another prediction that the collapse of the "empire" would not take place if the center held, see Laitin, "The National Uprisings in the Soviet Union," pp. 173–5. For the opposite viewpoint, see Robert Conquest (ed.), *The Last Empire: Nationality and the Soviet Future* (Stanford, CA: Hoover Institution Press, 1986).

Like many other fashionable turns in Sovietology, the post-Soviet move toward including the non-Russians was dictated by policy requirements and the interests of funders. As during the Cold War, so after the fall of Communism, the policy tail often wagged the scholarship dog. Yet in the post–Cold War environment, nonconformist thinking was more easily tolerated, and members of the academy who might have been marginalized or disregarded in the more frigid years of East–West confrontation found themselves addressing official audiences. Whether ideology was dead or not was less important than that policymakers believed that formerly marginalized politics were no longer relevant in a period of democratic capitalist triumph. With the Communist menace buried, officialdom was willing to listen to a wider range of dissonant voices to help them understand the current power of nationalism, predict the future of the decolonized Soviet bloc, or foresee new dangers from postnationalist fundamentalisms. Thus, the effect of policy requirements was not universally pernicious. Besides funding much academic research of great quality and value, the US government sponsored the activities of investigators, like Paul Goble, formerly of the Department of State, and Murray Feshbach, formerly of the Department of Commerce, whose publications provided valuable information to academic researchers. But the agenda of government was never innocently supportive of the full range of independent scholarship, which might have included work subversive to the policies of particular states and critical of cherished assumptions of people in power.

Paradigm Shift: From Primordialism to Constructivism

In the decade before the end of the USSR a fundamental paradigm shift had taken place in nationalism studies: the move from primordial to constructivist conceptions. In its largely atheoretical treatment of nationality, much of Sovietological thought had either accepted uncritically a commonsensical view of nationality as a relatively observable, objective phenomenon based on a community of language, culture, shared myths of origin or kinship, perhaps territory, or not thought about the question at all. Nationalism was seen as the release of denied desires and authentic, perhaps primordial, aspirations. This "Sleeping Beauty" view of nationality (a term that originated with a key theorist of the modernist, constructivist approach, Ernest Gellner) was challenged in the seminal work of Elie Kedourie, Benedict Anderson, Eric J. Hobsbawm, Miroslav

Hroch, and others, by a more historicized view that gravitated toward a postmodernist understanding of nationality as a constructed category, an "imagined community." This "Bride of Frankenstein" view of nationality and nationalism, a term suggested to me by the historian Reginald Zelnik, soon dominated academic writing outside of Sovietology after the publication of key texts in 1983.[53] Far from being a natural component of human relations, something like kinship or family, nationality and the nation were seen as created (or invented) in a complex political process in which intellectuals and activists play a formative role. Rather than the nation giving rise to nationalism, nationalism gives rise to the nation. Rather than primordial, the nation is a modern sociopolitical construct.

The emphasis in Soviet studies on a priori nations that were suddenly reawakened in the Gorbachev era and unexpectedly put forth their long-repressed demands had the regrettable effect of suppressing study of the formative influence of the seventy-year-long Soviet period. Seldom adequately evaluated, except negatively, by most Western writers and by the nationalists who came to power in many of the non-Russian republics, the Soviet period was in fact the incubator of new nations that were formed in part as a result of contradictory Soviet policies (for example, *korenizatsiia* followed by Stalinist Russification) and in spite of them.[54] At the very moment when opportunities for more interesting research opened up, when the possibility of working more closely with colleagues in the post-Soviet world became a reality, the triumph of anti-Communist nationalism also meant the victory of a certain reading

53   Ernest Gellner, *Nations and Nationalism* (Oxford: Basil Blackwell, 1983); Benedict Anderson, *Imagined Communities: Reflections on the Origin and Spread of Nationalism* (London: Verso, 1983: revised edition, 1991); Eric Hobsbawm and Terence Ranger (eds.), *The Invention of Tradition* (Cambridge: Cambridge University Press, 1983); Miroslav Hroch, *Social Preconditions of National Revival in Europe: A Comparative Analysis of the Social Composition of Patriotic Groups among the Smaller European Nations*, trans. Ben Fowkes (New York: Cambridge University Press, 1985); Eric J. Hobsbawm, *Nations and Nationalism Since 1780: Programme, Myth, Reality* (Cambridge: Cambridge University Press, 1990). An influential earlier text was Elie Kedourie, *Nationalism* (London: Hutchinson, 1960; 4th edition: Oxford and Cambridge: Blackwell Publishers, 1993).

54   For early elaborations of this thesis, see these works by Ronald Grigor Suny: "Nationalist and Ethnic Unrest in the Soviet Union: Gorbachev's Search for Accommodation," *World Policy Journal* VI, 3 (Summer 1989), pp. 503–28; "The Revenge of the Past: Socialism and Ethnic Conflict in Transcaucasia," *New Left Review*, no. 184 (November–December 1990), pp. 5–34; and "State, Civil Society, and Ethnic Cultural Consolidation in the USSR: Roots of the National Question," in Alexander Dallin and Gail W. Lapidus (eds.), *The Soviet System in Crisis: A Reader of Western and Soviet Views* (Boulder, CO: Westview Press, 1991), pp. 414–29.

of history and the potential exclusion of other readings. New political requirements at the moment of establishing ethnic claims to territory and statehood foreclosed conceptualizations that threatened the essentialist understanding of the antiquity and solidity of nations.[55]

Journalists and governments attempting to understand the explosion of nationalist violence sought the easy answer to their question in "ancient tribal struggles." In an article on the Armenian–Azerbaijani conflict, Serge Schmemann of the *New York Times*, for example, referred to

> images of unavenged deaths and ancient hatreds, of tribal passions that 70 years of enforced Communist harmony failed to quell. ... Artsakh, [Khachatur B. Simonyan] declares, using the ancient Armenian name for Nagorno-Karabakh, is indisputably Armenian and nonnegotiable. "Do you know when the first Turk set foot on Karabagh?" he thundered with disdain. "Only in 1752! How can they claim that these are their lands?"
>
> That he should consider 240 years so negligible begins to explain why a mere 70 years of Soviet peace failed to still ancient passions ...
>
> To Nagorno-Karabakh belongs the distinction of being the first tribal conflict to break through the enforced Soviet peace. That was four years and more than 2,000 casualties ago.[56]

Rather than an "ancient tribal" conflict, the war in Karabakh can be read as a multilayered struggle over territory and national identity that has as much to do with cultural and social constructions of what makes up Armenia and Azerbaijan in the twentieth century as it does with older narratives, with who Armenians and Azerbaijanis conceive themselves to be after seventy years of Soviet state-making, and how each people defines the "other" that it is ready to annihilate. Though there have been numerous conflicts between Armenians and Azerbaijanis in this region, they were not the same conflict with the same causes, and Armenians and Azerbaijanis had long periods of coexistence and collaboration as well. Few historians would excuse Serge Schmemann if he attributed the first and second world wars, fought within twenty years of one another and by the same adversaries, to ancient tribal antagonisms that can be read back into primordial Gallic or Gothic origins.

55   For a more extended discussion of the nationalist turn in the Caucasus and Central Asia and its effect on scholarly discourse, see Ronald Grigor Suny, "Constructing Primordialism: Old Histories for New Nations," *Journal of Modern History* LXXIII, 4 (December 2001), pp. 862–96.

56   Serge Schmemann, "In the Caucasus, Ancient Blood Feuds Threaten to Engulf 2 New Republics," *The New York Times*, July 8, 1992, p. A3.

Today it is generally understood that ethnic and other groups, as well as communities that imagine themselves to be nations, may be difficult to characterize in terms of essential characteristics, though they do exist within discursive constructions about who they are and who the others are. Such shared and shifting constructions are embedded in various emotions, which may range from affection and pride to anger, fear, and hatred. Ethnicities and nations can be thought of not only as imagined communities but as affective communities. Such groups may experience a collective disposition that shapes their emotional reactions and behavior, a disposition of anxiety about the future or the other, insecurity about their current position, suspicion of neighbors, and anxiety about the unknown future. This disposition can be understood in both meanings of the term: a shared and enduring mood and a tendency toward certain feelings and actions. Armenians and Azerbaijanis, for example, live in different discursive universes and different collective affective dispositions, even as they share general notions about the legitimacy of the nation-form, the role of the international community, the Soviet legacy, and other matters.

For Armenians, the world is one in which they have been victims of greater powers, most importantly the Turks. After decades of war and tens of thousands of deaths, the image of the other has been drowned in blood. The Turkic-speaking Azerbaijanis are routinely referred to by Armenians as "Turks," linking them to the Anatolian Turks who carried out the Genocide of 1915. For Azerbaijanis the world has also been one in which their agency has been sharply limited by the empires that have dictated their fate, but among the agents of empire have been the Armenians, whom they see as favored by the outside forces that have imposed themselves on Azerbaijan. As the proximate and more vulnerable victimizers, the Armenians are the ones on whom Azerbaijanis have turned their wrath—in the pogroms of 1905, the wars and massacres of 1918–19, and the interethnic killing of 1988 and 1990. Both peoples have cloaked themselves in tropes legitimized by the discourse of the nation: we were here first, therefore this is our historic homeland usurped by the other; we are the real victims of the predations of our neighbors and the ambitions of imperial powers.

By the early 1990s, the constructivist paradigm had been introduced into Soviet nationalities studies and by the end of the decade had become the principal approach of Western scholars to the histories of the non-Russian peoples. Scholars of Russia, the Soviet Union, and the post-Soviet space embraced the increasing interest in ethnicity and culture that accompanied the "Cultural Turn."[57] But there were holdouts who rejected the constructivist model. For the distinguished French scholar and member of the Académie Française, Hélène Carrère d'Encausse, the "nation" is natural and inevitable, and, therefore, in the Soviet case she does not need to explain the peculiar way in which nations formed—or did not form—in the USSR or account for the source of their consciousness and power in the Gorbachev years, except as the natural reaction to oppression and humiliation.[58] With her primordialist perspective, she was able to say categorically in 1990 that the breakup of the Soviet Union was irreversible. Her view conforms to the widely accepted nationalist narrative, while, for constructivist scholars, nationalism in the late Soviet Union is related to the effects of Soviet nationality policy in consolidating nations within the political structures of the Soviet federation and to the particular conjuncture of unfulfilled expectations and the consequences of economic decline. The rise of nations in the Soviet Union was, at one and the same time, the story of the erosion of central state power and the inability of the government to realize its own promises and overcome the contradictions of a modernizing program and a petrified state structure. The triumph of the nations is less the tale of an inevitable dawn than of the complex interplay of rival ambitions and visions, unpredictable contingencies, and the different capacities of national elites and populations to seize unprecedented opportunities.

In the West, at least before the Gorbachev years, the Soviet Union was frequently referred to as Russia. Sports stars, like Igor Ter-Ovanesyan, or politicians, like Anastas Mikoyan, were invariably called Russians, which had the effect either of denying the country's multinational character or reinforcing the point that Soviet policies and practices were aimed at Russification and homogenization of the whole Soviet people. This

---

57   See particularly, Suny, *The Revenge of the Past*; Yuri Slezkine, "The USSR as a Communal Apartment, or How a Socialist State Promoted Ethnic Particularism," *Slavic Review* LIII, 2 (Summer 1994), pp. 414–52; Geoff Eley and Ronald Grigor Suny (eds.), *Becoming National: A Reader* (New York: Oxford University Press, 1996); Terry Martin, *The Affirmative Action Empire: Nations and Nationalism in the Soviet Union, 1923–1939* (Ithaca, NY: Cornell University Press, 2001); and Francine Hirsch, *Empire of Nations: Ethnographic Knowledge and the Making of the Soviet Union* (Ithaca, NY: Cornell University Press, 2005). A major contribution by an anthropologist was Bruce Grant's ethnohistory, *In the Soviet House of Culture: A Century of Perestroikas* (Princeton, NJ: Princeton University Press, 1995), a study of the Nivkhi of Sakhalin Island and their complex interrelationships with Russian and Soviet cultures.

58   See, for example, her book *The End of the Soviet Empire: The Triumph of the Nations*, trans. Franklin Philip (New York: Basic Books, 1993).

erasure of the individuality of non-Russians was matched from the other side by the work of nationalist historians, who overplayed the singularity of their own nation's history, isolating it from the larger environment of empire and interrelationships with other peoples. In the 1980s, as non-Russians in the South Caucasus and Baltic region began agitating for autonomy and independence, a few historians and political scientists began to reconsider the dominant Cold War view that the nationalities policy of Lenin, while proudly proclaiming "national self-determination" of all peoples, was in actuality disingenuous and dedicated exclusively to the aggrandizement of the central state's power. Bolshevik attempts to foster ethnonational cultures, promote leaders from non-Russian nationalities, and organize the first state composed of national territorial units were re-examined by a small group of younger scholars—Yuri Slezkine, Jeremy Smith, Terry Martin, and Francine Hirsch among them—who attempted to move beyond nationalist and narcissistic accounts to place nationality in its wider, more comparative context.

Without omitting the negative and destructive aspects of Soviet nationality policy, post-Soviet scholarship on non-Russians in the USSR accepted the constructivist paradigm shift to consider the ways in which nations were made or remade within the body of the empire. In his unique account *The Jewish Century*, Yuri Slezkine argued that, until World War I and the anti-Semitic campaigns under Stalin after the war, Soviet Jews thrived, becoming a primarily urban population largely assimilated into the multinational Soviet people. By World War II almost 90 percent of Soviet Jews lived in cities, most of them in the largest eleven cities, making up a large and influential segment of the "Soviet bourgeoisie." Highly represented in the party leadership and the secret police, in the intelligentsia, among artists, in higher education, the diplomatic corps, and the spy service, Jews were among the most loyal Communists well into the 1950s. "In effect," writes Slezkine, "the role of the Jews in the prewar Soviet Union was similar to the role of the Germans in imperial Russia (or the role of Phanariot Greeks in the Ottoman Empire, among other instances)."[59] Jews were prominent in Bolshevism, and many gentiles identified Bolshevism with the Jews. By the 1930s, Soviet nationality policies moved steadily toward an essentialization, even biologization, of nationality, which became relatively fixed, a matter of identification at every stage of life and a line in one's internal passport. Even as they left

59 Yuri Slezkine, *The Jewish Century* (Princeton, NJ: Princeton University Press, 2004), p. 237.

the shtetl and Yiddish behind and assimilated into their beloved Russian culture, Jews remained Jews. The Nazi invasion only reinforced their Jewish identification, and both war and the creation of the State of Israel re-ethnicized Soviet Jews.

> The two trends—the ethnicization of the Soviet state and the national-ization of ethnic Jews—kept reinforcing each other until Stalin and the new Agitprop officials made two terrifying discoveries. First, the Jews as a Soviet nationality were now an ethnic diaspora potentially loyal to a hostile foreign state .... Second, according to the new Soviet definition of national belonging and political loyalty, the Russian Soviet intelligentsia, created and nurtured by Comrade Stalin, was not really Russian—and thus not fully Soviet. Russians of Jewish descent were masked Jews, and masked Jews were traitors twice over.[60]

The usual explanation of the anti-cosmopolitan campaign of the late 1940s usually starts with Stalin and his native anti-Semitism, but such an explanation does not explain the successes of Jews in the heyday of Stalinism before the war. Slezkine's explanation gives us a richer model: Jewish success along with the rise of educated Russians coupled with the emphasis in all walks of life of the importance of ethnicity (not class any longer) led to a situation in which it was no longer acceptable that Jews dominate the very realms into which Russians and others aspired to move. Anti-Semitism only increased with the emphasis on ethnicity and the re-ethnicization of Soviet Jews. Stalin in turn began to see Soviet Jews as an internal danger and decided to destroy them. The dictator essentially reflected the interests of the upwardly mobile new Russian educated class, the backbone of the regime. The older elite was deci-mated to allow a new one to emerge. In a nationalized Soviet Union, the Jews became Jews once again. And though Jews recovered some-what after Stalin's death, Slezkine's epitaphs are telling: "The Russian and Jewish Revolutions died the way they were born—together" and "Communism lost out to both liberalism and nationalism and then died of exhaustion."[61]

In her work Francine Hirsch shows that the state's efforts led to a "double assimilation": the coalescing of unstructured populations into

---

60   Ibid., p. 297.
61   Ibid., pp. 330–1, 359.

nationalities and the further assimilation of these nationalities into a Sovietized society. Referring to the Soviet Union as an "empire of nations," she demonstrates how ethnographers from the former tsarist regime collaborated with Leninists to shape the new state. Hers is the tale of a modernizing, self-styled scientific state that imposed categories, names, and programs on ethnic populations with relatively little say in their own fate. The whole enterprise is reminiscent—indeed, parallels —what European imperialists, like the British in India, did to their conquered and colonized subjects. Yet Hirsch is careful not to subscribe to the older view that Lenin was driven by power alone. Rather, she sees the building of the Soviet multinational state as the product of a joint intelligentsia project, at times enthusiastically backed by ethnographers and others, to liberate a benighted population and propel them along the evolutionary path toward modernity. Sometimes, the consideration for ethnicity gave way to other more compelling interests, like economics or defense, but the Soviet state never abandoned its official commitment to nation-making.

Hirsch is particularly insightful on how Soviet "race science" differed from that of the Nazis. Whereas the Hitlerites saw biological race as immutable and a fundamental determinant of a people's abilities, Soviet ethnographers saw "race" as a product of history, therefore changing and developing. All peoples, in their view, were capable of progressing through time. They advanced most rapidly in socialist society, and there they would eventually form a multicultural community—the Soviet people. Her account of the Soviet Union as a "work in progress" that neither began with a blueprint nor achieved completion reaffirmed the now widely accepted view of nation formation as a continuous process of human intervention and invention.

The "constructivist" view that nations are made in modern times and are the product of conscious efforts to piece together elements of shared language or culture in defense of the right to political freedom takes on a particular inflexion in the Soviet experience. As Terry Martin has shown, the socialist state played a particularly forceful role in delineating and consolidating nations within its fold, alternating nation-making with the most vicious destruction of ethnicities and nationalities during the Stalin years.[62] One of the great ironies of Soviet history is that the

---

62   One of Martin's most revealing findings is that much of the Stalinist Terror of the 1930s was directed against non-Russian nationalists. See Martin, *The Affirmative Action Empire*, particularly pp. 311–43. See also the beautifully written and argued study

regime's very success in creating and fostering nations led eventually to the union's disintegration once the central government began loosening its hold over the empire's peripheries. Thinking of nations as primordial, however, is still common among post-Soviet peoples. Most citizens of present-day Russia, Armenia, or Uzbekistan are certain that they are distinct and different from their neighbors precisely because of their ancient origins and unique cultural characteristics. This legacy of the long Soviet experiment is clear in the ethnic violence and interstate warfare that has marked the post-Soviet decades, evidence that the Soviet Union continues to unravel. Besides inclusion in and allegiance to a particular nation, post-Soviet peoples share the mentalities and habits of another unique cultural formation, the culture that can only be described as Soviet. Apparently you can take people out of the Soviet Union, but you may not, at least for a long time, take the Soviet out of the people.

of the western borderlands, Kate Brown, *A Biography of No Place: From Ethnic Borderland to Soviet Heartland* (Cambridge, MA: Harvard University Press, 2004).

4

Living in the Soviet Century:
Moshe Lewin, 1921–2010

"The history he wrote," a colleague said at his memorial, "was insepara-
ble from his life."[1] Another added, "He didn't fit in the world in which
he lived. He was always trying to save the Soviet Union, which was the
country that had saved him." His convictions were as strong as his biceps,
which he enjoyed showing off to friends. And so was his heart. We at that
small, intimate gathering, fellow travelers along the pathways of Soviet
history, recognized the man, Moshe Lewin, as a maestro in his field,
more a guru than an academic mentor, a teacher and scholar of enormous interpretive power who introduced novel conceptualizations into
the understanding of Russia's experience. Self-absorbed, a talker rather
than a listener, Misha (as almost all of us called him) was a pioneer in the
Western writing of Soviet social history, a singular light for many younger
scholars in the intellectually obscure years of the Cold War, a contrarian
who offered alternative ways to understand what had happened to the
emancipatory aspirations of 1917. Without much provocation, he poured
out deeply founded ideas and strongly held opinions on how a popular
revolution of extraordinary ambition had degenerated into the nightmare of Stalinism. He lived most of his life alone but never complained of
loneliness. He loved long late-night calls from his friends and was always

    1   My thanks to Geoff Eley, James Heinzen, Peter Holquist, and Lewis H. Siegel-
baum for reading earlier versions of this essay and making important suggestions for
improvement. An earlier version of this chapter was published as "Living in the Soviet
Century: Moshe Lewin, 1921–2010," *History Workshop Journal*, LXXI, 1 (Autumn
2012), pp. 192–209.

ready to receive visitors, plied them with schnapps and sausages, and held forth with his puckish humor on the latest possibilities for change (for better or worse) in Russia and (why not?) the rest of the world. His death at nearly eighty-nine left a personal vacuum, but his work remains as a foundation for present and future generations to ponder. Though he was firm in his convictions, as one of the principal "revisionists" in Soviet historiography, he would have appreciated that his own oeuvre like that of his admired predecessors—E. H. Carr, Isaac Deutscher, Naum Jasny, and Lev Trotsky—would be debated, contested, and revised.

Saved by the Soviets

Born in Wilno (Vilno), Poland, on November 6, 1921, Moshe Lewin was the product of a unique cosmopolitan culture in which Jews, Poles, Lithuanians, and Russians lived uneasily together. His own family reflected the cosmopolitanism of the city: his father was Jewish, his mother a Russian-speaking Ukrainian, and though he would self-identify throughout his life as a Jew, Misha defined his "nationality" autonomously from any of the standard categories. Certainly not religious, his ethnic culture was broadly eastern European and his intellectual culture self-consciously internationalist. His own city of birth would pass in his lifetime from Poland to Lithuania to German occupation to the Soviet Union and finally to become the capital of the independent Lithuanian republic, Vilnius. In a city where Jews were the second largest ethnicity, behind Poles but well ahead of Lithuanians, anti-Semitism was rampant. As Misha later told an interviewer, because it was frequently expressed in physical violence, Jews referred to it as "zoological."[2] Life in a place of such intense ethnic conflict and political activity forced one to choose one's movement literally as an act of self-defense. For young Misha, the choice was *Hashomer Hatsa'ir* (Youth Guard), a Zionist socialist youth movement that proposed a non-nationalist, bi-national state for Arabs and Jews in Palestine. "Zionism," he later said, "offered a dignified and honorable way out of the predicament, a way to save one's sanity as well as one's physical and cultural identity, and to say loudly 'no' to a virulent national and human discrimination."[3] Experiencing the pain inflicted by

---

2   "Moshe Lewin," in *Visions of History* (New York: Pantheon Books, 1976), p. 281. The interviewer was early Russian historian Paul Bushkovitch.

3   Ibid., p. 282.

national chauvinism, Lewin came "to understand the power of nationalism without acquiring any taste for it."[4]

When his home city, then the capital of Soviet Lithuania, was invaded by the Germans, Lewin escaped eastward. He tried to join fleeing Soviet soldiers but an officer refused to allow him to board the evacuating truck. The ordinary peasant conscripts, however, winked at him and pulled him up. He never saw his family again. Both his Russian-speaking mother and his father, whom Misha described as a real "Hercules," were murdered by the Nazis. As he told the story, when the Germans came to take them, his father wrested a machine gun from one of the soldiers and took several with him as they shot him and his wife. In another version of the story, related by Alain Gresh in *Le Monde diplomatique*, the arresting soldiers were actually members of a right-wing Lithuanian militia, who acted even before the Germans had entered the city.[5]

Misha eventually reached the Urals, where he worked on farms, in factories, and a mine before joining the Soviet Army in 1943 and moving westward back toward Poland. Years later, when a fellow leftist scholar scolded intellectuals who did not understand the labors of the proletariat and stared at Misha as he said it, Misha said, "Would working in a foundry do?"[6] When he reached Vilno, he spoke to his neighbors, who were frightened that he had come to take revenge on them. It was they who related the story of his parents' death. Sometime later, as an officer, he witnessed the victory parade on Red Square in May 1945. With experiences unique for a future historian, he returned to Poland, soon moving to Paris where he worked to facilitate Jewish migration to Palestine. His party, *Hashomer Hatsa'ir*, merged in 1948 with *Ahdut Ha'Avodah* (Labor Unity) to form *MAPAM* (United Workers' Party). Around this time, he met the influential Moshe Sneh, a leftist Zionist whom Misha deeply respected. He emigrated to Israel in 1951 as a committed Zionist and lived for a time in a kibbutz and worked with Sneh on the daily newspaper *Al Hamishmar* (On Guard). He eventually joined *MAKI*, the Communist Party, the only joint Jewish–Arab party in Israel.

Those who tried to marry Marxism, an internationalist, class-oriented vision of history and politics, with Zionism, deeply nationalist and committed to preserving a particular culture, were unusually vulnerable in the new Jewish state. Lewin's disillusionment with Zionism began, as he

---

4   Ibid., p. 283.
5   *Le Monde diplomatique*, August 16, 2010.
6   Personal communication from Dorothy Thompson, September 8, 2010.

told the story, when he was shocked by Ariel Sharon's raid into Jordan in 1953 that ended in a massacre of sixty people in the village of Qibia. Later, while serving in the Israeli army in the 1956 war with Egypt, he witnessed the killing of Egyptian prisoners of war and concluded that his original Zionist ideals diverged too much from the actuality of the state of Israel.[7] The Cold War had reshaped the political world, turned Israel into a Western ally, and the Soviet Union into a pariah state. Lewin felt his old formulae no longer explained enough. "Having read volume one of *Capital* at age fifteen, I felt unbeatable …. At the end of 1956 when I was thinking about next steps in my life[,] it was clear that my Marxist political past was unfolding without my understanding Marx."[8] He turned to scholarship, first at Tel Aviv University, where he studied economics and received his BA in 1961, and then at the Sorbonne, where in 1964 he completed the doctoral thesis under Roger Portal that became his first book, *La Paysannerie et le pouvoir soviétique: 1928–1930.*[9]

An Academic Odyssey

Deeply influenced by the social historical *Annales* school and by his friend, the sociologist Basile Kerblay, Lewin taught in Paris at the École pratique des hautes études before moving to the University of Birmingham (1968–78), one of the premier centers in Britain for studying Russia and the Soviet Union. There he developed friendships with colleagues like R. W. Davies, Edward and Dorothy Thompson, Christopher Hill, and Rodney Hilton, historians who shared his political enthusiasms and his appreciation of innovative Marxist approaches to the study of history. E. H. Carr invited Lewin to collaborate with him in writing the volumes of his *History of Soviet Russia* on the 1920s, the New Economic Policy (NEP) years. Misha declined, thinking he was not yet sufficiently prepared for the task, only to regret his decision in later years.

In 1978, he joined the faculty at the University of Pennsylvania, where he and his colleague, Alfred Rieber, organized a highly influential series of seminars—the National Seminar for the Study of Russia in the

---

7   Much of the material on Zionism and Lewin's years in Israel comes from personal conversations with Moshe Lewin and from Omer Bartov, "Moshe Lewin's Century," *Kritika* XII, 1 (Winter 2011), pp. 115–25.

8   "Moshe Lewin," *Visions of History*, p. 290.

9   Moshe Lewin, *La Paysannerie et le pouvoir soviétique: 1928–1930* (Paris: Mouton, 1966).

Twentieth Century—that brought a generation of younger historians from the study of imperial Russia into the post-1917 period. Since he had once been a member of a Communist Party, the American Congress had to pass a special bill, sponsored by Senator Edward Kennedy, to demonstrate that he was a "national resource" and therefore deserving of a permanent visa. Despite his disappointment that the promises made by the university administration for an elaborated program in Soviet studies were never fulfilled, Misha became an important presence in American historiography on the USSR. The seminars he inspired produced a series of volumes—on the Russian Civil War, the NEP, and Stalinist industrialization—at a time when there was very little reliable scholarship in English free from Cold War polemics. His co-founder of the seminar, Al Rieber, notes that "Misha was in his element, for he was always more effective as a 'teacher of teachers' than a teacher of students."[10] Eventually, the failure to secure funding for the project, in part the product of resentments and jealousies toward those included in the seminars from others left out, led to the demise of the effort. Once again disappointed, Misha found refuge in his crowded study on the top floor of his apartment, there surrounded by books, reprints of documents and articles, and drawers of notes, primarily in Hebrew. Among the graduate students who benefited from his mentorship were James Heinzen, David Kerans, and David Shearer.

While dedicated to his scholarship, Misha Lewin was not content simply to contemplate the world. He looked for ways to change it. Along with Ken Coates, Dorothy and Edward Thompson, he initiated the influential European Nuclear Disarmament movement in the early 1980s.[11] In the Gorbachev years, he travelled to the Soviet Union, the first time since he had left during the war. In 1987 and 1989, he carried out research in the newly opened archives, and, while in Moscow, gave a number of lectures, which were warmly received. For a brief time, he played the role of public intellectual in Russia, a unique bridge between Western and Soviet scholarship at the very moment when the petrified orthodoxy of communism was being abandoned and before the new orthodoxy of anti-communism would take hold. Friendships with Soviet historians, like the scholar of peasants Viktor Danilov and of nationalities Albert Nenarokov, enriched his life, and younger scholars, like Oleg Khlevniuk, and newly empowered archivists, like Larissa Rogovaia, embraced Mikhail Lvovich as a

10   Alfred J. Rieber, "Moshe Lewin: A Reminiscence and Appreciation," *Kritika* XII, 1 (Winter 2011), pp. 130–1.

11   Personal communication from Dorothy Thompson, September 8, 2010.

recovered uncle. In September 1991, months before the end of the Soviet Union, he organized a major conference in Philadelphia to move beyond the totalitarian model and find novel ways of comparing (and contrasting) Stalinism and Nazism. Working with the historian Ian Kershaw, he eventually co-edited a collection of papers from the conference as *Stalinism and Nazism: Dictatorships in Comparison.*[12]

Lewin retired from Penn in 1995. Despite a full life in Philadelphia, which included long walks through the city, concerts, museums, and restaurants, he complained about the distance from his friends in Europe and his isolation from the mainstream of Soviet studies in America. He was a man of strong likes and dislikes, and those of us who had discussions with him about the field of Soviet history remember well his unyielding assessments of other scholars. "A stinker," he would proclaim, "a *goniff*," using the Yiddish for "thief" or "dishonest scoundrel." Listening to an eminent historian who was discoursing far too long and seemed not to be making a point, he leaned over to his neighbor and in a quite audible stage whisper said, "The man is asleep!" His work was the vital center of his life, and he chastised an itinerant scholar like myself who accepted too many lectures and went to too many conferences. In his impeccable Yiddish he gently scolded, "*Men ken nit tantsn oyf tsvey khasenes mit eyn tukhes.*" (You can't dance at two weddings with one backside.) His colleagues, many of whom disagreed with his values and approaches, nevertheless recognized his extraordinary achievements and bestowed upon him the American Association for Slavic Studies award for Distinguished Contribution to Slavic Studies in 2006. A year later, he moved to Paris and set himself up in a beautiful apartment in the Pigalle area, where he was always ready to receive and entertain friends. Sadly, however, despite his vigor, regular exercise, and impressive physical strength, he did not have much time left. The decline was swift. He suffered from dementia, paranoia, and hallucinations. Friends distanced themselves. Among the few who came by was his longtime and loyal friend, the Israeli painter Raffi Kaiser, whose delicate, enigmatic landscapes hung on Misha's walls in Philadelphia and Paris. Moshe Lewin died on August 14, 2010, in many ways out of touch with the world he left behind.

---

12   Ian Kershaw and Moshe Lewin (eds.), *Stalinism and Nazism: Dictatorships in Comparison* (Cambridge: Cambridge University Press, 1997).

The Work: Lewin's Vision of Soviet History

For the first fifty years after the Bolshevik Revolution, very few professional historians in the West ventured into Russian history and fewer still crossed the revolutionary divide into the history of the Soviet Union. Among the few who did were the prolific former diplomat Edward Hallett Carr and the dissident socialist Isaac Deutscher. In the United States in particular the field was left to political scientists, the so-called Sovietologists or Kremlinologists, while university history departments contented themselves with students of pre-Petrine or imperial Russia. Interestingly enough, the first two major scholars to break through the barrier of 1917 and pioneer the historical study of Soviet socialism were neither American nor British, but Moshe Lewin, a refugee from Poland and the USSR, and Sheila Fitzpatrick, an Australian from a prominent leftist family. Working independently, each shaped the burgeoning generation of social historians of the Soviet Union that populated the profession in the last few decades. Both were critics of the dominant Cold War models, most notably totalitarianism, that oriented researchers toward the political heights of the Soviet state and away from the everyday and mundane behaviors and attitudes of ordinary and even well-placed social actors. Turning out her own empirically grounded studies of administration, culture, and the everyday, Fitzpatrick trained a cohort of students who delved into the Soviet archives as they became available. To her fox—borrowing here the ancient metaphor, later employed by Isaiah Berlin—Lewin was the hedgehog.[13] His legacy was a stunning series of original works from which flowed bold conceptual formulations of the great processes and patterns of Soviet social transformation. Often impressionistic and tentative, his syntheses provided a coherence to what he often referred to as the chaos and confusion that characterized the Soviet experience.

Lewin's scholarly work centered on three broad subjects: the Russian peasantry and its relationship to the Soviet state, the Soviet bureaucracy, and the limits of leadership. From the beginning, he considered himself a "historian of society," rather than simply of a regime. "It is not a state that has a society but a society that has a state."[14] His *Russian Peasants and*

---

13   In this metaphor taken from the Greek poet Archilochus, the fox knows many things, the hedgehog one big thing. Isaiah Berlin, *The Hedgehog and the Fox: An Essay on Tolstoy's View of History* (London: Weidenfeld and Nicholson, 1953).

14   Personal communication with the author, March 13, 2004.

Soviet Power: A Study of Collectivization was the first serious empirical investigation in the West of the decision to collectivize Russia's peasants.[15] *Lenin's Last Struggle* presented a portrait different in all ways from the Cold War stereotype of a power-hungry and dogmatic despot. What was striking at the time to this reader, then a graduate student, was how the author revealed a Lenin with serious doubts about the direction in which his experimental regime was moving and who tried desperately but futilely to shift to another path. Rather than a fatalistic line drawn from Marxism or the revolution to Stalin's despotism, Lewin saw alternatives to Stalinism within Bolshevism, contingencies and choices, as well as the deep social structures, determining what the Soviet Union would become. "Stalin," Lewin wrote, "worked hard, in fact, to eliminate ideologically and physically both Bolshevism as a political party and Leninism as its guiding strategic orientation."[16] Rather than a continuation of Leninism, Stalinism was a reversion to an older, prerevolutionary despotic statism and traditional peasant, prebourgeois culture that the revolution proved impossible to overcome in its first decades. As a one-time Communist, Lewin was interested in how a leftist revolutionary dictatorship could be socially transformative in a progressive direction but not degenerate into a "personal, despotic and irrational dictatorship."[17] In many ways, this book was addressed as much to leaders in Cuba and China as to his fellow scholars or a more general public.

Lewin never completed an ambitious project about which he often spoke—a social history of the Soviet Union. Yet from his prolific production it is possible to reconstruct a rough account of his major arguments about the most significant developments, their causes and effects, in the seventy years of Soviet power. For Lewin, 1917 was full of positive potential, but the revolution was embedded in "a connected chain of crises, in part 'imported' from abroad."[18] What more conservative historians would fail to admit, Lewin pointed out, was that in this "unhinged country," "the Bolsheviks stepped into a morass that nobody else could face—and a new system emerged that allowed the country to survive."[19] The Bolsheviks' initial success in winning state power in October 1917 was followed by an even greater achievement—turning a massive peasant

---

15   Moshe Lewin, *Russian Peasants and Soviet Power: A Study of Collectivization*, trans. Irene Nove (Evanston, IL: Northwestern University Press, 1968).

16   Moshe Lewin, *Lenin's Last Struggle* (Ann Arbor: University of Michigan Press, 2005), p. xxvii.

17   Ibid., p. 136.

18   Ibid., p. xxvi.

19   Ibid.

jacquerie into a proletarian revolution and in the face of foreign inter-vention and White, nationalist, and liberal opposition to create a state in the midst of civil war. The seizure of power by the Bolsheviks had been a risky gamble predicated on the idea that a socialist revolution would succeed in Russia once the European proletariat came to its rescue. But Europe's workers did not play the role that Lenin had written for them, and instead of a rapid move toward socialism, Russia was fated to a long period of holding out against capitalist forces—*proderzhatsiia*—until revolutionary reinforcements, perhaps from colonized Asia if not from Europe, came to the rescue.

Surrounded by enemies and at war for the next three-plus years, the Bolsheviks abandoned the vision elaborated in Lenin's *State and Revo-lution* of worker self-rule in favor of bureaucratic management, which in the devastated landscape of civil war ended up with the Communist Party losing "the support of the mass of its troops" and "suspended in the void."[20] The long years of war contributed to centralization of power and the erosion of democratic practices; appointment from above was substituted for election from below. The Civil War had brought certain kinds of people into the party and state apparatus, people who knew how to be harsh, how to organize, and how not to be too scrupulous as they used "the enormous powers that a wartime dictatorship [had] conferred on them."[21] Bolshevism evolved into Leninism. Lewin follows Trotsky and Deutscher in describing the sociopsychological makeup of this new generation of party activists who had not lived outside of Russia and were not as deeply attached to the earlier vision of socialism. They were less idealistic, more pragmatic, "less attached to the dream and more concerned with power."[22] Instead of a Russian workers' republic administered by soviets and factory committees, a dictatorship of the party was established.

Lenin, who had long touted the ability of workers to make a revo-lution, discovered to his dismay that they were too few in number and not educated enough to govern the country. Without a definite level of *kul'tura* (culture), the building of socialism was impossible. He feared that the workers and their party would be overwhelmed by *petit bour-geois* decline, the traditionalist influence of the overwhelming majority of the population, the peasantry. In March 1921, when "the prevailing psychology was one of a struggle for existence," Lenin made what would

20   Ibid., p. 8.
21   Ibid., p. 32.
22   Ibid., p. 60.

prove to be a fatal error: he proposed a ban on factions within the party.[23] Misjudging the degree of danger to the party from both outside and inside its ranks, he limited the freewheeling discussions that the party had tolerated during the war but now in peacetime found to be dangerously divisive. "Lenin's views," Lewin writes, "did not conceal a thirst for personal power, and in fact, the Party machine that Lenin and Trotsky helped to build turned against both of them."[24] In contrast to what Stalin would become, Lewin emphasized that though Lenin was "'master of Russia'... he was not a dictator in his own party, but its leader. His leadership was incontestable and uncontested but it demanded of him a constant effort of thought and organization; he had to act as if he was reaffirming and reconquering it each day."[25]

While not uncritical of Bolshevism, Lewin was genuinely sympathetic to Lenin, an admirer of his strategic brilliance as well as his ambitions for Russia. His own historical narrative paralleled that of Lenin and Trotsky, and he was unable to accept the criticisms of the NEP that a younger generation of scholars derived from the archives.[26] He was convinced that the revolution might have realized a far more just and egalitarian society than it did and that much suffering and excess repression might have been avoided if Lenin had lived and Stalin had been removed from his post. Lewin's dominant emotion throughout was regret that things had not turned out differently. Yet, even as he recognized contingency, chance, and accidents, he occasionally expressed a more tragic judgment that the earlier promise of the revolution could not be realized given conditions outside the control of any leader or party.

Lewin not only took Marxism seriously as a powerful analytical lens but also considered the ideology of the Bolsheviks an influential if not all-determining element. The party had certain expressed intentions, but without a reliable social base, it was unable from quite early on to impose its "pure political power" on the spontaneous dynamic that under the NEP was moving in a direction opposite from what the leaders favored. Lewin used as an epigram for *Lenin's Last Struggle* the famous caution of Friedrich Engels that an "insolvable dilemma" arose when a leader took over government at a time that the "movement was not ripe for the domination of the class which he represents .... What he can do contradicts all his previous actions, principles, and immediate interests of his

23   Ibid., p. 32.
24   Ibid., p. 15.
25   Ibid., p. 42.
26   Personal communication from James Heinzen, January 3, 2012.

party, and what he ought to do cannot be done …. Whoever is put into this awkward position is irrevocably doomed."[27] But, again in contrast to more conservative historians, like Martin Malia, Lewin took Lenin at his word and concluded that "Leninist doctrine did not originally envisage a monolithic state, nor even a strictly monolithic party; the dictatorship of the Party *over* the proletariat was never part of Lenin's plans, it was the completely unforeseen culmination of a series of unforeseen circumstances."[28] Once victory had been consolidated in the Civil War, the next task was to create an economic infrastructure to underpin Soviet political power and to raise the cultural level of both the party cadres and, through literacy campaigns, the people. In a country like Russia where (as the Mensheviks had warned) the necessary preconditions for the kind of social order envisioned by Marx simply did not exist, Lenin proposed cultural revolution and the formation of all kinds of cooperatives as indispensable steps toward socialism.

The NEP, Lenin's most distinctive innovation to Marxist economic practice—and one that Lewin later argued was the essence of Deng Xiaoping's reforms in China—was based on a deal that the regime made, first with independent producers, and then with the peasants: they would be allowed to retain much of their surplus production and engage in commercial relations in the countryside but would not contest the Bolsheviks for political power. Peasants could not live and produce without capitalism, Lenin wrote; he added, however: "We promise neither freedom nor democracy."[29] NEP was "a pact with the devil," salutary for the patient but potentially fatal for the doctor.[30] By conceding a limited degree of capitalism to the masses of peasants, the party potentially was encouraging the growth of capitalist rather than collectivist sentiments among agriculturalists as well as nurturing the rise of all kinds of petty tradesmen and merchants to the detriment of the workers. The greatest dangers to the regime were the potential fracturing of the putative "alliance" of the workers and peasants (the *smychka*) and the personal and political divisions among the leaders at the top, most importantly between Stalin and

---

27   Lewin, *Lenin's Last Struggle*, p. v; the original quotation is from Engels, *Der deutsche Bauernkrieg* (*The Peasant War in Germany*), written in 1850.

28   Lewin, *Lenin's Last Struggle*, p. 17.

29   Ibid., p. 41; V. I. Lenin, *Polnoe sobranie sochineniia*, XLIV (Moscow: Izdatel'stvo politicheskoi literatury, 1970), p. 54. Lenin was speaking to the Third Congress of the Comintern (Communist International), July 5, 1921, explaining the tactics of the Russian Communist Party. The whole sentence reads: "And we say: 'In war we act as one does in war: we do not promise any kind of freedom nor any kind of democracy.'"

30   Lewin, *Lenin's Last Struggle*, p. 22.

Trotsky. Lenin's last struggle was against the bureaucratic mentalities and practices epitomized by Stalin, particularly in the conflict over nationality policy (the famous "Georgian Affair"), the degree of centralization of the multinational Soviet state, and the increasing power of the General Secretary and his Secretariat. For political and personal reasons, Lenin came to the stunning conclusion that Stalin had to be removed from his position as head of the Secretariat, but a series of strokes made it impossible for him to carry out his will.

Suspended as it was above the social forces below, the party leadership had to rely on itself to maintain Soviet power. What Lenin did not realize was that "the bureaucracy would become the true social basis of power."[31] Here, Lewin engages in his own form of middle level political theory (again essentially indebted to Trotsky and Deutscher).

> There is no such thing as "pure" political power, devoid of any social foundation. A regime must find some other social basis than the apparatus of repression itself. The "void" in which the Soviet regime had seemed to be suspended had soon been filled, even if the Bolsheviks had not seen it, or did not wish to see it. The Stalinist period might be defined, therefore, as the substitution of the bureaucracy for the original social basis of the regime, namely, the working class, a section of the poorest peasants and certain strata of the intelligentsia.[32]

The Communist Party was transformed from "a political party into a state apparatus. Stalin seized on this tendency and, instead of controlling it as Lenin wished, accepted it, based his own power upon it and developed it."[33]

In his master work, *The Making of the Soviet System: Essays in the Social History of Interwar Russia*, Lewin brought together sprawling seminal essays on early Soviet history, enveloping great social processes in pungent phrases: "quicksand society," "the contamination effect," "'superstructure' rushing ahead" of the social base, a "ruling class without tenure."[34] Such innovative and suggestive interpretations continued in what might be considered its sequel *Russia, USSR, Russia: The Drive and Drift of a Superstate*.[35] Here, too, the contingency and evident

---

31   Ibid., p. 124.
32   Ibid., pp. 124–5.
33   Ibid., p. 126.
34   Moshe Lewin, *The Making of the Soviet System: Essays in the Social History of Interwar Russia* (New York: The New Press, 1985; 1994).
35   Moshe Lewin, *Russia, USSR, Russia: The Drive and Drift of a Superstate* (New York: The New Press, 1995).

improvisation of the Bolsheviks challenged the monophonic view of a rigid consistent ideology from which the regime could find formulae for the future. Lewin's histories stood between the highly deterministic accounts that seem to posit that what happened had to happen—and was probably for the best or as good as it could be—and highly speculative "if histories," which wistfully conjectured what might have been "if only."[36] His conversation was primarily with other leftists—those who like Maurice Dobb or R. W. Davies (at least for a time) saw the Stalinist choice as necessary and unavoidable or Carr, who appeared enthralled by victors, as well as Trotskyists and Bukharinists, who were convinced that their heroes would certainly have provided a viable and preferable alternative to Stalinism. For Lewin, Nikolai Bukharin, the champion of the NEP, offered a more rational path to socialism, but he was hardly uncritical of "the darling of the party." Bukharin misunderstood Stalin until it was too late; he displayed a "lack of character" and "weakness as a politician."[37] The historian, Lewin emphasized, must lay out the what and why of history, the reasons for the choices made and the alternatives to the path taken, which for others might be instructive for learning from the past and avoiding errors. "Is not this, after all, one of the primary reasons for embarking on any study of history?"[38]

Lewin's method was to sketch in the social background of the events and decisions that he would examine. He began with the peasantry, and his portrait is a powerful one of a superstitious, largely illiterate mass holding Russia back because of what Lenin called its "semi-Asiatic *bez-kul'turnost'*" (lack of culture). Hardly an inert or irrational population, the peasants were the hardworking machine generating what economic production Russia enjoyed. The peasantry, after all, had in part made the victory of the revolution possible by wiping out the power of the landlords in the countryside and ultimately siding with the Reds against the Whites. Until the last years of the 1920s the "alliance" between the Soviet government and the villagers held. "The peasants identified the Soviet regime with NEP, and NEP with socialism. They accepted the regime, but without enthusiasm, for since the revolution they had not yet had sufficient opportunity to determine what real advantages it had to offer."[39] In its own Marxist vision, the party feared that the *muzhiki* were gravitating toward capitalism, but Lewin subjected this Communist

36   Lewin, *Russian Peasants and Soviet Power*, p. 15.
37   Ibid., pp. 12–13.
38   Ibid., p. 16.
39   Ibid., p. 36.

sociology to devastating criticism. "Kulak" was a vague and dangerous category that was applied to the hardest working and most productive farmers. In no way, he wrote, should they have been considered capitalist, semi-capitalist, or petty capitalist. Here, Lewin draws close to the views of Bukharin, who emphasized a gradual, rather slow progress toward socialism through the cooperatives and the demonstration of the economic superiority of socialist practices. But he chides Bukharin for his fierce opposition to Evgenii Preobrazhenskii's arguments that the peasants would have to bear a greater tax burden in order to industrialize the country rapidly. Russia was so backward that a "primitive socialist accumulation" was the only road to modernity. Bukharin himself came to realize the importance of the peasants' contribution to industrialization, but factional politics and personal animosities kept those around Preobrazhenskii and Trotsky from effecting an alliance with Bukharin and those who would be labeled "the Right."

NEP realized its potential for restoring the Soviet economy by 1926–27, and, by 1927–28, a serious grain procurement crisis compelled the party leaders to consider alternatives to the generally pro-peasant policy they had favored a few years before. Now dominant politically, Stalin pushed through a radical program of forced grain requisitions that were reminiscent of the years of civil war. "*The truth was that NEP, in its 'classic' form, was virtually dead.*"[40] Stalin had concluded that the peasantry constituted a capitalist class, and in short order he eliminated the last major opposition to his personal power, the so-called "Right Opposition." While Bukharin rejected the use of force against the peasants, echoing Engels and Lenin, and proposed guiding them through the cooperative movement toward socialism, Stalin was prepared to resort to coercion, effectively ending the *smychka*. Collectivization and the campaign against the kulaks constituted a new revolution that would create a novel political and economic formation—Stalinism. But, Lewin argues, the Stalinists were prepared to abandon NEP "*before any alternative forms or structures had taken shape, even in the minds of the leadership.*"[41]

The first, but hardly the last, victims of the precipitous drive to industrialize by Stalin and his supporters were the Soviet Union's peasants. Himself a survivor because of some insubordinate peasants, Lewin was profoundly sympathetic to what had been done to their countrymen, the unnecessary repression of millions of people and a whole way of life. Yet

40   Ibid., p. 235 (emphasis in original).
41   Lewin, *The Making of the Soviet System*, p. 91 (emphasis in original).

at the same time he coolly considered their customary social relations, their values and beliefs, and their mode of production to have been both archaic obstacles that had to be overcome in order to modernize Russia and the resistant foundation that insidiously made Stalinist autocracy possible.

The Stalinists had come to power during the NEP period when the system remained based on informal "social contracts" with the peasantry, bourgeois specialists, and various non-Communist intellectuals. Now, in the ferocious struggle with the peasants and the accelerated, forced industrialization of the country, Stalinism as a system came into being, eliminating market relations in the economy and increasing the power of the political and economic elite. Coercion marginalized consultation and negotiation. In the process the leader soon metastasized into an autocrat with absolute power of life and death over his subordinates. The Communist Party ceased to be in any meaningful sense a political party and became an administrative bureaucracy under a single, despotic *vozhd'* (leader). Politics was subjugated to economics, and all aspects of the system—cultural and artistic as well—were "economized." This was a regime built on layers of dangerous myths—"the myth of the 'foreign conspiracy,' the myth of the 'saboteur in foreign pay,' the 'kulak menace,' or again the 'danger from the right' and the 'right-wing appeasers,'" and eventually the myth of "Stalin the invincible."[42] A program of rebuilding and restructuring a whole society was undertaken without adequate materials, at tempos impossible to realize, with great waste of resources and human beings, creating what Lewin characterized as a "permanent crisis." While industrialization in Russia required both "tribute" from the people and a tough, resolute dictatorship, it did not need a terroristic autocracy subject to repeated excesses.

His deeply textured analysis of Stalinism, profoundly critical of the system, at the same time belied the mythologies of the totalitarian model. There was no atomized population, little screws being turned by an all-powerful regime. He had this to say to an interviewer:

It was clear to me ... from conversations with workers, peasants, officials, and soldiers—when I lived there—that people reacted to the world in their own way, with their own words .... You couldn't come to a worker and tell him in private that he was a member of a ruling class. When I worked in the Urals, workers knew who they were and that it was the

42   Ibid. p. 100.

nachalstvo, the bosses, who had the power and the privileges. How many times did I hear from fellow workers that the *nachalstvo* [the bosses] take care of themselves but very little of "our kind"? The engineers and administrators had their own restaurant in the factory, and they came out from it clearly having eaten quite enough. Even their waitresses were fatter than the ones that served us.[43]

Dictatorial Stalinism failed to impose a single all-encompassing ideology on all; many mentalities coexisted along with the embalmed ideology of Stalin's own history of the Communist Party of the Soviet Union, the infamous *Short Course* [*Kratkii kurs*].[44] Society was "not an appendix to the Politburo."[45]

Not only was Stalinism not mature Leninism for Moshe Lewin, it was the opposite of Leninism, even though it had grown out of the earlier ideology. "Now with respect to the original Leninism," he wrote,

> Stalinism not only changed strategy but also reoriented the system toward quite different objectives. It was no longer a matter of constructing a society in which the classes and the state would disappear, passing through a stage of "socialism," as that term had been understood by Marx, Engels, Lenin, and also many Western socialists. It was now a matter of "statizing," that is, of crowning the whole with an all-powerful, dictatorial state in order to preserve the class system and such privileges as had been put into place during the period of forced industrialization.

Political isolation, both at home and internationally, the backwardness of Russian society, and the mismatch between ideology and social realities led agonizingly toward the tragedies and triumphs of the 1930s. The upward mobility of peasants into the working class and workers into management was matched by downward mobility, the elimination of whole classes of people and the decimation of elites in the Great Purges. Stalin's fear was that the routines and secure tenure required by the bureaucracy might constrain his absolute power, and he used fear and terror to discipline his subordinates. Lewin tells us, however, there was an alternative bureaucratic culture and practice throughout the years

---

43   "Moshe Lewin," *Visions of History*, p. 295.
44   For a full treatment of the gestation of this work, see David Brandenberger and Mikhail Zelenov (eds.), *Stalin's Master Narrative: A Critical Edition of the History of the Communist Party of the Soviet Union (Bolsheviks): Short Course* (New Haven, CT: Yale University Press, 2019).
45   "Moshe Lewin," *Visions of History*, p. 304.

of Stalinism that needed regulation and regularity, and ultimately with the tyrant's death that bureaucracy came into its own. The last decades of Soviet power were oligarchic and bureaucratic, authoritarian to be sure, but no longer terroristic and despotic. That post-Stalinist system, however, generated its own contradictions and crises that ultimately led it into a reformist frenzy that brought down the whole structure.

The great divide among Western Sovietologists and historians of Russia has been between those who collapsed the whole of the Soviet experience into the Stalinist phase and those who distinguished between Bolshevism, Stalinism, and the hybrid regime that emerged after 1953. While he was as critical of Stalin and Stalinism as any liberal or conservative, Lewin warned historians not to "'over-Stalinize' the whole of Soviet history by extending it backwards and forwards ... , a common practice that serves a variety of purposes—but not that of historical inquiry."[46] Lenin's gamble that seizing power in Russia would spark a revolution abroad and provide international aid for the building of socialism in a peasant country did not pay off. "That Russia was not ready for any form of Marxian socialism was a self-evident truth to every Marxist."[47] But when masses of new recruits came into the party who did "not know the difference between Marx and Engels and Marks & Spencer," the way was open for a plebeian "propensity for authoritarianism" to take over.[48] This was no "failure of socialism," Lewin wrote, "because socialism was not there in the first place. Devastated Russia was fit neither for democracy as Pavel Miliukov [the leader of the Liberals] understood it, nor for socialism, as Lenin and Trotsky knew full well."[49] Socialism remained an ideal for Lewin—"ownership of the means of production by society, not by a bureaucracy. It has always been conceived of as a deepening—not a rejection—of political democracy. To persist in speaking of 'Soviet socialism' is to engage in a veritable comedy of errors," he wrote.[50] This hippopotamus should not be confused with a giraffe! He summed up his own position on both the USSR and its historiography as "anti-anti-Communism."

While history and politics were tightly intertwined for Moshe Lewin, he continually warned that research and historical writing must be kept

---

46   Moshe Lewin, *The Soviet Century*, edited by Gregory Elliot (London: Verso, 2005), p. 322.
47   Ibid., p. 308.
48   Ibid., p. 291.
49   Ibid., p. 309.
50   Ibid., p. 379.

free from partisanship. Both Zionism and Marxism were initial inspira-
tions that set him on a path toward rethinking the world as it was and
attempting in whatever way he could, with the limited resources he had,
to improve things for Jews, for Russians, for whomever. Both projects
ended up, for quite different reasons, as states and societies with which
Misha could not fully identify. "The more friendly you are toward systems
or movements," he said, "the more vigilance you should exercise."[51] Still,
he was never like those unreconstructed Communists or Zionists who
continued to defend the actuality long after it had metamorphosed into
the opposite of its ideal. But neither did he turn 180 degrees into an
anti-Communist, as so many former leftists had, or an anti-Zionist. His
dialectical skepticism about the permanence of the present kept him
open to the possibilities of change. In the preface to *Lenin's Last Struggle*,
he revealed that this little book is not merely a rediscovery of Lenin's
futile attempt to rescue his life's work of emancipating the masses but
also a warning to socialists in power to heed lessons from the Soviet past.
Unusually confident about the effects his ideas might have, he consistently worked toward a more détentist attitude toward the Soviet Union,
elaborated "revisionist" views about totalitarianism as an explanation of
Soviet behavior, and questioned facile deductions from ideology to the
imperatives of real politics.

Although he was not at all sentimental about the actuality of the Soviet
system, as a socialist deeply influenced by Marxism, Lewin maintained a
profound optimism about the possibility of a more humane outcome for
the Soviet Union. At a time when almost no historians engaged in serious
work on the post-Stalin period, he assiduously read esoteric and deliberately obscure economic texts that revealed an intense debate among
scholars and policy makers in the 1960s over the relationship of market
mechanisms to a planned economy. His view of a more pluralistic Soviet
society with conflicting interests contrasted with the standard Western
vision of Soviet politics as uniform and homogeneous. In his *Political
Undercurrents in Soviet Economic Debates: From Bukharin to the Modern
Reformers,* he argued that ideas generated by Bukharin in his struggle to
preserve NEP had once again become relevant to the discussions among
reformers in the USSR and were even being revived in disguised forms.
Since the death of Stalin, a civil society had emerged in the USSR that
in turn generated critical views on the system, and though the efforts
at reform had been blunted they could not be stopped forever. Noting

---

51   "Moshe Lewin," *Visions of History*, p. 289.

the deep tensions and contradictions in Soviet society that had led to an ongoing series of "thaws" and "freezes," he concluded, nevertheless, that there was "a democratic stream that is trying, within the framework of a planned economy, to open the way for substantial changes in the Soviet system."[52] Almost no other journalist or scholar in the West perceived the existence or the power of that underground current that would pour forth after 1985.

In *The Gorbachev Phenomenon: An Historical Interpretation*, he reiterated that the Soviet system, born out of rural backwardness, profoundly changed in the decades before and after World War II. Just as ruralization and archaization had helped produce Stalinism, in the years after 1953 urbanization and the society it created enabled intellectuals and ordinary people to question and criticize the system. Growing out of the newly emerging civil society, democracy was "firmly placed on the Russian historical agenda," and it made its appearance with Gorbachev.[53] Society moved ahead, but the state system born in earlier eras remained embedded in the old agrarian despotism. Whereas in much of Russian history the state had been the agent of modernization, it eventually fell behind the transforming society and became (to employ a favorite Marxist term) a "fetter" on further development. Lewin was convinced that a Bukharinist model, a neo-NEP, was about to become a reality, this time not only with a mixed economy but with democratic politics. But his optimism was misplaced, and—though he did not explicitly make the conclusion— the fatal dialectic that ran through so much of his work played itself out. The interplay of the modernizing state and backward society that he had used to explain the rise of Stalinism had been turned on its head. An archaic state prevented the possible transition to a democratic polity and a socialist economy. Gorbachev also bears much of the blame for the demise of Lewin's beloved Soviet Union and the possibility of a socialist alternative. In every other way different from the Stalinists, Gorbachev, nevertheless, repeated their error of bringing down the existing system "*before any alternative forms or structures had taken shape, even in the minds of the leadership.*"[54]

In his last book, *The Soviet Century* (originally published as *Le siècle soviétique* in 2003), Lewin provided a powerful counternarrative to the

52   Moshe Lewin, *Political Undercurrents in Soviet Economic Debates: From Bukharin to the Modern Reformers* (Princeton, NJ: Princeton University Press, 1974), p. 352.

53   Moshe Lewin, *The Gorbachev Phenomenon: An Historical Interpretation*, Expanded Edition (Berkeley: University of California Press, 1991), p. 158.

54   Lewin, *The Making of the Soviet System*, p. 91 (emphasis in original).

dominant post-Soviet story of Soviet socialism as a utopian attempt to do the impossible. Russia's twentieth century, he wrote, involved a "collision between a developing industrial society and the reaction—or lack of reaction—of the peasantry, as well as the impact of this complex mix on the political regime."[55] When the regime coerced the country-side to abandon its traditional ways, the peasantry found ways to exact "its revenge, as it were, by compelling the regime further to strengthen its already imposing administrative-repressive machinery."[56] What had been a participatory and radically democratic regime in the first year of the revolution metastasized into an autocracy with an exaggerated sense of what it could do.

For many post-Soviet historians, Lewin's insistence on preserving the idea of socialism as distinct from the Soviet system may seem an irrelevant exercise and the regrettable consequence of his own ideological preferences. But, one may ask, which is more ideological and less historical—to conflate all the possible meanings and practices of socialism into the single case of Stalinism or the USSR or to distinguish between the different aspirations, possibilities, and actualities of socialist endeavors? His engagement with the history of social transformation unavoidably involved an evaluation of the worthiness of such an attempt despite the unpredictability of consequences. For Moshe Lewin socialism was fundamental to his vision of historical possibilities.

> However vague, the concept of socialism is not a dustbin into which any tyrant or ignorant can throw any thoughts. It is a complicated but very serious reflection about lifting political democracy to a higher level by allowing the citizenry to master not just the political but also the economic environment and to eliminate the glaring disparities of economic power between social classes, allowing equal rights to such classes, (in this sense "eliminating" them). It is also a tool to loosen or break the power of too rigid structures such as classes, bureaucracies and oppressive dogmas, and to open up a larger space for individual freedom and creativity. This definition can be challenged, changed or expanded, but without such features, and especially in an environment that is practicing exactly the opposite, the term is an abuse or a plain fraud.[57]

---

55   Moshe Lewin, *The Soviet Century*, edited by Gregory Elliott (London: Verso, 2005), p. 69.

56   Ibid.

57   Moshe Lewin, *Stalinism and the Seeds of Soviet Reform: The Debates of the 1960s* (London: Pluto Press, 1991; Armonk, NY: M. E. Sharpe, 1991), p. xxv.

Values are a close cousin of even the most neutral, ostensibly objective historical writing, and it is naive as well as hubristic to think that historical interpretation can free itself from ethical or political commitment or ideology in the broadest sense.

Intellectual fashions come and go, and Lewin did not care much for more recent approaches to Soviet history, once coining the neologism "deconstraction" to denote his displeasure. He once signed a letter to me: "Misha (Director, Upside Down Studies Institute)." He loved to rail against or sometimes just gently poke fun at his various homelands, reminding me once that every one of them had grandiose, messianic aspirations to save the world. I ran through the list and it seemed right: Poland, the Soviet Union, Israel, France, Britain, the United States. "But," I asked, "What about Lithuania? "Yes," he quickly replied, "even Lithuania!" Al Rieber remembers Misha saying that as soon as he arrived in a new country, it began to decline.[58] He certainly felt that way about the United States and remained to the end a rootless internationalist.

58   Rieber, "Moshe Lewin," p. 127.

5

Writing Russia: Sheila Fitzpatrick and the History of Stalinism

Historians, unlike some postmodern anthropologists, usually efface their own personality when writing up their work.[1] The political views of the person are seen as an encumbrance, a limit on objectivity and neutrality, and the unreachable ideal for the true historian ought to be like a filter through which the archival effluvia seeps with the minimum of subjective clogging. Most practicing historians know, of course, that selectivity, interpretation, emphasis, and even artistry makes complete objectivity impossible, even as the best of them work as artisans careful about not allowing the personal and political to overwhelm the evidence. Historians cannot stand outside of history, free from time and place. Someone had to educate the educator. Therefore, when evaluating the contributions of a major historian like Sheila Fitzpatrick, where she came from, what influences shaped her, and how she chose to deal with her own past should not be seen as merely a superfluous addendum to her intellectual biography but a window through which the products of her creative efforts can be understood.

---

1 First given as a talk at a Festschrift conference for Sheila Fitzpatrick in Melbourne, Australia, an earlier version of this chapter was published as "Writing Russia: The Work of Sheila Fitzpatrick," in Golfo Alexopoulos, Julie Hessler, and Kiril Tomoff (eds.), *Writing the Stalin Era: Sheila Fitzpatrick and Soviet Historiography* (New York: Palgrave Macmillan, 2011), pp. 1–19.

Her Father's Daughter

Sheila Fitzpatrick was born in Melbourne, Australia, on June 4, 1941, the daughter of Brian Fitzpatrick and Dorothy Mary Davies. She grew up and was educated in that southern hemisphere city, graduated from its premier university, where she first became interested in Russian history, and then took her rich life experience in an extraordinary family into her work and the wider world. The unique amalgam of three English-speaking countries, three university systems, and three distinct though not unrelated professional cultures has given her work a special quality, which I would call "detached engagement." By that I mean that, throughout her writing, Sheila has maintained, in so far as they are possible to achieve, the highest scholarly standards of objectivity, neutrality, faithfulness to the sources (archival if at all available), and careful, thoughtful reconstruction of a complex and elusive past. At the same time, she is deeply engaged in the central questions affecting Soviet history, fearlessly treading on the toes of sacrosanct orthodoxies, forcing reluctant readers to rethink what they thought they knew, resisting easy categorization into this group or that (she does not want to be "ascribed"), and undermining the facile generalizations and essentialist understandings of Soviet history in general and Stalinism most particularly that have marred Western scholarship on the USSR.

She is, without doubt, her father's daughter, and yet her work exists in an acute tension with the thrust of much of his writing and activity.[2] Brian Fitzpatrick was a very public intellectual, a renegade journalist and later historian, at the edge of respectable academia. Neither a Marxist nor a Communist, he seems to have been a dedicated anti-anti-Communist. His biographer, Don Watson, writes: "Fitzpatrick did not see Russia as the socialist fatherland but for many years he saw it as an experiment worth supporting and he was convinced that it saved Western democracy in World War II. In many ways he was a 'fellow traveller.'"[3] A gregarious man, fond of pubs and the people in them, seeking there a special fellowship and community, Brian Fitzpatrick was a democrat, a civil libertarian, a socialist, and a radical nationalist, never a Leninist.

---

2   For a full and personal account of growing up with Brian Fitzpatrick, see Sheila Fitzpatrick, *My Father's Daughter: Memories of an Australian Childhood* (Melbourne: Melbourne University Press, 2010).

3   Don Watson, *Brian Fitzpatrick: A Radical Life* (Sydney: Hale & Iremonger, 1979), p. xvii.

He suffered, however, according to Watson, from a "Soviet blind spot" and was willing to "turn a blind eye to Stalinism's totalitarian abuses of all the ideals he professed."[4] His daughter "asked him early on (though without getting a serious answer) why we didn't move to Russia, if, as he seemed to think, things were better there."[5] As a historian, he was convinced of the fundamental importance in historical explanation of economic factors (more Charles Beard than Karl Marx) and to the end of his life "continued to believe in both the concept and the existence of 'class'," even berating C. Wright Mills once for rejecting the term in favor of 'power elite'."[6] Above all, he was highly suspicious of all authority. In her account of her father, Sheila Fitzpatrick quotes appreciatively his core belief expressed at the height of the Cold War in 1953: "First, power corrupts men wielding it, whether Communists or Catholics, Marxists or Mennonites. And secondly, all governments are bad, and some worse."[7]

What a home that must have been to have grown up in! Certainly, engagement comes out of it, and given all the heat and controversy, perhaps also the imperative to cultivate detachment as well. Growing up in a leftist family in anti-Communist Cold War Australia, at a time when any sympathy displayed toward the Soviet project, combined with criticism of one's own country, placed one outside the comfort zone of acceptable views and may have stimulated a life-long search in Sheila Fitzpatrick to try to get the Soviet story right, to see it in all its varied hues, and to shrug off the accusations of partisanship that would likely follow anyone working toward that noble aim.

She graduated from the University of Melbourne in 1961 and went on to St. Antony's College, Oxford, where she earned her D. Phil. in 1969, working with Max Hayward, known derisively in the Soviet Union as the "not unknown Max Hayward."[8] Examined by Leonard Shapiro, she

4   Ibid., pp. xx, xvii. "If Fitzpatrick's initial affection for Russia stemmed from faith in the revolution, his continuing defence of it in the face of overwhelming evidence of appalling aberrations was sustained by his distaste for the politics of its detractors. Rationality suffered on more than one score: not only did anti-communism serve to shore up the irrationalities of capitalism but it took a quite irrational attitude to Russia. To paint Russia as all bad was to be as unreasonable as the *apparatchiks* who painted it as all good" (p. 213).

5   Sheila Fitzpatrick, "Diary," *London Review of Books* XXIX, 3 (February 8, 2007), p. 34.

6   Watson, *Brian Fitzpatrick*, p. 255.

7   *The Australian News-Review. Brian Fitzpatrick's Monthly Digest of Australian, U.N., World Events* III, 20 (May 1953), p. 3.

8   Sheila Fitzpatrick, "A Student in Moscow, 1966," *The Wilson Quarterly* VI, 3 (Summer 1982), p. 134.

met and befriended E. H. Carr and R. W. Davies, thus coming to know the broad and contentious Pleiades of British academic experts on the USSR. She first went to the Soviet Union briefly as a tourist and later that same year, 1966, to do her dissertation research, "having just acquired a husband [Alex Bruce] (who was studying in Tokyo)." She spent some eighteen months there and grew close to Igor Aleksandrovich Sats, a member of the *Novyi mir* (New World) editorial board in its liberal period under Aleksandr Tvardovskii, but much earlier Lunacharskii's literary secretary (and brother-in-law).[9] She regarded him as an important influence and even "a lately acquired parent."[10] Sats and *Novyi mir* were formative in Fitzpatrick's ambivalence toward the USSR and the Russian Revolution. Sats was an Old Bolshevik upset by the path that the revolution had taken and hopeful that the work of Tvardovskii and those loyal to a Leninist humanism would redeem the promise of 1917. Given her innate skepticism, Fitzpatrick stood apart from such a commitment but felt a greater allegiance to the ambitions of *Novyi mir* ("a Soviet allegiance, on the face of it, but a tremendously ambiguous one") than she did to her anti-Soviet mentors at St. Antony's.[11]

Sheila Fitzpatrick went on to teach at Melbourne, Birmingham, St. John's University in New York, Columbia University, the University of Texas at Austin, the University of Sydney, and the University of Chicago (1990–2012), where we were colleagues for eleven years. As the Bernadotte E. Schmitt Distinguished Service Professor in Modern Russian History at Chicago, her honors are many. In recognition of her body of work, she was awarded something like a Nobel Prize in history, the Mellon Distinguished Achievement Award. She is the author of twelve books to date and the editor or co-editor of another seven, as well as over eighty articles. Today, it is simply impossible for anyone seriously interested in Soviet history not to know and to have read Sheila's work, and our understanding of Stalinism in particular would be deeply impoverished without her contributions. Sheila was a pioneer in moving the profession from its earlier concentration in imperial Russian history into the current renaissance of Soviet history. For a time, she was the only younger historian doing serious research into postrevolutionary Russia, alongside a handful of older men, some of them quite cranky and possessive about their hold on the field. Her sheer productivity made her

---

9   Ibid., p. 135.
10   Ibid., p. 141.
11   Sheila Fitzpatrick, *A Spy in the Archive: A Memoir of Cold War Russia* (London: I. B. Tauris, 2015), pp. 342–3.

the leader in the study of the darkest period of Soviet history, and she has even taught many of us Russian! Before Sheila mentioned them, how many of us had ever heard of *vydvizhentsy* (upwardly mobile workers) or *obshchestvennitsy* (Soviet women social activists)?

The Work: Fitzpatrick's Soviet Union

Sheila's work builds from the ground up, not from grand theory or master narrative or modernist or Marxist teleology. Her work is very often ethnographic, the fieldwork done largely in the archives. She loves the archives, knows them better than anyone else in the West, and is probably rivaled in Russia only by the prodigious pioneer Oleg Khlevniuk. To generalize very broadly, she has been more interested in varieties of approaches to history than to confirming or disconfirming a particular model or paradigm. When one reads through her work, one finds a rich, complex story of the Soviet experience that defies reduction to a simple formula. She eschews the idea that there is a magic key, an essential factor, that explains Soviet history—whether it be the totalitarian model, *What Is to Be Done?*, Lenin or Stalin's personality, or (as has now become fashionable) modernity.

In this synthetic overview of her work, I would like to suggest what I take to be Fitzpatrick's Soviet story, how she explains why Russia and its revolution turned out as it did and what the causes and the consequences of the Bolshevik project were.

Sheila's writings first focused on the New Economic Policy period, with swings back into the revolution and civil war but generally progressing forward into the 1930s, World War II, and most recently the postwar and even post-Stalin and post-Soviet periods. At the same time, her methods and thematic interests have moved over time from institutional and political history, questions of culture and power, through social history, even at times an apolitical social history, and on into explorations of social identities and everyday life, returning often to various cultural themes. Culture was there from the beginning, in her study of Anatolii Lunacharskii, the relatively tolerant and intellectually sensitive People's Commissar of Enlightenment. Over the years, she has explored culture in a variety of modes: the cultural policy of the regime in the 1920s (which she referred to as the "soft line"); the transformation of popular and social culture in the revolutionary years of the First Five-Year Plan (the "Cultural Revolution") and after; the high culture of people like Dmitrii Shostakovich; and aspects of cultural practices and discourses that led her into looking at representations and emotions.

In her first published article, Fitzpatrick took as her topic a review of Soviet literature on the softest of Bolsheviks, Lunacharskii, whom she thought of as "one of the greatest Soviet compromisers."[12] She wondered, why Lunacharskii now? Why in the 1960s was there a revival of interest in this second-rank (not second-rate) Bolshevik? "Like so many of his contemporaries," she wrote, "Lunacharsky has acquired a symbolic importance: he stands for a relatively permissive policy towards art and literature, and as a mediator between the party and the intelligentsia."[13] She looked at novelist Ilya Ehrenburg and poet Kornei Chukovskii as memoirists who constructed a useful Lunacharskii through "a very sophisticated process of selection," who becomes in their hands a liberal responsible for the party's soft, neutral line on the arts. This was the Lunacharskii that certain intellectuals of the Sixties needed to support their claim for an art with integrity and room for diversity, if not deviance, within the larger context of a Marxist–Leninist regime. She applauds instead Lunacharskii himself, who in his *Siluety*, autobiographical portraits of Old Bolsheviks, does what a good historian should do—"demythologize, and to reoccupy the old historical ground between rumour and party history."[14]

Assessing the Bolshevik takeover in 1917, Fitzpatrick staked out her own position. In the debates over the October Revolution that divided Western historians in the 1960s and 1970s, first political historians, like Alexander Rabinowitch, and later a generation of young social historians had challenged the idea of the Bolshevik victory as the work of a cynical group of political manipulators who successfully and behind the backs of the working class carried out a coup d'état. The new historiography showed that the Bolsheviks had broad support among workers and, even more importantly, soldiers, and that the Petrograd Soviet held sway over the popular forces that determined much of the course of the revolution in the late summer and fall of 1917. The actual events of October were more a coup de grace than a coup d'état in that real power had already passed to the Soviet once it had secured control of the Petrograd garrison through September and into October "in effect disarming the Provisional

12   Ibid., p. 17.
13   Sheila Fitzpatrick, "A. V. Lunacharsky: Recent Soviet Interpretations and Republications," *Soviet Studies* XVIII, 3 (January 1967), p. 270.
14   Ibid., p. 289.

Government without a shot."[15] In the actual fighting in the October revolution (October 24–26), fewer than fifteen people were killed.

In her reading of October, Fitzpatrick recognizes the overwhelming support that the Bolsheviks had among key constituencies in the city; however, she speaks of a coup d'état. She argues that Lenin was determined to set up a one-party government no matter what the Soviet or some of his closest comrades desired. Although he was ultimately forced to compromise and admit a small number of Left Socialist Revolutionaries into a coalition government, Lenin's own intentions, she contends, played the key role in the eventual creation of a one-party state. She shares Engels's warning that "a socialist party taking power prematurely might find itself isolated and forced into repressive dictatorship," a risk that "the Bolshevik leaders, and Lenin in particular, were willing to take."[16]

The requirement to hold power in a largely peasant country in which their support from workers grew fragile presented the Bolsheviks with a dilemma: how could they gain and hold the loyalty of ordinary people while at the same time relying on repression to stay in power? Revolutionary violence and terror were built into the revolution. Fitzpatrick, like Robert C. Tucker, Moshe Lewin, and Stephen F. Cohen, sees the Civil War experience as far more formative in the Bolshevik style of rule than the long history of prerevolutionary Social Democracy. Actual social experience supplemented ideology. The attitudes and habits of Bolsheviks had to be factored in. Soviet authoritarianism stemmed, first, from the irreducible fact that "a minority dictatorship was almost bound to be authoritarian, and those who served as its executants were extremely likely to develop the habits of bossing and bullying that Lenin often criticized in the years after 1917."[17] Second, the followers of the Bolsheviks—the bulk of Russia's soldiers, sailors, and workers—were less concerned with the niceties of lawful rule than Old Bolshevik intellectuals and were more willing to crush opposition and use force. Civil war certainly shaped what Bolshevism was becoming, but, it also must be noted, Lenin and the Bolsheviks welcomed civil war. Their October seizure of power, followed by the forceful dispersal of the Constituent Assembly, threw down the gauntlet to the liberals and moderate socialists and "gave the new regime

---

15   Alexander Rabinowitch, *The Bolsheviks Come to Power: The Revolution of 1917 in Petrograd* (New York: W. W. Norton, 1976), pp. 313–14.

16   Sheila Fitzpatrick, *The Russian Revolution*, 2nd ed. (Oxford: Oxford University Press, 1994), p. 67.

17   Ibid., p. 71.

a baptism by fire ... the kind of baptism the Bolsheviks had risked, and may even have sought."[18]

A key question for Soviet historiography has been the role (even the meaning) of ideology. Fitzpatrick does not deduce the flow of Soviet history from ideology, a historiographical practice well established during the Cold War by authors like Bertram Wolfe and resurrected in the new modernist school of Martin Malia, Stephen Kotkin, and others that holds that ideas going back to the Enlightenment or earlier to Tomasso Campanello play a key determining role. For the modernists, the Soviet Union flows from an Enlightenment project carried to an extreme. The USSR is a gardening state in which the cultivators plan and plant and brutally cut down the weeds. Fitzpatrick does not neglect the mind-set and preferences of the Bolsheviks. But, rather than positing that the Bolsheviks successfully carried out their ideological aims, she sees their plans as fundamentally utopian fantasies that were thwarted by a clash with reality. There was no international revolution to come to the aid of Russia; the Polish workers did not rise up in 1920 to aid the Red Army; *State and Revolution* was an absurd manual for running a government; *The ABC of Communism*, which depicted a society in which "all will work in accordance with the indications of the statistical bureaux" and there "will be no need for special ministers of State, for police or prisons, for laws and decrees" was patently improbable. The Bolsheviks talked about ending exploitation of workers, women, and colonized nationalities and spreading the revolution to the West, all the while fighting a civil war and dealing with famine and hundreds of thousands of wounded men and women and parentless children. Ideas and understandings were certainly important and had enormous consequences, but, in Fitzpatrick's story, they have to be integrated into the social reality that undermined them at every step. She is convinced that Marxist analysis was inappropriate to Soviet social reality—too crude and too foreign—and, among other errors, led the Bolsheviks into false understandings of the "maturity" of the working class and the development of proletarian consciousness. Marxist prescriptions for a socialist transformation of Russia had to be adjusted. "The Bolsheviks," according to Fitzpatrick, "had made an absurd, undeliverable promise to the working class when they talked of a 'dictatorship of the proletariat.' The oxymoron of a 'ruling proletariat,' appealing though it might be to dialectical thinkers, was not realizable in the real world."[19]

18   Ibid., p. 72.
19   Sheila Fitzpatrick, "The Bolsheviks' Dilemma: Class, Culture and Politics in the Early Soviet Years," *Slavic Review* XLVII, 4 (Winter 1988), pp. 599–613.

Given the heavy-handed practice of both Western sectarians and many Soviet historians, the wariness of Fitzpatrick to use Marxist concepts is understandable. A tendency to force Russian society into a rigid structure determined by a quite different historical evolution in the West has more often closed avenues of investigation than offered fruitful new conceptualizations. Fitzpatrick's objections to the practice of past proponents can be understood as an appropriate critique of historical explanations that treated Marxism as an infallible text, a dogma or recipe book, from which prescriptions for analysis and action could be drawn. That text was thought to be fixed and scientific. Fitzpatrick opposes notions of historical teleology or fixed laws of history (*zakonomernost'*). On her acquaintance with Marxism in Western Soviet scholarship, she writes:

> The existence of Marxist revisionism in American Soviet studies (as represented by Ronald Grigor Suny and others of the 1917 revisionism cohort) was an oddly late discovery for me: for some years after my arrival in the United States, I thought that when people talked about Marxist revisionists (including me in that category) it was just a Cold War smear tactic .... Marxism, like the related issue of left-wing politics, was a problem for me, and looking back I see how badly I handled it ... . For those on the Left, there was the puzzle, why if I was on the Left too, I kept disagreeing with them—and doing so, moreover, with a sharpness that no doubt arose from my private resentment at being so misclassified. The sharpness was in evidence in the 1988 article in *Slavic Review* about my article, "The Bolsheviks' Dilemma," when Suny protested that I had gone on a personal crusade against Marxist "class analysis," while I accused him of having ideological blinkers.[20]

Setting Marxism aside, from the mid-1970s through the early 1980s she explored alternative social scientific explanations of Soviet dynamics, influenced by her second husband, political scientist Jerry Hough. Along with bureaucratic politics and the play of interest groups, she was most interested in the phenomenon of social mobility, and a central theme in her work revolved around the concept of class. Fitzpatrick's own dilemma about class, as she acknowledges, was that it is difficult to do early Soviet history and not take seriously that one concept that the Bolsheviks took

---

20   Sheila Fitzpatrick, "Revisionism in Retrospect: A Personal View," *Slavic Review* LXVII, 3 (Fall 2008), pp. 688–9; the original comments were published in *Slavic Review* XLVII, 4 (Winter 1988), pp. 614, 625.

very seriously, namely class, while, at the same time, not falling victim to their particular classifications. Class was their sociology: society, indeed the world, was divided into antagonistic classes, exploited and exploiting classes. The Soviet dictatorship of the proletariat would not be an egalitarian society; it would favor the exploited classes and wage war against the exploiters and their international allies—a cartoon Lenin sweeping the globe of the bourgeoisie. This dictatorship would soon change its meaning. Instead of "a collective class dictatorship exercised by workers who remained in their old jobs at the factory bench," it became "a dictatorship run by full-time 'cadres' or bosses, in which as many as possible of the new bosses were former proletarians."[21]

Along with her reluctance to accept class as a useful analytical category, one receives from Fitzpatrick's early work two different impressions of class: first, that class is an artificial concept imposed by Marxists on a complexly differentiated social reality; and second, that class is helpful as an objective sociological entity susceptible to such simple forms of analysis as counting. Both of her views were locked in an objective sense of class that missed the quality of human intervention and invention in the making of social categories and identities. As historians and theorists began to suggest that class be seen as one of the social identities available to individuals and groups, either to represent themselves or others, Fitzpatrick moved from a more objective to a more subjective notion of class. Although a history of perceptions would never substitute for social history in her work, she became ever more influenced by social theory that underlined the importance of ideology, the burdens of *mentalités*, representations, and the limits and restraints of discourse in shaping, not only the way people understand their social environment, but how that environment is produced as well. But that came later.

Whatever support among the workers the Bolsheviks may have enjoyed in the summer and fall of 1917, they lost the allegiance of significant parts of city dwellers during the Civil War. The disintegration of the working class in the years 1918–21 left behind its vanguard "like the smile of the Cheshire cat."[22] The party, especially at its upper levels, was made up largely of intellectuals and was hardly representative of workers even in its lower ranks. In the absence of either a coherent working class or an adequate class culture, the Bolsheviks were forced to rely on other

21   Fitzpatrick, *The Russian Revolution*, 2nd ed., p. 92.
22   Sheila Fitzpatrick, "The Bolsheviks' Dilemma: The Class Issue in Party Politics and Culture," reprinted in Fitzpatrick, *The Cultural Front: Power and Culture in Revolutionary Russia* (Ithaca, NY: Cornell University Press, 1992), p. 19.

social groups, like the so-called "bourgeois specialists." Antagonisms ("class tension" in Fitzpatrick's language) developed between the displaced workers and those who favored using the *spetsy* (bourgeois and military experts).

The Bolshevik dilemma of a revolutionary Marxist party holding power in a largely peasant society was to be resolved, in the Bolshevik view, by aid from more advanced countries in Europe—another utopian fantasy as it turned out. Thus, the dilemma became acute in the last years of the Civil War when despair about the workers gripped many party leaders, including Lenin, and the pointed attacks of the Workers' Opposition seemed to undermine the very sense of legitimacy of the Marxists who had made the revolution. "By 1920, a large part of the industrial proletariat had disintegrated, and the old capitalist bourgeoisie had been expropriated and ceased to exist as a class. In effect, the great 'class struggle' was waged by a surrogate proletariat (the Red Army and the Communist Party) against a surrogate bourgeoisie (the White Armies and the urban intelligentsia)."[23] But, just as the impossibility of creating a dictatorship of the proletariat was becoming apparent, a provisional solution was found. The introduction of the New Economic Policy encouraged the revival of industry and the reconstitution of the working class in 1923–24. The "Lenin Levy" brought thousands of "workers" into the party, and a class base for Bolshevism was reconstituted in the first half of the 1920s. Rather than trying to achieve a party majority of actual bench workers, the Bolshevik dilemma of proletarian identity was resolved by bringing more former workers into the ruling apparatus.

The Communists "patched up the marriage with the working class" during the New Economic Policy years, but during "the First Five-Year Plan, relations soured again because of falling real wages and urban living standards and the regime's insistent demands for higher productivity. An effective separation from the working class, if not a formal divorce, occurred in the 1930s."[24] Fitzpatrick's principal innovation in our thinking about the Soviet working class is that it actually benefited from the Soviet revolution by being recruited into the party, into the educational system, and into management. The Communists "created a broad channel for working-class upward mobility, since the recruitment

---

23   Sheila Fitzpatrick, "New Perspectives on the Civil War," in Diane P. Koenker, William G. Rosenberg, and Ronald Grigor Suny (eds.), *Party, State, and Society in the Russian Civil War: Explorations in Social History* (Bloomington: Indiana University Press, 1989), p. 6.

24   Fitzpatrick, *The Russian Revolution*, 2nd ed., pp. 10–11.

of workers to party membership went hand in hand with the promotion of working-class Communists to white-collar administrative and managerial position .... It was not workers that mattered in Stalin's regime but *former* workers—the newly-promoted 'proletariat core' in the managerial and professional elites."[25] This is clearly not what Marx and many Marxists had in mind when they envisioned the dictatorship of the proletariat. Changes in the forces of production and worker upward mobility were not accompanied by any essential changes in the relations of production or empowering the producers. Stalin pushed through a program of affirmative action for workers at the end of the 1920s,

> a very bold and imaginative policy which did in fact serve to consolidate and legitimize the regime .... Despite the relatively short duration of the affirmative action policy, the regime gained lasting credit as a sponsor of upward social mobility. The Bolsheviks never tried to fulfill the Marxist promise that the workers would rule. But they did fulfill a simpler and more comprehensible promise of the revolution—that workers and peasants would have the opportunity to rise into the new ruling elite of the Soviet state.[26]

Even this mildly positive assessment of the fruits of the revolution was enough to have Fitzpatrick accused from the Right of being an apologist for Stalinism and from the Left for not assessing positively enough the promise and potential of the revolution and its betrayal by the Stalinists. For her, the standard Trotskyist formulation of the bureaucracy standing over and dominating society was far too simplistic, for the lower echelons of the bureaucracy were as much dominated as dominating.[27] Fascinated by the upward social mobility into the elite that characterized early Soviet society, Fitzpatrick introduced Western audiences to the *vydvizhentsy* (those thrust upward from the working class).[28] In contrast to those Western scholars, and consistent with Trotsky and Isaac Deutscher, who argued that the erosion of the working class was key to the eventual evolution of the Bolshevik regime from a dictatorship of the proletariat to a dictatorship of the bureaucracy, Fitzpatrick contended that the real

25 Ibid., p. 11.
26 Sheila Fitzpatrick, *Education and Social Mobility in the Soviet Union 1921–1934* (Cambridge: Cambridge University Press, 1979), pp. 16–17.
27 Sheila Fitzpatrick, "New Perspectives on Stalinism," *Russian Review* XLV, 4 (October 1986), p. 361–2.
28 Fitzpatrick, *Education and Social Mobility*.

meaning of the revolution was the coming to power of former workers who occupied the key party and state positions in significant numbers.

> The way in which workers became "masters" of Russian society after the October Revolution was not by an abolition of the old status hierarchy. It was by moving in very large numbers into the old masters' jobs. Thus the essence of the special relationship between the party and the working class after 1917 was that the regime got "cadres" (administrators and managers) from the working class, and workers got responsible, high-status jobs from the regime .... Although it took some time for the Bolshevik leaders (being good Marxists) to realize it, the regime's commitment to the working class had much less to do with workers in situ than with working-class upward mobility.[29]

Fitzpatrick saw the *longue durée* of the revolution as encompassing modernization (escape from backwardness), class (the fate of the workers), and revolutionary violence (how the regime dealt with its enemies).[30] Clustered together with all its other more ephemeral utopian dreams, the Bolsheviks had two

> overriding imperatives to which policy debate continually returned. It was imperative that the Soviet Union should industrialize; and it was imperative that the new regime should create its own elite by promoting and educating workers, peasants and their children. Within the Communist Party, these were universally accepted truths ... which had substantial endorsement in the society as a whole, and this must surely be a factor in any explanation of Soviet achievement in these areas.... For the *vydvizhentsy*, industrialization was an heroic achievement—their own, Stalin's and that of Soviet power—and their promotion, linked with the industrialization drive, was a fulfillment of the promises of the revolution.[31]

Even as she focused on the social transformations of the early Soviet years, Fitzpatrick warned against moving too far from ideology and

---

29   Sheila Fitzpatrick, *The Russian Revolution 1917–1932* (Oxford: Oxford University Press, 1984), p. 8.

30   Fitzpatrick, *The Russian Revolution*, 2nd ed., pp. 9–13. Fitzpatrick's interpretation of the revolution took a darker tone in the second edition, published after the collapse of the Soviet Union. Revolution here is about illusions and disillusions, euphoria, madness, and unrealized expectations (pp. 8–9).

31   Fitzpatrick, *Education and Social Mobility*, p. 254.

political culture toward the notion (then quite popular) of "improvisation." Certainly, the Bolsheviks built their state on the run, with the materials at hand, and without precise blueprints, but they also did not build a pluralistic, inclusive state but one they proudly proclaimed was a "dictatorship." Bolsheviks were not Mensheviks, and they certainly were not liberal democrats. (Even liberal democrats, as her father repeatedly experienced, were often neither liberal nor very democratic.) Ideology might be what people "think and say about what they do," but it is most productively studied in relationship with political practice, "what they do."[32]

For most people even slightly acquainted with the historiography of the Soviet Union, Sheila Fitzpatrick would be identified as a "revisionist" and a "social historian." Revisionism, in its simplest definition, included those scholars (then young) in the late 1960s and through the 1970s who rejected the totalitarian model and sought a more complex (or in the vocabulary of the day, "nuanced") understanding of Soviet society and politics. Although she was among the strongest advocates of social historical methodologies, from the beginning Fitzpatrick was critical of certain tendencies among revisionists. Stephen Cohen's sharp distinction between Leninism and Stalinism as completely different phenomena, in his words "an essential discontinuity," appeared too stark for Fitzpatrick and was expressed too polemically.[33] "I thought he was whitewashing 'original Bolshevism,'" she wrote, "and he thought I was whitewashing Stalinism."[34] Here, she took a radical middle position between those who, on the one hand, saw an essential continuity between Marxism, Leninism, and Stalinism, an inevitable outgrowth of the system out of its ideological origins, and those, on the other, who spoke of a "revolution betrayed" and viable alternatives. Critical of the older school of historians whose work was often directed at indicting the Soviet experiment, she worried about revisionists moving toward exculpation. Once the initial cohort of revisionists who wrote on 1917 demonstrated that the Bolsheviks had popular support by October and, at times, proposed radically democratic institutions and practices, even within their own party, another source of Stalinism had to be found. Since 1902 and 1917 were no longer sufficient to explain how the revolution turned out, maybe it was the Civil War, or the peasantry, backwardness, perhaps the bureaucracy?

32   Sheila Fitzpatrick, "Politics as Practice: Thoughts on a New Political History," *Krtika*, V, 1 (Winter 2004), p. 37.
33   Ibid., p. 50.
34   Fitzpatrick, "Revisionism in Retrospect," pp. 687–8.

She demurred from those revisionists who sought "to exonerate Lenin and the revolution for responsibility for Stalinism."[35] Rather than alternatives or roads not taken, she was more interested in the "revolution fulfilled," how the coming to power of the working class was realized, not in terms of its dominant position in the state but how that state carried out the industrialization of the country, so enamored by Marxists. In *The Russian Revolution*, she traced

> lines of continuity between Lenin's revolution and Stalin's .... But the issue here is not whether 1917 and 1929 were alike, but whether they were part of the same process. Napoleon's revolutionary wars can be included in our general concept of the French Revolution, even if we do not regard them as an embodiment of the spirit of 1789; and a similar approach seems legitimate in the case of the Russian Revolution.[36]

The concept of the revolution ought to include both the originating upheaval and the consolidation of the new regime. Responding to criticism from Cohen, Fitzpatrick added to her initial take on the Russian Revolution, which, in the first edition of her text ended in 1932, and included Stalinism of the 1930s as part of the revolution in future editions. The Great Terror, she argues, lies at the boundary of the revolution and postrevolutionary Stalinism. In its rhetoric, the *Ezhovshchina* was revolutionary terror, but, in its practice, "totalitarian terror in that it destroyed persons but not structures, and did not threaten the person of the Leader." Still, 1937–38 must be included in the revolution for "dramatic reasons alone."[37] Along with A. L. Unger and Kendall E. Bailes, Fitzpatrick showed how a new "leading stratum" of Soviet-educated "specialists" replaced the Old Bolsheviks and bourgeois specialists.[38] The largest numbers of beneficiaries were promoted workers and party rank-and-file, young technicians, who would make up the Soviet elite through the post-Stalin period until Mikhail Gorbachev took power. Stalin, wrote Fitzpatrick, saw the old party bosses less as revolutionaries

---

35 Fitzpatrick, "New Perspectives on the Civil War," p. 388.
36 Fitzpatrick, *The Russian Revolution*, 2nd ed., p. 3.
37 Ibid., p. 4.
38 A. L. Unger, "Stalin's Renewal of the Leading Stratum: A Note on the Great Purge," *Soviet Studies* XX, 3 (January 1969), pp. 321–30; Kendall E. Bailes, *Technology and Society Under Lenin and Stalin: Origins of the Soviet Technical Intelligentsia, 1917–1941* (Princeton, NJ: Princeton University Press, 1978), pp. 268, 413; Fitzpatrick, "Stalin and the Making of a New Elite," *Slavic Review* XXXVIII, 3 (September 1979), pp. 377–402.

than "as Soviet boyars (feudal lords) and himself as a latter-day Ivan the Terrible, who had to destroy the boyars to build a modern nation state and a new service nobility."[39]

Defining and Explaining Stalinism

The term "Stalinism" has its own genealogy, beginning in the mid-1920s even before the system that would bear its name yet existed. Trotsky applied the word to the moderate "centrist" tendencies within the party stemming from the "ebbing of revolution" and identified with his opponent, Stalin.[40] By 1935, Trotsky's use of Stalinism gravitated closer to the Marxist meaning of "Bonapartism" or "Thermidor," "the crudest form of opportunism and social patriotism."[41] Even before Trotsky's murder in August 1940, Stalinism had become a way of characterizing the particular form of social and political organization in the Soviet Union, distinct from capitalism, but, for Trotskyists and other non-Communist radicals, not quite socialist. Not until the falling away of the totalitarian model, however, did scholars bring the term Stalinism into social science discussion as a sociopolitical formation to be analyzed in its own right. For Robert C. Tucker, Stalinism "represented, among other things, a far-reaching Russification of the already somewhat Russified earlier (Leninist) Soviet political culture."[42] For Cohen, "Stalinism was not simply nationalism, bureaucratization, absence of democracy, censorship, police repression, and the rest in any precedented sense .... Instead Stalinism was excess, extraordinary extremism, in each."[43] Taking a more social historical perspective, Lewin saw Stalinism as "not only a specific and blatant case of development without emancipation," but "in fact, a retreat into a tighter-than-ever harnessing of society to the state bureaucracy, which became the main social vehicle of the state's policies and ethos."[44]

39   Fitzpatrick, *The Russian Revolution*, 2nd ed., p. 159.
40   Robert H. McNeal, "Trotskyist Interpretations of Stalinism," in Robert C. Tucker (ed.), *Stalinism: Essays in Historical Interpretation* (New York: W. W. Norton, 1977), p. 31.
41   Ibid., p. 34.
42   Robert C. Tucker, "Introduction: Stalinism and Comparative Communism," in Tucker (ed.), *Stalinism*, p. xviii.
43   Stephen Cohen, "Bolshevism and Stalinism," in Tucker (ed.), *Stalinism*, p. 12.
44   Moshe Lewin, "The Social Background of Stalinism," in Tucker (ed.), *Stalinism*, p. 126.

Stalinism was now a way of describing a stage in the evolution of non-capitalist statist regimes in developing countries dominated by a Leninist party, as well as an indictment of undemocratic, failed socialist societies. The cohort of social historians of Stalinism that emerged in the 1980s was not particularly interested in broad synthetic interpretations of Stalinism or Marxist-inspired typologies. Their challenge was directed against the top–down, state intervention into society approach and proposed looking primarily at society, while at the same time disaggregating what was meant by society. They looked for initiative from below, sources of support for radical transformation, as well as popular resistance to the regime's agenda.[45] Some stressed the improvisation of state policies, the chaos of the state machinery, the lack of control in the countryside. Others attempted to diminish the role of Stalin. As they painted a picture quite different from the totalitarian vision of effective dominance from above and atomization below, these revisionists came under withering attack from more traditional scholars, who saw them as self-deluded apologists for Stalin at best and incompetent, venal falsifiers at worse.[46]

In her 1986 review of social historical work on Stalinism, Fitzpatrick isolated three approaches within the revisionism challenging the T-model. The first emphasized "that the regime had less actual control over society than it claimed, that its actions were often improvised rather than part of a grand design, that implementation of its radical policies often diverged from the policy-makers' intentions, and that the policies had many unplanned and unanticipated social consequences."[47] Here, the idea of a Stalinist "revolution from above" was preserved, though amplified by reference to social restraints and consequences. The work of Moshe Lewin fits this description. The second approach focused on the social constituencies, responding to social pressures and grievances, and liable to be modified in practice through processes of informal social negotiation."[48] Vera Dunham is an exemplary representative of this approach. And the third approach went furthest of all and argued that the Stalin revolution was more a revolution from below than from above, that popular initiative "from below" was decisive in shaping policies in

---

45   For a bold attempt to find support for state policies from below, see Sheila Fitzpatrick (ed.), *Cultural Revolution in Russia, 1928–1931* (Bloomington: Indiana University Press, 1978).

46   See, for example, Richard Pipes, *Vixi, Memoirs of a Non-Belonger* (New Haven, CT: Yale University Press, 2003), pp. 126, 221–3, 242.

47   Sheila Fitzpatrick, "New Perspectives on Stalinism," *Russian Review* XLV, 4 (October 1986), p. 368.

48   Ibid.

the 1930s. Gábor Rittersporn made such an argument in his study of the Great Purges.[49] Fitzpatrick came closest to the third approach in her introduction ("Cultural Revolution as Class War") to her edited volume, *Cultural Revolution in Russia*, where she emphasized the participation in the revolution of "forces within the society," while conceding that initiative came from above.[50] The radical thrust of that introduction was not carried through by the contributors to the volume, and Fitzpatrick herself soon shifted toward recognition of the much greater importance of the "revolution from above." As an "iconoclastic revisionist" resistant to any orthodoxy, whether it be the T-model or Marxism, her revisionism aimed at finding new ways of interpreting the Soviet past, and she feared the foundation of a revisionist orthodoxy and revisionist scholars who would "take themselves too seriously, exaggerate their contributions, underestimate those of their predecessors, and speak as if they were replacing error with truth."[51] In response, several of her fellow revisionists felt betrayed by the apostasy of their mentor.[52]

In the 1990s, with Soviet archives open and available, Fitzpatrick turned to close studies of the everyday life of urban dwellers and peasants under Stalin.[53] These pointillist accounts, careful ethnographic reconstructions of how ordinary people dealt with the tumultuous changes and brutal repressions of the 1930s, must surely be counted as her most original and powerful monographs. Rich in anecdote and telling detail, they were informed by a number of social theories then in vogue: James Scott's ideas of "everyday resistance" and "hidden transcripts," the *Alltagsgeschichte* school of Alf Ludtke and others, the Subaltern Indian historians, and the work of the sociologist Erving Goffman. These two books, along with accompanying articles, changed the way the profession understood Soviet life under Stalin, bringing the reader down to the household, the family table, the marketplace, demonstrating how people survived and made out in an economy of chronic shortage, a political arena marked by a relentlessly expanding state, the elimination of older

---

49   Gábor Tamás Rittersporn, *Stalinist Simplifications and Soviet Complications: Social Tensions and Political Conflicts in the USSR, 1933–1953* (Chur, Switzerland: Harwood Academic, 1991).

50   Fitzpatrick, *Cultural Revolution in Russia, 1928–1931*, pp. 8–40.

51   Sheila Fitzpatrick, "Afterword: Revisionism Revisited," *Russian Review* XLV, 4 (October 1986), p. 412.

52   Fitzpatrick, "Revisionism in Retrospect," pp. 690–1.

53   Sheila Fitzpatrick, *Stalin's Peasants: Resistance and Survival in the Russian Village After Collectivization* (New York: Oxford University Press, 1994); *Everyday Stalinism. Ordinary Life in Extraordinary Times: Soviet Russia in the 1930s* (New York: Oxford University Press, 1999).

forms of social support like the church, severe disruptions of traditional networks and hierarchies, and blows to the family. She postulated that class became less meaningful under Stalinism than it had been in the revolution and 1920s. This was social history with the state as a hulking presence.

> What mattered was the relationship to the state—in particular, the state as an allocator of goods in an economy of chronic scarcity.... Production no longer served as a meaningful basis of class structure in Soviet urban society. In fact, the meaningful social hierarchies of the 1930s were based not on production but consumption. "Class" status in the real world was a matter of having greater or lesser access to goods, which in turn was largely a function of the degree of entitlement to privilege that the state allowed.[54]

In these works, there is no apology for the horrors that ordinary people in the USSR had to endure in the 1930s; genuine heroism had been replaced by official heroes and heroics; and the sacrifices and suffering were all the more unbearable. But, somehow, people managed. "There were fearful things that affected Soviet life," she wrote, "and visions that uplifted it, but mostly it was a hard grind, full of shortages and discomfort. *Homo sovieticus* was a string-puller, an operator, a time-server, a freeloader, a mouther of slogans, and much more. But above all, he was a survivor."[55] In a later article published in Australia, she noted that happiness was part of the official script, the acceptable public expression of positive emotion, "a kind of civic requirement," while grief, suffering, and *toska* (melancholic longing) were decidedly non-Soviet emotions that "might carry overtones of ingratitude, even disloyalty, to the beneficent state."[56] They were the private expression of feelings found in diaries. In Fitzpatrick's vision of everyday Soviet life, themes of achievements and legitimacy had been left far behind, and the personal suffering and misery of the ordinary Soviet men and women had been now brought to the fore.

54   Fitzpatrick, *Everyday Stalinism*, pp. 12–13.
55   Ibid., p. 227.
56   Sheila Fitzpatrick, "Happiness and *Toska*: An Essay in the History of Emotions in Pre-war Soviet Russia," *Australian Journal of Politics and History* L, 3, (2004), pp. 357–71; 371.

The Cultural Turn and the Deconstruction of Class

By the early and mid-1990s, the social historical wave had receded, and cultural history became "the dominant force in the modern Russian historical field," though a new interest in political history, enriched by the available archives, also was lapping at the shore.[57] Fitzpatrick's work continued to express the variety of Soviet experiences. Her work on class identities flowed naturally into a concern with the conventions of self-presentation and the reinvention of personae in revolutionary and postrevolutionary societies. In her co-edited volume on Soviet women with her former graduate student Yuri Slezkine, she emphasized how diverse the life paths of the memoirists were.[58] While the subjectivity enthusiasts were concerned with individual identities and sensibilities, Fitzpatrick remained concerned with collective responses and diversity of experience. Soviet subjectivity could not be captured with a single diary or encapsulated in an easy formula.

Fitzpatrick began to deconstruct the notion of class in a stunning series of articles that paralleled the work that feminists were doing with gender categories and theorists of nationalism were doing with the nation. Class as "a matter of classification" presented a far more intriguing problem to her than the idea of class as a reified social category. For the Bolsheviks, identification with the proletariat was an ideological sine qua non, but in actuality, as Fitzpatrick emphasized, that identity in any meaningful sociological sense became a mirage soon after October. After the revolution, people needed to fashion new identities and even to challenge the identities of others. In her work on denunciations, she investigated how individual Soviet citizens attempted "to discredit the class self-presentation of others."[59] This led to investigations of petitions and appeals in which people tried to present themselves with positive class identities complete with life stories.

While already previewed in earlier pieces, the turning point in her work on class came with the 1994 piece in *The Journal of Modern History* (of which she was one of the editors), "Ascribing Class: The Construction

57   Sheila Fitzpatrick, "A Response to Michael Ellman," *Europe/Asia Studies* LIX, 3 (2002), p. 475.

58   Sheila Fitzpatrick and Yuri Slezkine (eds.), *In the Shadow of Revolution: Life Stories of Russian Women from 1917 to the Second World War* (Princeton, NJ: Princeton University Press, 2000).

59   Sheila Fitzpatrick, *Tear Off the Masks!: Identity and Imposture in Twentieth-Century Russia* (Princeton, NJ: Princeton University Press, 2005), p. 8.

of Social Identity in Soviet Russia."[60] Here, she showed how the Bolsheviks essentially invented class categories in the absence of actual, clear class identifications and turned them into legal categories that afforded people particular advantages and disadvantages. A Marxist idea of class as positioning in relation to the means of production gave way to state ascription of class-belonging that was akin to the prerevolutionary classification of the population by *soslovie* (legal estate). What is most dramatic in this picture is the active construction of social reality by the state, the making of class in the absence of clear class positions or class consciousness (*pace* Edward Thompson). While it is easy enough to trace the genealogy of such an approach to the work of Leopold H. Haimson on social identities, Gregory Freeze on *soslovie*, Moshe Lewin on the artificial category of the *kulak*, Teodor Shanin on the awkwardness of applying class analysis to the peasantry, and (if I might add immodestly) Ronald Suny on the state production of nationality, Fitzpatrick's story is rich in its emphasis on "class stigma," the real costs of being ascribed to the wrong class. Once ascribed to a class, which might become an alien class that then became an enemy class, a person's identity became indelible, fixed on passports (or not worthy of receiving a passport). The consequences could be catastrophic, literally a matter of life and death. Class ascription helped solidify a new social hierarchy in Stalin's Soviet Union. A new elite with new privileges, a kind of "service nobility," emerged, a *soslovie* that would remain in power almost to the last days of the USSR.

Who Was *Homo Sovieticus?* Pavel Morozov or Ostap Bender?

Reading through Fitzpatrick's corpus, one is struck foremost by her inventiveness, her constant exploration of new materials and new ways of interrogating them, her deep interest in variation as well as constancies. For those like myself who tend to think of history as a special form of science—a *nauka* that is about discovery, as in ecology or biology, of variations—and a social science—that is about regularities, patterns, and generalizations, if not universal or natural laws—Fitzpatrick's work, like all good science, moves our understanding forward by producing new knowledge of change and constancy over time. When she takes up a question like the forms of citizen's supplications to state authority,

---

60   Sheila Fitzpatrick, "Ascribing Class: The Construction of Social Identity in Soviet Russia," *Journal of Modern History* LXV, 4 (December 1993), pp. 745–70.

her apparent pleasure in discovery is matched by her consideration of their various genres: *ispoved* (confession) of "what is in my heart," cries for help, denunciations, complaints, opinions, suggestions, advice, the particular form of the *annonimka* (anonymous letter). She notes the regularities in language, in greetings, and the consistent performative elements. In the debate between the modernists, who see the USSR as an extreme example of the pathologies of modernity, and the neotraditionalists, who recognize the remnants of custom and practice in the maelstrom of modernization, Fitzpatrick is closer to the neotraditionalists. Her investigations on patron/client networks, *blat* (pull, influence), *proteksiia* (protection, patronage), *semeistvennost'* (family ties, favoritism) show the persistence of older practices even in the throes of state-driven transformations. Rather than atomized or individualized, family bonds were strengthened in the 1930s (despite what we thought we had learned about Pavlik Morozov, the boy supposedly murdered by relatives for denouncing their crimes to the authorities). The only sexual offense to feature frequently in denunciations, even after homosexuality was outlawed in 1934, was female promiscuity. Denunciation was a practice, like patronage and favoritism, which operated where law and bureaucracy functioned poorly. Russia and the Soviet Union may have been modernizing; the regime may have had a modernist ideology; but when the rubber industry hit the muddy dirt road, older ways of doing things found a new life.

The closer Fitzpatrick took us to the ordinary Soviet person, the more her dissection of Stalinism undermined the rather rigid model of totalitarianism propagated during the Cold War. "It is difficult," she writes, "to see a society in which con men and imposture flourished to this extent as being under effective totalitarian mobilization and control." Rather, the Soviet Union of the 1930s "was characterized … by poor communications, lack of effective accountability, institutional habits of hoarding, and 'off-budget' distribution, credulous and ill-educated officials, and personalistic practices."[61] Soviet citizens, motivated primarily by the drive to survive, are in her view rational actors rather than idealistic socialists or dedicated patriots. In her discussion of the infamous Pavlik Morozov, the poster boy denunciator, she explains the rarity of such behavior not by the affective ties of parents to children or husbands to wives but from "practical reasons." To denounce a close family member would taint and endanger all who were closely related to the traitor.

---

61   Fitzpatrick, *Tear Off the Masks*, p. 280.

Fitzpatrick's skepticism extends to a critique of the notion of a distinct Soviet subjectivity. A number of younger scholars have proposed that Bolshevism and Stalinism produced a particularly nonliberal sense of self and purpose, a desire to fashion oneself as an authentically "Soviet Man" or "Woman," instead of self-absorbed egoism and personal satisfaction. A true Soviet person, they argue, would aim to become a politically conscious builder of the new socialist society, and generations of those who lived under Stalin's iron fist strove, not to forge individualistic identities, but to merge with the collective.[62] The quintessential Soviet for Fitzpatrick, on the other hand, was a shrewd manipulator able to adapt to shifting opportunities, maneuver through ever-present dangers, and "con" the authorities when necessary. Actual and fictional Soviet con men were read as Jews, she claims, and the immensely popular novels of Ilf and Petrov, with their trickster hero, Ostap Bender, were banned in the late Stalin period as an anti-Semitic campaign targeted intellectuals, doctors, and other professionals. By the time the ban was lifted in 1956, Stalin was gone, and the Soviet Union had become a much more mundane society, routinized and bureaucratic, with its revolutionary pretensions nothing more than pretensions. Soviet citizens, in the words of the dissident writer Andrei Siniavskii, had imbibed Bender's survival skills, and, Fitzpatrick adds, "The Jewish trickster, in short, had become the personification of really existing Soviet Man."[63] In the very last sentence of her book she concludes, "On the road to new post-Soviet identity, the impostor, Janus-faced, was once again in the vanguard."[64]

Is There a Sheila Fitzpatrick (or Chicago) School of Soviet History?

Solidly empirical, indebted to what she could find in the archives, Fitzpatrick has been wary of many of the fashionable theoretical approaches that accompanied the cultural turn. She has expressed her "low tolerance for totalizing theory, including Marxist and Foucauldian (though sharing with Marx an ingrained suspicion of ideology as false consciousness)."[65]

---

62   See Jochen Hellbeck, *Revolution on My Mind: Writing a Diary under Stalin* (Cambridge, MA: Harvard University Press, 2006).
63   Fitzpatrick, *Tear Off the Masks*, p. 300.
64   Ibid., p. 317.
65   Ibid., p. 8.

Historians in general tend to be atheoretical in contrast to anthropologists, sociologists, and political scientists, and in the decade (1994–2005) that Sheila, Richard Hellie, and I taught together in the University of Chicago Russian History Workshop, I encountered a general hostility to theory, especially Marxism. At the time, I was a superannuated student of political science, pulled by my home department in one direction and the association with die-hearted empiricists in the workshop in another. I frequently tried to insinuate some social science, Foucault, or Marx into the discussion, usually against considerable skepticism. Over time, resistance faded away—less from any particular pressure from me—and more from general trends in the profession like the cultural turn and the turn away from the cultural turn that impelled students to think through their own take on the larger epistemological issues posed by theorists and historians in other national fields. The study of history, while suspicious of, if not hostile to, the methodological individualism (rational choice), quantification, and formal modeling of political science, was imbibing the concerns with language, representations, subjectivities, and self-reflexivity of anthropology, historical sociology, and literary studies in particular. And by simple osmosis our students enriched their own research with the insights of other historiographies.

Rather than being a producer of theory, Sheila Fitzpatrick is a consumer, an employer and deployer of theory. Her instincts, it seems to me, take her to the concrete, the particular, the empirically and archivally demonstrable. But she does not stop there: rather than just cheese and worms, she makes sense of diversity and variety, finds patterns and meanings, and enriches our understanding as any good biologist would do in a rain forest.

The question has been posed: Is there a Sheila Fitzpatrick school of Soviet history?[66] After all, her considerable achievements and the training of a generation of students at the University of Texas and the University of Chicago certainly auger well for the formation of such a school. The first question to be asked about the question is: what is a school? Arguably, the cadre (to use a favorite Soviet word) of historians who came out of her courses and workshops make up a stellar generation of scholars teaching and training another generation of historians. But do these scholars share a single approach to history, a common intellectual agenda, be it social history or the history of categories or a hostility to

---

66   The following section of this essay is taken from my contribution to "Roundtable: What Is a School? Is There a Fitzpatrick School of Soviet History?," *Acta Slavica Japonica* XXIV, pp. 240–1.

the Marxist concept of class? On first glance, it is not easy even to argue that two historians of Soviet nationalities policies, like Yuri Slezkine and Terry Martin, one who deals with discourses and representations among other things, the other who focuses on policies and institutions, employ a common approach to their shared subject. School, it appears, is too narrow a term to encompass the variation among Fitzpatrick's students or the colleagues most influenced by her.

What distinguishes both Sheila Fitzpatrick's scholarship and teaching has been its broadness, inclusiveness, and willingness to adapt to and adopt new approaches and evidence. There is no orthodoxy here, no commitment to a single explanation. Consistently committed to varieties of approaches rather than confirming or disconfirming a particular model or paradigm, she moved from studies of bureaucracy through social history on to cultural study of discourses and categories, from the world of what is to what does it mean; she explored emotions and the everyday, and after retiring from the University of Chicago and returning to Australia, to political history and autobiography.[67] When one reads through her work, one finds a rich, complex story of the Soviet experience that defies reduction to a formula. If that openness and commitment to hard thinking about hard problems constitutes a school, then one could argue there is a Fitzpatrick (or Chicago) school, but such broad inclusiveness would belie the very notion of a school. A more fruitful question might be: What characterizes the work of Sheila Fitzpatrick and in which ways are those qualities captured in the work of one, more, or many of her students and colleagues?

The first characteristic both of Fitzpatrick and the great majority of her students is the affection for, the infatuation with, the archives. Even before it was customary or easy for Western historians of the USSR to use Soviet archives, she managed to push through the door, overcome the myriad obstacles placed in her way, and endure the tedium necessary to find the gems that gave clues and insights to a darkly understood society. Her work builds from the ground up, not from grand theory or master narrative or modernist or Marxist teleology, but from the sources. Often ethnographic, the fieldwork done largely in the archives, her dedication and *Sitzfleisch*, and her skepticism about facile formulations have been emulated by those students and colleagues most closely associated with

---

67   Sheila Fitzpatrick, *On Stalin's Team: The Years of Living Dangerously in Soviet Politics* (Princeton, NJ: Princeton University Press, 2015); *My Father's Daughter*; *A Spy in the Archives*; and *Mischka's War: A Story of Survival from War-Torn Europe to New York* (London: I. B. Tauris, 2017).

Sheila Fitzpatrick. In the Chicago workshop, there was no orthodoxy, no insistence on conformity, and no unchallenged hierarchy. We were all students, Sheila Fitzpatrick not least of all.

The second characteristic of Fitzpatrick and many of those closest to her illustrates one of the great ironies of our profession. While Sheila has been vilified as an apologist of the Soviet project, even a Stalinist, while she has been calumniated by the most conservative critics of Soviet historiographical revisionism for changing her mind over time, the great consistency in her work has been a coolness rather than an emotional attachment to the USSR or Marxism, on the one hand, and a reluctance to adopt the easy Soviet-bashing of aspiring organic intellectuals of the American state, on the other. Here again, her students and close colleagues have shared with her a critical attitude toward the practices and aspirations of the Soviet regime but not the visceral hatred or disdain that passed for judgment in the Cold War years and has been transferred to Russia more recently.

Sheila Fitzpatrick has called herself a British-style "positivist at heart," who believes "that historians ought to keep their value judgments and prejudices out of their writing." History may be subjective but one must strive to discipline "the subjective impulse." She is against "ponderous scholasticism," "semantic orthodoxy (conformity to a particular intellectual jargon)," and ideologies of all sorts. She does not see teleological progress in history but a great cycle "where one relative truth succeeds another in a sequence that is not pre-determined."[68]

Perhaps a good place to end this exploration of the life and work of Sheila Fitzpatrick is to remember that one of her great pleasures has long been the violin. Music has been a big part of her life and has given her great joy, companionship, even solace at hard times. Those of us who were at Chicago remember how she enjoyed making music with her friends and even, on occasion, with her students and how important her playing in the University of Chicago orchestra was after the loss of Michael Danos, her beloved "Misha," a faithful attendee at the Russian History Workshop. Reading through her memoirs, one is struck by how sad Sheila was at so many times of her life. The ten years she was married to Misha, she indicates, were the happiest in her life, but, as she writes, her homecoming theme music—"Schubert's 'Rosamunde' quartet—is sad. The sadness was for happiness coming so late."[69]

---

68   Fitzpatrick, "Afterword," pp. 411, 410, 412.
69   Fitzpatrick, *Mischka's War*, p. 251.

At Chicago, she made a wonderful kind of music with those in the weekly workshops. There she worked through sometime cacophony toward some kind of harmony, tolerant of dissonance, trying to find the right note. Fidelity to evidence was the right key in which to play. And new melodies were always being sought. "Historical interpretation," she once wrote, "means finding patterns. But none of these patterns fit completely, so we keep looking for new ones."[70] If there is one conclusion to be made about her work to date, it is that Sheila Fitzpatrick is always learning; she is always open to new ideas, new ways of looking at the world, new challenges to comfortable orthodoxies. Even in her most unMarxist moments, she would probably feel quite at home with what Marx claimed was his motto, probably borrowed from Aristotle: *De omnibus dubitandum*, "Doubt everything."[71]

70   Ibid., p. 412.
71   Karl Marx's "Confession" (1865), first published in the original English in the *International Review of Social History* (1956), marxists.org.

Part II
Detours, Dead Ends, Ways Out

6

The Evil Empire Revisited: Stephen F. Cohen and the History and Politics of the USSR

The privileges of material resources, state support, and perceived national interest made the US Sovietological establishment the most prolific and influential purveyor of information on the Soviet Union and its allies outside the USSR and the former Soviet states.[1] All during the years of the Cold War, a veritable army of government employees, journalists, scholars, and private consultants were hard at work analyzing and pronouncing on the Soviet Union. In a real sense, the view of the other side forged in America not only shaped the policy of one great superpower but determined the limits of the dialogue between "West" and "East." While the interpretations produced by US journalists and professional Sovietologists were by no means uniform, the usual choice of adjectives to describe the other great superpower was consistently negative—aggressive, expansionistic, paranoid, corrupt, brutal, monolithic, stagnant. Ordinary language itself reproduced the sense of Russia's alien nature, its inaccessibility, its opaqueness. Exchange students going to the USSR for a year of study routinely spoke of "going into" and "out of" the Soviet Union, as into and out of a prison, instead

---

1   An earlier version of this chapter was published as "The Evil Empire Revisited," *Michigan Quarterly Review* XXV, 3 (Summer 1986), pp. 590–9, as a review of Stephen F. Cohen's books *Sovieticus: American Perceptions and Soviet Realities* (New York: W. W. Norton, 1985) and *Rethinking the Soviet Experience: Politics and History Since 1917* (New York: Oxford University Press, 1985).

of the conventional "to" and "from" used for travel to other countries. Long after coexistence and detente moderated the excesses of Cold War rhetoric, most of those studying the USSR in the United States remained either openly hostile or barely tolerant of Soviet peculiarities. Even after the disintegration of the USSR, much of the same rhetoric continued to be deployed, now against the Russian state and its leaders, often by the same people. It has long been the contention of a coterie of scholarly critics that the distortions of a superannuated orthodoxy have been and still are in desperate need of revision.

Stephen F. Cohen, long-time professor of Soviet politics and history at Princeton University and later at New York University, is a rare combination of scholar, journalist, and public intellectual able to write both for his university peers and the broader, informed public. His scholarly credentials were secured in the early 1970s with the publication of a well-received biography of the Soviet leader Nikolai Bukharin, one of the most prominent victims of Stalin's purges of the 1930s. Soon after, he turned his attention to the dissident movement and the limits of reform within the USSR and edited a number of books on various aspects of the Soviet past.[2] From October 1982, he was a regular, then an occasional, columnist for the left liberal weekly *The Nation*, edited and published by his wife, Katrina vanden Heuvel. In the mid-1980s, he was represented by two collections of his articles—*Sovieticus: American Perceptions and Soviet Realities* and *Rethinking the Soviet Experience: Politics and History Since 1917*. Taken together, these two slim volumes constituted a reprise of the failings of Sovietology and the media in explaining the nature and aims of the Soviet Union and a challenge to those who had produced the existing record. Cohen continued his dissent against journalists and Russophobe scholars into the years when Russia was governed by Mikhail Gorbachev, Boris Yeltsin, and Vladimir Putin.[3]

---

2   *An End to Silence: Uncensored Opinion in the Soviet Union* (New York: W. W. Norton, 1982); with Robert C. Tucker (ed.), *The Great Purge Trial* (New York: Grosset & Dunlap, 1965); and with Alexander Rabinowitch and Robert Sharlet (eds.), *The Soviet Union Since Stalin* (Bloomington: Indiana University Press, 1980).

3   With Katrina Vanden Heuven (eds.), *Voices of Glasnost: Interviews with Gorbachev's Reformers* (New York: W. W. Norton, 1989); *Failed Crusade: America and the Tragedy of Post-Communist Russia* (New York: W. W. Norton, 2000); *The Victims Return: Survivors of the Gulag after Stalin* (Exeter, NH: Publishing Works, 2010); *Soviet Fates and Lost Alternatives: From Stalinism to the New Cold War* (New York: Columbia University Press, 2009, 2011); *War with Russia? From Putin and Ukraine to Trump and Russiagate* (New York: Hotbooks, 2019); and *Why Cold War Again?: How America Lost Post-Soviet Russia* (New York: I. B. Tauris, 2020).

Cohen's historical writings are intimately connected to issues of political relevance. His biography of Bukharin was more than a life and times
of its hero; it was, at the same time, an argument against the "necessity" of
Stalinism and a case for the viability of Bukharin's program of moderate
economic growth based on encouraging peasant production. Profoundly
revisionist in the best sense of the word, Cohen's biography shifted the
focus from the well-known Stalin–Trotsky rivalry to insist that Bukharin
was the far more significant political figure as an alternative to Stalinism
and as a potential influence in the post-Stalin Soviet Union. Although
the book was written more than a decade before Gorbachev's *perestroika*,
his notion that Bukharin's approach represented a milder form of Soviet
socialism seemed to be vindicated by the policies of the last Communist
General Secretary. The unbroken line between Lenin and Stalin was thus
broken, and as in the work of Moshe Lewin, alternatives were visible in
the fierce infighting that characterized the Bolsheviks until the advent
of Stalin's dictatorship.

Bukharin was almost two decades younger than Lenin and a decade
younger than Trotsky and Stalin. But this never stopped him from participating vigorously in the inner party discussions from his mid-twenties
and making major contributions to Marxist theories of the nature of
capitalism, imperialism, nationalism, and the state. He fearlessly, though
sometimes reluctantly, confronted Lenin during World War I, and Lenin
brutally characterized him as insufficiently Marxist and "soft as wax." His
youthful leftism remained intact through the revolutionary year and into
the Civil War. As a Left Communist, he led the movement against the
Treaty of Brest–Litovsk, opposed Lenin's disenchantment with workers'
control and promotion of "state capitalism" in 1918, and remained faithful to the idea of a commune state long after Lenin had turned to a
more authoritarian form of the dictatorship of the proletariat. With the
regime thrown into bitter struggle for survival, Bukharin became a chief
spokesman for the improvised and pragmatic economic program later
known as "war communism." With Evgenii Preobrazhenskii, he wrote
The ABCs of Communism (1919–20) as a primer outlining the party's
program, a short history of how it came to power, and a rationalization of the new power of the proletarian state in the development of
the economy. Justification of the need for rigorous discipline and state
violence to build socialism in a backward country was even more evident
in his next major work, *The Economics of the Transition Period* (1920),
where he boldly stated that "proletarian coercion in all its forms, beginning with shooting and ending with labor conscription ... is a method

of creating communist mankind out of the human materials of the capitalist epoch."[4]

As "Sovieticus," writing at the moment of transition from Brezhnevian stagnation to Gorbachev's *perestroika*, Cohen experimented with what he calls "scholarly journalism," applying his specialist's knowledge to the analysis of current events connected with East–West relations. He took up journalism, he tells us, because of his discontent with the one-dimensionality of the media's presentation of the USSR as a stagnant, crisis-ridden society that was also and simultaneously corrupt, reckless, and paralyzed. He characterized the US mood as "Sovietophobia," the "exaggerated fear of [the] Soviet threat," and located its causes, neither in the visceral anti-Communism of the US leadership nor in a lack of knowledge, but in the denial of the legitimacy of the Soviet Union as a great power.[5] At the same time that the USSR was seen as a global threat, "the focus of evil in the modern world," its internal system was perceived to be in serious danger, its citizens disillusioned and indifferent, its economy unable to provide basic needs for the population. Alcoholism, minority nationalism, corruption, bureaucratism, and the persecution of dissidents and Jews were the principal subjects of popular writing on Soviet domestic life to the near exclusion of other aspects of Soviet reality. While the all-too-familiar negative side of the Soviet political order remained a palpable indictment of that system, Cohen set himself the Promethean task of confronting the one-sidedness of the available picture and introducing a more complex vision.

In the essays that make up *Rethinking the Soviet Experience*, Cohen extended his critique to the scholarly professionals who study the Soviet Union. Here his claim is that Anglo-US Sovietology is beset by an intellectual crisis, a loss of vigor and purpose brought on by "a scholarly consensus on virtually all major questions of interpretation. Soviet studies has been inadequately historical, concerned with an "unbroken continuity" throughout Soviet history, and "largely excluding the stuff of real history—conflicting traditions, alternatives, turning points, and multiple causalities."[6] Like his one-time mentor and Princeton colleague, Robert C. Tucker, Cohen rejected the hegemonic concept of totalitarianism, which held nearly unchallenged sway over Western analyses of the USSR from World War II into the late 1960s. That model, which had

---

4   Stephen F. Cohen, *Bukharin and the Bolshevik Revolution: A Political Biography, 1888–1938* (New York: Alfred A. Knopf, 1973), p. 92.

5   Cohen, *Sovieticus*, p. 19.

6   Cohen, *Rethinking the Soviet Experience*, pp. 4, 7.

few detractors within the US academic community for nearly a quarter of a century, "turned out to be wrong, or seriously misleading, on all counts"—most importantly because it failed to see the potential for change within the Soviet system.[7]

As a product of the Cold War, academic Sovietology from the beginning was highly politicized in its practice. The real fear of Communism, the sense of embattlement with the Soviets, and the needs of policymakers compromised the independence of scholars. The first Soviet study center in the United States (founded in 1946), Columbia University's Russian Institute (from which both Steve Cohen and I graduated), was producing more specialists for the government than for academia in its early years, but two of its founders, Soviet legal expert John N. Hazard and specialist in Soviet literature Ernest J. Simmons, were named by Senator Joseph McCarthy as members of the "Communist conspiracy." Under enormous political and intellectual pressures and with little chance to do real research in the Soviet Union, scholars evolved a "Cold War consensus" according to which the Soviet Union was depicted as a monolithic system of rule by terror that might be transformed only by being overthrown.

The orthodoxy of the Cold War years proclaimed the "inner totalitarian logic" that linked the heady days of the revolutions of 1917 to the Stalinist horrors of the 1930s and 1940s. All phenomena led inevitably to Stalinism in a perverse mockery of a Whig interpretation of Russia's history. According to the prevailing interpretation, the October Revolution was the result of Lenin's cynical maneuvers against the democratic aspirations of the Russian people; Bolshevik victory in the Civil War was due to the ruthlessness and superior organization of the Communists. The New Economic Policy (NEP), the retreat into state capitalism after 1921, was seen, Cohen says, "as a cunning programmatic bivouac by the increasingly totalitarian party."[8] Politicized history was also narrowly political history, the exclusive investigation of elites and political infighting, with research into society largely left out. Such an emphasis on politics was inherent in the totalitarian model, which in its initial incarnation was designed to link conceptually the regimes in Nazi Germany and Stalinist Russia. "Because the Soviet system is totalitarian," John Armstrong wrote in a 1961 study, "the examination of the ruling party tends to embrace the entire history of the USSR."[9] Soviet

---

7 Ibid., p. 25.
8 Ibid., p. 22.
9 John Armstrong, *The Politics of Totalitarianism: The Communist Party of the Soviet Union from 1934 to the Present* (New York: Random House, 1961), pp. xi–xii.

studies construed "political dynamics" as something exceedingly narrow, unitary, and static. Politics meant only the high regime of the Communist Party—its leadership, proffered ideology, apparatus, and "quest for absolute power."[10] The party, treated as if it did not change very much over time, stood "outside of history" as well as outside of society. Essentially the party acted, and the people were acted upon. Though Cohen did not specifically make the point, others have commented that the evident dissimilarities between a highly developed capitalist industrial economy in crisis (Germany) and an underdeveloped peasant society engaged in a chaotic program of rapid industrialization under noncapitalist conditions (USSR) were largely neglected by the totalitarian model that looked narrowly at the political structure of the two countries.

Cohen maintained that poor historical analysis is linked to poor political analysis and, by extension, to poor policymaking. The emphasis on a static, unchanging political system devoid of a social dimension led to the failure of Sovietologists to notice the profound changes in the mid-1950s as Soviet society began the long, fitful move away from Stalinism, and the government turned outward away from isolation and confrontation to international—and domestic—détente. According to Cohen, the thaw in Sovietology dates from the late 1960s and was an outgrowth of the improvement in Soviet–US relations under Eisenhower and Khrushchev and the destalinization within the USSR that made the system look less "totalitarian" than in its Stalinist phase. Moreover, a new post–Cold War generation of scholars emerged, freer of the old conceptions, able to work in the Soviet Union, and—one might add to Cohen's list—much more critical of the underlying liberal–conservative assumptions about the US system. When many of the crop of young professors and researchers teaching about the Soviet Union in the Gorbachev years were undergraduates or graduate students, the liberal architects of US foreign policy had carried the Cold War consensus about Communism into the hot war in Southeast Asia, and serious questioning of both the Soviet threat and the vulnerabilities of the "Free World" dominated the political and intellectual discourse in universities.

The revisionists whom Cohen cites were neither of a single generation nor of a single mind. In no sense did scholars like Moshe Lewin, Robert C. Tucker, Alexander Rabinowitch, Sheila Fitzpatrick, or William G. Rosenberg create a unified consensus to replace the old. But their collective challenge was serious, and in certain subfields, like the study of

10   Cohen, *Rethinking the Soviet Experience*, p. 23.

1917, the revisionist view became the dominant interpretative paradigm. Cohen did not ask for new orthodoxies but rather for "competing perspectives, approaches, and interpretations grappling with the changing multicolored complexity of the Soviet experience."[11] The eloquent and wide-ranging critique presented in Cohen's essays, however, found fault with almost all of his scholarly predecessors who had written on Stalinism, with the clear exception of Tucker and Lewin, to whom he was indebted intellectually. Even those like E. H. Carr, the author of the fundamental multivolume history of the Soviet 1920s, and Isaac Deutscher, the Marxist biographer of Trotsky and Stalin, neither of whom was ever part of the academic Sovietological establishment, were swept into the orthodoxy of the "continuity thesis." At times, Cohen fudged the differences that existed within scholarship even during the Cold War and the conformist 1950s. In addition to Carr and Deutscher, the work of Alec Nove and the people around the British journal *Soviet Studies* prepared the way for the next generation's assault on the Cold War consensus. Yet his general point that the dominant view was of an unbroken continuity in Soviet history remains a powerful insight.

Cohen offered in his own work an alternative analysis of early Soviet history that built on his reading of Tucker and Lewin. For him, Stalinism had its roots in earlier experiences, but it was qualitatively different from anything that went before it or came after. "Stalinism," he wrote, "was excess, extraordinary extremism." It was "a virtual civil war against the peasantry," "a holocaust by terror that victimized tens of millions of people for twenty-five years," "an almost fascist-like chauvinism," and the "deification of a despot."[12] Original Bolshevism, on the other hand, had been a diverse political movement (in which Leninism was but one strain).[13] A more tolerant and pluralistic social order had been established in the period of NEP, and Bolsheviks were far from united in their plans for the future socialist society. "Stalin's new policies of 1929–33, the 'great change' as they have become known, were a radical departure from Bolshevik programmatic thinking."[14] This moment represented the rejection of the Bukharinist program of slower but steady growth within the framework of NEP and (following Lewin here) the creation piecemeal of a new state that

11 Ibid., p. 37.
12 Ibid., p. 48.
13 This point was conclusively demonstrated in a classic but regrettably neglected book by Robert C. Daniels, *The Conscience of the Revolution: Communist Opposition in Soviet Russia* (Cambridge, MA: Harvard University Press, 1960).
14 Cohen, *Rethinking the Soviet Experience*, p. 62.

took shape as makeshift solutions to the social chaos, the "quicksand society," generated by the destruction of NEP institutions and processes during the initial revolution from above .... The Stalinist system was less a product of Bolshevik programs or planning than of desperate attempts to cope with the social pandemonium and crises created by the Stalinist leadership itself in 1929–33.[15]

The argument of a break between Bolshevism and Stalinism had not only the advantage of explaining the subsequent murders of the former Leninist leadership in the party but also of opening up Soviet historiography to new and interesting questions. Cohen's discussion remained largely on the level of description of the differences between two sociopolitical orders and did not provide a full analysis of the transformation of one into the other. He rejected the bureaucracy-as-ruling-class or caste arguments associated with Trotsky and his followers, claiming instead that in this new personal despotism "the bureaucracy did not ultimately rule."[16] It is left to the Trotskyists to explain why this ruling bureaucracy "committed suicide" in the Great Purges of the late 1930s. In Cohen's view, Stalinism was a political response to a social crisis that had been created by Stalin. Stalinism was neither inevitable nor the only outcome of Bolshevism. Rather, it was the policy adopted when the far more sensible, practical, and humane Bukharinist alternative was abandoned. Here is the great drama of Soviet history—not the stereotyped Stalin–Trotsky conflict of the 1920s, but the martyrdom of the "favorite of the whole party," Nikolai Bukharin. And the memory of that loss, driven underground by official history, insistently made itself felt after Stalin's death in the renewed debates over NEP within the Soviet intelligentsia. To explain full-blown Stalinism, Cohen nodded toward Tucker and the elusive notion of Russia's political culture. Traditional values were resurrected in the 1930s along with Russian nationalism, and the gargantuan cult of the leader was at one and the same time an expression of genuine popular support and religious traditions. Stalinism in its inception had been a catastrophic revolutionary upheaval, directed by the state against society; in its full realization it metamorphosed into a rigid, conservative, traditionalist system.

After reading the Cohen critique of orthodox Sovietology, it is difficult not to turn impatiently to the contributions of the revisionist and social

15   Ibid., p. 64.
16   Ibid., p. 66.

historical scholarship that took the T-model as its foil. With totalitarianism on the defensive and social historians studying everything from patterns of work organization in Stalin's factories to the "25,000ers" who poured into the countryside in the campaign for collectivization, one would have expected Cohen to be gratified by the contemporary practitioners of revisionist history. Instead, he found the 1970s–80s writings of postorthodoxy less than compelling. He mentioned Fitzpatrick, Jerry Hough, Arch Getty, and George Yaney as some who "tend to emphasize what they consider to have been modernizing or otherwise progressive developments, such as industrialization, urbanization, social mobility, mass culture, and administrative rationalism, while minimizing or obscuring the colossal human tragedies and material losses caused by Stalin's brutal collectivization of the peasantry, mass terror, and system of forced labor camps."[17] He went on to criticize three prominent representatives of an older generation—Theodore von Laue, Alec Nove, and E. H. Carr (very different historians)—for their continued adherence to a determinist analysis of Stalinism and to question those younger revisionists who may have "an unstated political desire to rehabilitate the entire Stalin era."[18]

Cohen certainly had a point that a full social history of the 1930s would require investigations of the Stalinist terror and the Gulag, but that would have to wait until the fall of the USSR and the opening of the archives. When he looked at rival interpretations, however, Cohen's polemical style, so effective against past practitioners of orthodox Sovietology, tended to be dismissive and had the effect of closing off a debate that at the time had hardly gotten off the ground. As compelling as his critique was, he would have few disciples.

The most startling example of his unwillingness to accept the kind of pluralism for which he seemed to be arguing was his rather cavalier sweep of E. H. Carr into his general condemnation of historians of the Cold War period. Carr, who never wrote systematically on the 1930s, disagreed in print with Cohen over the role of Bukharin and the possibility of a Bukharinist alternative to Stalin. In a long review of the Bukharin biography, Carr took issue with what he called the US "cult of Bukharin," the elevation of a sympathetic party leader into the major opponent of Stalin. Whatever one may think of Carr's views on the inability of the NEP to solve the grain-delivery problem of the late 1920s, his criticism of

---

17   Ibid., p. 33.
18   Ibid.

Cohen was serious, substantive, and based on great erudition.[19] Cohen used these essays as an opportunity to get back at Carr but without really engaging the arguments of his critic.

> For Western historians now to obscure those profound and enduring tragedies ... is to return to the anticold-war, but deeply flawed, scholar-ship of E. H. Carr, the British historian whose voluminous and valuable writings grew into a tacit justification of the whole Stalin era through a selective periodization and choice of facts, by the use of Soviet-style euphemisms to characterize major events, and by excluding a full evalu-ation of both alternatives and outcomes. Ironically, that approach leads, as it led Carr, to the cold-war axiom that Stalinism was the only rational and feasible fulfillment of the Bolshevik revolution.[20]

Leaving aside the fact that Carr never systematically dealt with the Stalinist 1930s in the same detail as he did the period of NEP, the Cohen attack ironically resurrects memories of the kinds of rhetoric associated with the orthodox scholarship he so convincingly condemns. What more disabling accusation can be made against a historian of the Soviet Union than that he has fallen prey to "Soviet-style euphemisms" and through his selectivity and choice of facts, has come to justify, albeit tacitly, the whole Stalin era. Even if one disagrees that Bukharin's solution would have worked or believes that there were compelling reasons for wide support for Stalin's program within the party, does this mean that one also justifies the purges, the Nazi–Soviet Pact, and the Doctors' Plot? Cohen himself has urged that historians continue their analysis of Stalin-ism to investigate the evolution within the Stalinist period. The defeat of Bukharin and the abrogation of NEP marked a great turning point, but the formation of the Stalinist autocracy came after the great losses of col-lectivization. This is a connected but distinct historical problem, and an unwillingness to accept Cohen's estimation of a Bukharinist alternative does not "inevitably" make one an apologist for Stalinism.

Cohen's history is as present-minded as those whom he attacks, but then writing on the Soviet past is seldom wholly free from the political context in which it is being created. Since 1917 at least, Russian studies has been an engaged field without the luxury of detachment enjoyed by less relevant areas of investigation. Cohen could not resist drawing

19   E. H. Carr, "The Legend of Bukharin," *Times Literary Supplement*, no. 3785, September 20, 1974, pp. 989–91.
20   Cohen, *Rethinking the Soviet Experience*, p. 34.

out the significance, as he sees it, of the broken debates of the 1920s for the discussions of reform in the last decades of the USSR. In the final two essays in *Rethinking the Soviet Experience*, he traced the development of Soviet thinking about Stalin since the dictator's death and its continued weight in the movement for reform. Despite the lively discussion of Stalinism following Khrushchev's "secret speech" of 1956 and the Twenty-Second Party Congress in 1961, the Brezhnev regime was effective in partially rehabilitating the memory of Stalin, particularly as a wartime leader. By the 1970s Stalin's crimes were largely forgotten by all but the survivors and their relatives. Though there was no rebirth of Stalinism, that "system of personal dictatorship and mass terror," "the product of specific historical circumstances and a special kind of autocratic personality" that "have passed from the scene," sometimes covertly, other times openly expressed pro-Stalin sentiments became part of the conservative resistance to further reform in the structure he bequeathed his successors.[21] Ironically, both Soviet conservatives and reformers in the post-Stalin decades have their roots in the dual nature of Stalinism, a system of radical change and conservative restoration. But the agent of change (and conservation) has not been the working class, as Marxists might have anticipated, but the bureaucracy created by Stalin. Approaching what would be its last decade, Soviet society and its ruling elite (now that the bureaucracy had become something like a ruling class) were deeply conservative, Cohen asserted, and two conditions were required for successful reform—a coalition between reformers and conservatives in Soviet officialdom and détente with the West. With the advantage of hindsight, we now know that such a coalition never really coalesced; the reformers were few, though they briefly held the top positions in the land; and the conservatives within the Communist Party attempted in vain, and to the destruction of the very system they hoped to preserve, to carry out a coup and bring reform to an end.

The Cohen argument ends up, in a sense, where it began in the columns of *The Nation*, with the vital necessity, both for human survival and Russia's development, of a more cooperative, less confrontational relationship between the superpowers. The Cold War was and remains the enemy, both in scholarship and in international relations. Cohen wrote in opposition to the Cold War, then and on a number of future occasions when it appeared to be revived. His words written just before Gorbachev took power remain relevant: "Let 1983 be remembered as the

21   Ibid., p. 123.

year our cold warriors led us, in the name of national security, to the greatest insecurity in the history of American–Soviet relations .... The only way back from this nuclear Rubicon is to recognize and repudiate the myopic thinking that has led us there."[22] His policy recommendations —détente and the end of Sovietophobia—were consistently, intimately related to his scholarly agenda: the abandonment of models of the Soviet Union that did not understand its variety, complexity, and capacity for significant change. Cohen tried and continues to try to understand the USSR and Russia without hostility but also without apology for the genuine horrors of its past. There is great sympathy here for the victims and the dissidents, but it does not descend into despair about the rigidity of the system.

Leaving behind fatalism, Cohen in his historical writing and political interventions introduced a more open-ended and optimistic reading of both the Soviet past and Russia's potential futures. His call for a more social historical approach opened the way for a deeper analysis of the sources of stability and change in the Soviet Union and a more comprehensive understanding of the inputs into Soviet domestic and foreign policies. Though Cohen's own readings of the Soviet experience remained on the political level, referring almost exclusively to leaders, ideology, and the influence of the East–West conflict, and did not realize his own program for new approaches, he set a formidable agenda for his colleagues both in scholarship and the media. In subsequent books and articles Cohen continued to perform as the gadfly of Sovietology and as a critical public intellectual fiercely swimming upstream against US clichés about the Soviet Union and post-Soviet Russia. He repeatedly warned against those whom he believed were engineering a renewal of the Cold War. His self-confidence armored him against the often vicious attacks by colleagues, politicians, and pundits. He remained convinced that the Soviet experience, and Russia today, deserve more balanced and serious treatment than has been evident in the work of unreconstructed Cold Warriors, theirs and ours.

22   Cohen, *Sovieticus*, pp. 131–2.

7

Socialism, Post-Socialism, and the Appropriately Modern: Two Competing Paradigms

James Scott and the Gaze of the State

In a widely read and influential book, *Seeing Like a State: How Certain Schemes to Improve the Human Condition Have Failed*, James C. Scott argues that a pernicious combination of "an aspiration to the administrative ordering of nature and society" (which he calls "high modernism," borrowing the term from the geographer David Harvey), "the unrestrained use of the power of the modern state as an instrument for achieving these designs," and "a weakened or prostrate civil society that lacks the capacity to resist these plans" has marked the most tragic episodes of state development in the last two centuries."[1] With apparent regret, he notes that most of these massive state engineering schemes have in the twentieth century been the work of progressive or revolutionary elites committed to changing existing society but often with no commitment to democracy or civil rights. The prophets of high modernism—and the villains in this book—are Walter Rathenau, Vladimir

1 James C. Scott, *Seeing Like a State: How Certain Schemes to Improve the Human Condition Have Failed* (New Haven, CT: Yale University Press, 1998), pp. 88–9.

This chapter began as a talk at the Program in Comparative Study of Social Transformations, University of Michigan, on October 7, 1998, and was later published in *The Journal of the International Institute* VI, 2 (Winter 1999) and in Russian as "'Sotsializm, post–sotsializm i normativnaia modernost': Razmyshleniia ob istorii SSSR," in *Ab Imperio* 2 (2002), pp. 19–54; this chapter is a much revised and expanded version of those earlier essays. The section on "Thinking About Ideology" is from an essay written for a Festschrift for my colleague at the University of Chicago, Richard Hellie: "On Ideology, Subjectivity, and Modernity: Disparate Thoughts About Doing Soviet History," *Russian History/Historie Russe* XXXV, 1–2 (Spring–Summer–Fall–Winter 2008), pp. 251–8.

Lenin, Joseph Stalin, Le Corbusier, and Julius Nyerere; their worthy opponents are Rosa Luxemburg, Alexandra Kollontai, Jane Jacobs, and E. F. Schumacher. Small, personal, idiosyncratic, local, and spontaneous are all beautiful, while attempts to create full high modernist state legibility leads to perverse outcomes like the Soviet collective farms, the Tanzanian *ujamaa* villages, Brasilia, concentration camps, and the strategic hamlets of Vietnam. Instead of planning from above and outside by all-knowing, all-seeing elites, Scott advocates *metis*, by which he means practical skills and acquired intelligence that respond to constantly changing natural and human environments.

The case that Scott makes is a powerful one, a warning against the intellectual hubris that seems to be rooted in rationalist social engineering and rides over the diversity and particularities of actually lived lives. For a historian of the Soviet Union, the critique has a familiar ring, for conservative critics from Richard Pipes and Martin Malia have been making a similar argument about the Enlightenment and intelligentsia origins of the Russian Revolution, the Soviet dictatorship, and the horrors of Stalinism. Scott strains against the accusation that his argument easily blends into a conservative Burkean apologetic defending uncritically inheritances from the past. But it is hard not to notice that Scott's principal foes are on the Left and that, at the time he wrote the book, the debris of post-Communism was cluttering the rush to the market. In the decade after the disintegration of the USSR, his targets seemed too easy to hit. He takes aim at the Soviet Union in two chapters, one on the revolutionary party, the other on Soviet collectivization. Scott claims that Lenin's version of the revolutionary vanguard, in contrast to Luxemburg and Kollontai's, left little room for the *metis* of actual workers and peasants or even for that other Lenin who, at times of revolution, celebrated the self-generated activity of the people. As Scott shows in the chapters on Brasilia, collectivization, and the *ujamaa* villages, even in the harshest climates of imposed schematization and rationalization, ordinary people managed to thwart the high modernists and reassert their own improvised adaptations in order to survive.

This is a book rich in ideas and arguments that invite challenges. Alongside the failed imposed schemes to improve the human condition, one reflects on other devastating failures, like the US urban crisis, that were less about rationalist planning and more about the fallout of market forces inflected by racism.[2] In what ways are the imposed programs of

---

2   See the brilliant account by Thomas Sugrue, *The Origins of the Urban Crisis: Race and Inequality in Post-War Detroit* (Princeton, NJ: Princeton University Press, 1996).

privatization and marketization that have caused so much dislocation and pain in the former Soviet Union related to high modernism? Even as James Scott reveals a particular pathology in the history and practice of state-making, he is always aware that we are condemned to live with states, that they are "the ground of both our freedoms and our unfreedoms."[3] It is hard to disagree that "authoritarian disregard for the values, desires, and objections of their subjects" have marred many states in our times, but one wonders whether the choice between local knowledge and utopian schemes has to be presented as starkly as Scott does. The reliance on *metis* sounds at times too romantic, while the condemnation of rational planning in its authoritarian setting is not balanced by discussion of more democratic cases. The normative tone of the book is consistent throughout, and an important warning is being sounded. But at a time when the Soviet experience is being used universally to demonstrate that any alternatives to capitalism (and of a certain type!) is utopian, a "thicker," more textured elaboration of a variety of modernities would leave us with less despair about confronting the intractable social problems at the beginning of a new millennium.

A Brief Excursion in Soviet Historiography

Over the last several decades, two opposing schools of interpretation emerged in the media and among professional Sovietologists to explain the Soviet past and the reasons for the collapse of European Communism. At one pole are those who believe that the Soviet experience was a dangerous, wrongheaded, impossibly impractical, even evil, experiment on living human beings, in the words of Martin Malia, "the great utopian adventure of our century."[4] Though they never achieved their utopian vision, Soviet rulers created "a monstrous antireality, or an inverted world," the result of an ideological-driven attempt to create a "full or integral socialism," "full non-capitalism."[5] The Communist Party came to power in a coup d'état, behind the backs of the mass of the people, and as a minority regime attempting to maintain itself in power it required, not only a huge propaganda apparatus to perpetuate the Big Lie, not only a communications and cultural monopoly, but an omnipresent secret

---

3   Scott, *Seeing Like a State*, p. 7.
4   Martin Malia, *The Soviet Tragedy: A History of Socialism in Russia, 1917–1991* (New York: The Free Press, 1994), p. 1.
5   Ibid., pp. 8, 34.

police.[6] Russia appeared doomed by its own past and the hubris of its Soviet leaders. Some historians saw Soviet society and its seemingly omnipotent state as the reincarnation of the worst of Russian traditions, a carry-over of autocracy and aristocracy, serfdom and Siberian exile, into the twentieth century.[7]

Although there are differences among the liberal and conservative critics of the Soviet experiment—with some locating the cause of the tragedy in human nature, others in the Enlightenment, still others in the nature of the Russian character or society—the most influential "ideo-cratic" version of Soviet history was captured in the so-called totalitarian model, which linked Soviet Communism with fascism and condemned both as terroristic regimes bent on world conquest.[8] Imbedded in the model was the conviction that the State had essentially atomized the people, rendering them impotent and incapable of effective resistance. Unlike authoritarian regimes with which Western democracies could do business, totalitarian regimes were unchanging and unchangeable— except through their total destruction, either from without or from their own internal contradictions. From the perspective of this Cold War vision, one period of Soviet history was collapsed into the other, so that Stalin became, not the gravedigger of Leninism, but the fulfillment of the Leninist ideal. A revolution conceived in idealism and democratic aspiration was seen as the inevitable precursor of Stalinist terror. The evident changes in Soviet society after the death of Stalin were generally interpreted as mere window dressing; reform was not taken seriously, even as it unraveled the very threads that held the system together; and

6   Among historians close to this view, one should note Leonard Schapiro, *The Origin of the Communist Autocracy: Political Opposition in the Soviet State: First Phase, 1917–1922* (Cambridge, MA: Harvard University Press, 1955) and his *The Communist Party of the Soviet Union* (New York: Alfred A. Knopf, 1960); Richard Pipes, *The Russian Revolution* (New York: Alfred A. Knopf, 1990); Richard Pipes, *Russia Under the Bolshevik Regime* (New York: Alfred A. Knopf, 1993).

7   For the so-called "continuity thesis," see Nicholas S. Timasheff, *The Great Retreat: The Growth and Decline of Communism in Russia* (New York: E. P. Dutton, 1946); Edward L. Keenan, "Muscovite Political Folkways," *Russian Review* XLV, 2 (April 1986), pp. 115–81; Robert C. Tucker, *Stalin as Revolution, 1879–1929: A Study in History and Personality* (New York: W. W. Norton, 1973); Robert C. Tucker, *Stalin in Power: The Revolution from Above, 1928–1941* (New York: W. W. Norton, 1990).

8   Among the major works in the totalitarian school are Hannah Arendt, *The Origins of Totalitarianism* (New York: Harcourt, Brace, 1951); Barrington Moore, Jr., *Terror and Progress USSR: Some Sources of Change and Stability in the Soviet Dictatorship* (Cambridge, MA: Harvard University Press, 1954); and Carl J. Friedrich and Zbigniew K. Brzezinski, *Totalitarian Dictatorship and Autocracy* (Cambridge, MA: Harvard University Press, 1956)

the idea of a "democratic socialism" was characterized as an oxymoron, a "democratic Stalinism," according to Malia.[9]

This view bloomed fully in the Cold War, withered during the several decades of coexistence and détente of the 1960s and 1970s, and revived with the collapse of the Soviet Union to become, with some of the details shifted, the dominant understanding of the nature, evolution, and failure of the Soviet system. The overwhelming sense among the people who came to power in Russia in 1991 was that the revolution that established the Soviet republic had been a conspiratorial coup d'état that shunted the country off the track of democracy, prosperity, and modern civilization onto a tragic trajectory that took another seventy-four years to reverse. Indeed, the words that ever more frequently described the years of Soviet power included "tragedy," "utopia," and (with the sense of something that went drastically wrong) "experiment."[10] For many in the West as well, the Soviet experience has come to mean that alternatives to capitalism have been disposed on the "trash heap of history." Many in post-Soviet Russia's new elite adopted the West's Cold War synthesis and its two fundamental claims: Marxism leads to totalitarianism and real socialism is equivalent to Stalinism. To many Russians, looking about them at the debris and destruction of the old society, the Soviet Union appeared a deformed modernity, something to be overcome. The West, at least for a few short years, presented an alternative modernity, with free markets and democracy, prosperity and private property. Briefly, Western liberals and conservatives and much of the political elite of Russia shared a view of history and aspired to the same future. But by the end of the 1990s, those visions had themselves evaporated in the harsh air of economic collapse, criminality, corruption at the highest levels, and what was perceived in Russia as Western cultural and military arrogance.

---

9   Malia is critical of aspects of the totalitarian model and argues that it is unnecessary to use such a model to understand the USSR. He instead starts from his notion of full integral socialism, the impossibility of realizing this utopian vision, and the descent into terror that was necessitated by the effort to implement it. For revisions of the original totalitarian model within the totalitarian school, see Merle Fainsod, *How Russia Is Ruled*, revised ed. (Cambridge, MA: Harvard University Press, 1963) and Adam B. Ulam, *The New Face of Soviet Totalitarianism* (Cambridge, MA: Harvard University Press, 1963).

10   Malia, *The Soviet Tragedy*; Orlando Figes, *A People's Tragedy: A History of the Russian Revolution* (New York: Viking, 1996); Mikhail Heller and Aleksandr M. Nekrich, *Utopia in Power: The History of the Soviet Union from 1917 to the Present* (New York: Summit Books, 1986); and in a less condemnatory version, Ronald Grigor Suny, *The Soviet Experiment: Russia, the USSR, and the Successor States* (New York: Oxford University Press, 1998, 2011).

A second grand interpretation developed within the practice of Sovietology in the late Cold War years (1960s through the 1980s) and came under considerable challenge in the 1990s. Beginning in the 1960s, some social scientists looked at the USSR as an alternative model of social and economic development. Unlike earlier leftist enthusiasts for Soviet-style socialism, this "developmentalist" school acknowledged the brutal and costly excesses of Stalinism but was convinced that the Soviet Union had recovered from the practice of mass terror after 1953, was unlikely to return to it, and was slowly evolving into a modern, articulated urban society with many features shared with other developed countries. In the years when modernization theory (and its kissing cousin, convergence theory) held sway, the overall impression was that the Soviet Union was a much more benign society and tolerable enemy than had been proposed by the Cold Warriors.[11]

With the development in the late 1960s of social history, historians in the West began investigating the origins of the Soviet regime, most particularly in the revolutionary year 1917; they radically revised the view of the October Revolution as a Bolshevik conspiracy with little popular support. Rather, they argued that workers and soldiers, particularly though not exclusively in the capital city, Petrograd, were radicalized during 1917 by the ongoing war and economic collapse, the collaboration of moderate socialists with the "bourgeois" Provisional Government, and the effective mobilization by the Bolsheviks of workers and soldiers in support of a lower class soviet government. Other "revisionists" went on to challenge the degree of state control over society during the Stalin years and emphasized the procedures by which workers and others maintained small degrees of autonomy from the all-pervasive state.[12] Gradually the totalitarian model lost its potency, and because of its inability to explain change after 1953, its neglect of any serious investigation of society, and its attempts to homogenize Communism into Fascism, the T-model was largely rejected by younger generations of historians of the USSR.

---

11   Among the "modernization school," one might include Raymond A. Bauer, Alex Inkeles, and Clyde Kluckhohn, *How the Soviet System Works: Cultural, Psychological and Social Themes* (Cambridge, MA: Harvard University Press, 1956; New York: Vintage Books, 1961); Alex Inkeles and Raymond A. Bauer, *The Soviet Citizen: Daily Life in a Totalitarian Society* (Cambridge, MA: Harvard University Press, 1961); and Moshe Lewin, *Political Undercurrents of Soviet Economic Debates: From Bukharin to the Modern Reformers* (Princeton, NJ: Princeton University Press, 1974).

12   For revisionist scholarship on the 1930s, see Sheila Fitzpatrick, "New Perspectives on Stalinism," *Russian Review* XLV, 4 (October 1986), pp. 357–73, and the subsequent responses.

In Soviet studies, this second interpretation—what might be called the "developmental" or "modernization" model—was a welcome alternative to the fiercely anti-Communist T-model. Here, the Soviet Union was hardly a stagnant or unchanging society, but one characterized by constant reforms and even revolutionary transformations. Rather than an unbroken continuity between the policies and practices of Lenin and those of Stalin, many in this school saw a deep disjuncture, a reversal of Lenin's goals and methods—an abandonment of his internationalist program, the reduction of his promotion of national cultures within the Soviet Union, the jettisoning of his moderate policies toward the peasants in the drive toward forced collectivization—all of which necessitated in the 1930s the physical elimination of most of Lenin's closest comrades. The potential for democratic evolution of the system seemed to be confirmed by the efforts of Gorbachev to restrain the power of the Communist Party, to awaken public opinion and political participation through *glasnost'*, and to allow greater freedom to the non-Russian peoples of the Soviet borderlands. But the failure of democratic reforms and the collapse and disintegration of the USSR revived interest in the totalitarian model and encouraged a far more pessimistic reading of Soviet modernity.

Modernity

The question of modernity has long haunted Soviet studies. For many revisionists, modernization was a ubiquitous process, largely unavoidable, probably inevitable, and generally thought to be positive. But, in the years of Soviet collapse and the so-called "transition to democracy," modernity came to be employed in a much more equivocal sense by historians, many of them borrowing from the critique offered by postmodernism. Linking the Soviet program of social transformation to the intellectual and political influences of the Enlightenment, these historians noted how Bolsheviks, like other modernizers, attempted to create a modern world by scientific study of society, careful enumeration and categorization of the population, and the application of planning and administration. The frame of "modernity" presented an all-encompassing comparative syndrome in which the Soviet experiment was a particularly misguided effort that contributed to the unprecedented violence and state-initiated bloodshed.

Whereas the emphasis on the process of modernization of an earlier generation had "normalized" Russian and Soviet history by linking it to a universal teleology of progress toward industry and urbanity, many historians in the 1990s looking from the angle of modernity "normalized" Russia and the Soviet Union by underscoring the Enlightenment heritage that they shared with Western Europe. A number of post-Soviet generation historians considered the common context of different states and systems, effacing the great divide between Russia and Europe.[13] Instead of radically separating traditional imperial Russia from the modernizing Soviet Union, they similarly erased a second great divide, that of 1917, and read back into the tsarist past the modernizing practices of categorizing the population, rationalizing production, and subjecting society to experts' scientific knowledge. Instead of focusing on the way in which Russia or the USSR were "incompletely modern," the modernity school proposed that the Soviet Union was an extreme version of a darker modernity that it shared with the West.

Modernity is an unusually protean term. It has been used to explain everything from human rights to the Holocaust. At one end, it refers to everything in the modern world, even phenomena that are deeply opposed or contradictory to one another, and the whole modern age is contrasted to past eras as totalities. "Modern" is a term set against ancient, medieval, or traditional. But, within scholarship, "modern" has come to be used more selectively, as a description of a cluster of ideas and attitudes that came out of the Enlightenment—the privileging of reason over belief, reliance on science, and so on. Here the Enlightenment program remains an ideal type, a kind of utopia against which actual manifestations of modern times might be referred or judged. A struggle between modernity and non-modern elements, like religion and customary practices (exemplified in the peasantry), is highlighted. If the goal of the Enlightenment was in a sense a rational social order, Soviet "socialism" should certainly be included as a variant that attempted to realize that ideal.

But an even more useful way of looking at modernity would note the variety of adaptations to the model of modernity presented by the developed West. Rather than simply identifying modernity with the industrial, urban, capitalist West, one might consider other appropriate modernities that might include or reject aspects of the West or the Enlightenment program. In this way, post-Soviet Russia or revolutionary

13   For essays written in the spirit of a shared modernity, see David L. Hoffmann and Yanni Kotsonis (eds.), *Russian Modernity: Politics, Knowledge, Practices* (New York: St. Martin's Press, 2000).

Iran can be seen as adaptations to the dominant Western form of the modern, attempts to redefine modernity combining it with local or traditional elements, or indeed carrying certain aspects of the West's modernity further than the West itself. As Malia disapprovingly suggests (paraphrasing Alexis de Tocqueville), "If one is ruthlessly logical about the idea of democracy as equality, then one inevitably arrives at the concept of socialism."[14] Even those movements that seem most dedicated to the rejection of the modern, Afghanistan's Taliban or Syria and Iraq's Islamic State, in fact employ the tools of modernity (the AK-47, modern communications, social media) to turn their realms back to an ideal past, all the while attempting to find a political formula with which it can deal with the rest of the "modern" world. Postcolonial thinkers in particular have been caught between the inescapability of Western modernity, which includes such quintessentially modern forms as the nation and nationalism, and a search for selective adaptation of their own traditional to an appropriate modernity of their own.[15]

In fact, modernity is not a thing but a discourse—and a highly normative one that judges, evaluates, and grades societies, systems, and states. Modernity, in other words, is a modern discourse. My own approach is to begin by identifying a cluster of intellectual and political practices that made up this powerful discourse of politics and social organizing, one that became so hegemonic over time, so often simply assumed and unquestioned, that it took the self-reflexivity of what we call postmodernism to identify the relative coherence of this set of loosely held commitments and practices, which historically appeared first in seventeenth and eighteenth century Europe. I would identify the following elements as constituting the modern:

- the emergence of the idea of the "social," a separate and distinct sphere of activity that could be analyzed without reference to the divine, in material terms, to be rationally apprehended and explained. This elaboration of a separate realm of human activity, distinct from "nature" and the divine, in time gave rise to the "social sciences."

14   In the same spirit De Tocqueville wrote, "Can it be believed that democracy, after having overthrown aristocracy and the kings, will stop short before the bourgeoisie and the rich?" cited in Malia, *The Soviet Tragedy*, p. 33.

15   This is strongly felt in reading the work of the Indian political scientist Partha Chatterjee. See his *Nationalist Thought and the Colonial World: A Derivative Discourse* (Minneapolis: University of Minnesota Press, 1986) and *The Nation and Its Fragments: Colonial and Postcolonial Histories* (Princeton, NJ: Princeton University Press, 1993).

- the decline of religious worldviews and the rise of secularism and materialist culture, which at times moved to opposition to traditional religion (anti-clericalism). Growing numbers of intellectuals became committed to the idea that knowledge should be free from religious orthodoxies.
- the consequent dominance of secular forms of political power and authority; power was organized eventually in territorial nation-states existing in an international system of sovereign states.
- capitalist market economies based on large-scale production and consumption of commodities for the market. Private ownership of property was privileged over "feudal" tenures and communal holdings.
- replacement of traditional social orders of fixed social hierarchies by dynamic social and sexual divisions of labor; the replacement of estates by classes, which contributed to greater mobility in society. Commitments to egalitarianism undermined older hierarchies and distinctions.
- the idea of progress: the belief that by applying science and reason the natural and social condition of humans can be improved and that happiness and well-being of people will be increased.
- individualism: the idea that the individual is the source of all knowledge and action, that his/her reason is subject to no higher authority, and that society is the sum of the thought or action of a large number of individuals.
- rationalism: the idea that any thinking person has the capacity to think rationally, based on clear, innate ideas independent of experience; reason was the innate capacity of the mind, something that human beings came equipped with.
- empiricism: the notion that knowledge should be based on facts apprehended through sense organs.
- toleration: the conviction that humans everywhere are the same and deserve respect, freedom, and equal treatment, out of which developed a notion of human nature as universal.
- appreciation of liberty and opposition to traditional constraints imposed by power and religion.
- cosmopolitanism, rather than nationalism.

The original optimism about human possibilities and progress is well expressed in Peter Gay's characterization of the family of *philosophes*: "The men who were united on a vastly ambitious program, a program of secularism, humanity, cosmopolitanism, and freedom, above all freedom in its many forms—freedom from arbitrary power, freedom of speech, freedom of trade, freedom to realize one's talents, freedom of aesthetic response, freedom, in a word, for moral man to make his own way in the world."[16] Rationality provided individuals with the means to make calculated choices about what was best for them, to break through constraining traditions and institutions, and increase their freedom as active agents. But, as proposed by Max Weber (who was, along with Marx perhaps the principal theorist of Western capitalist modernity), modernity was marked not only by "disenchantment," the loss of religious wholeness, but by the "iron cage" constructed by rationalization and bureaucratization and the reduction of human beings to cogs in a machine.

In a darker light, Max Horkheimer and Theodor W. Adorno claimed that modernity was based on a pernicious logic that hides behind Enlightenment rationality, a logic of domination and oppression.[17] Rather than creating a new humanity, ideas of progress led to a new barbarism. The lust to dominate nature entailed the domination of human beings.[18] The very ideas and ideals that had been the central values of rationalist intellectuals for two hundred years were now to be questioned, for instead of emancipation they had led to an oppressive violent world. Whereas the earlier image of science had been as hero, now a mad scientist took its place. The idea that propositions can be tested, proved, and disproved by the experimental method and that knowledge thus will expand was now seen as a pretension to absolute and fixed truth, a bold and dangerous political project of universally applying reason and science everywhere and producing general laws that could govern the entire universe, both nature and society. Freeing oneself from such notions was very difficult given their pervasiveness, perhaps because Enlightenment ideas in fact empower intellectuals.

Clearly, from this perspective on modernity, socialism, particularly Soviet state socialism, was a modern project, indeed a particularly fiercely applied one. For some historians, like Martin Malia and Richard

---

16   Peter Gay, *The Enlightenment: An Interpretation* (New York: W. W. Norton, 1995), p. 3.

17   Max Horkheimer and Theodor W. Adorno, *Dialectic of Enlightenment: Philosophical Fragments* (Stanford, CA: Stanford University Press, 1972), first published in German in 1947.

18   David Harvey, *The Condition of Postmodernity: An Enquiry into the Origins of Cultural Change* (Oxford: Blackwell, 1990), p. 13.

Pipes, the agent of that modernity was the intellectual. For other analysts, like Scott or Zygmunt Bauman, it was the state, "the modern, obsessively legislating, defining, structuring, segregating, classifying, recording, and universalizing state [that] reflected the splendor of universal and absolute standards of truth."[19]

Modernization

Those who have adopted the modernity perspective reject the now largely discarded modernization theory of late Cold War Western social science, yet there is a strange affinity between the two. Modernization theory played an important role in Sovietology, proposing that the Soviet Union should be seen both as a part of the general process of modernization as well as a deviation from the modern as defined by the Western example. Modernization theory tried to link the developmental processes of socialist states with the general and necessary processes that went on in the First and Third Worlds. Like modernity, modernization attempted to break down the exceptionalism in the Soviet experience and eventually was criticized precisely for a failure to emphasize adequately the stark differences between the East and West, making what critics labeled a false "moral equivalence." One of the early writers on modernization, Daniel Lerner, indeed boldly emphasized that "there is a single process of modernization which operates in all developing societies—regardless of their colour, creed, or climate and regardless of their history, geography, or culture. This is the process of economic development, and ... development cannot be sustained without modernization."[20]

Modernization theory had a distinguished Weberian pedigree and was proposed as an alternative to Marxism, which, in its own way, was a theory of modernization but one that projected a revolutionary transcendence of capitalism and Western parliamentarianism. Both Marxism and what might be called liberal modernization theory were "modernist" in their acceptance of the basic progressive teleology of development; both practiced a materialist inevitability and, when applied to the Soviet Union, were criticized for apologizing for the worst excesses of Soviet socialism as having been necessary for development.

19   Zygmunt Bauman, *Intimations of Postmodernity* (London: Routledge, 1992), p. xiv.
20   As quoted in Charles Tilly, *Big Structures, Large Processes, Huge Comparisons* (New York: Russell Sage Foundation, 1984), p. 46.

Indeed, modernization theorists argued that the "continual changes in all spheres of a society [entailed by modernization] means of necessity that it involves processes of disorganization and dislocation."[21] Social disorder, violence, even genocide could be explained as part of the modernization process.

Martin Malia and the Soviet Tragedy

Within the first decade after the disintegration of the Soviet Union, a popular consensus had already developed that nothing less than history itself had decisively proven the Soviet experience a dismal failure, if not an unmitigated disaster, and that it was only a matter of time before the regimes that still ruled over more than a billion people in China, North Korea, Vietnam, and Cuba would come to realize that the future was knocking on a different door. Not surprisingly, then, as the funeral corteges of expired states passed by, lit up by fires of ethnic warfare, historians of Communist *ancien regimes* turned to summing up the history of the recent past. Among the first of these postmortems was an inspired polemic of grand theorizing by Martin Malia that replaced modernization with modernity. First published under the pseudonym "Z" as an essay in *Daedalus*—"The Road to Stalin's Mausoleum"—Malia expanded his thoughts into a book of over five hundred pages, *The Soviet Tragedy*, in which he laid out three major themes as a way of synthesizing Soviet history. As the title suggests, Malia understands Soviet history, first of all, as a tragedy "produced by the quest for that perfection of justice, equality, and peace which is 'socialism' and for that summum of Promethean technological power which defines 'modernity.'"[22] Second, he launches a sustained, ferocious attack on Western Sovietology, which, in his view, contributed to a fundamental misconception and misunderstanding of the Soviet system. This "pseudoscience," couched in the language and methodology of value-free social science, held that the Soviet Union was a variant of modernity and that socialism was still possible within the Soviet system. Sovietologists consistently elevated the centrality of society, a generalizable category across cultures and political systems, and reduced ideology and politics to reflections of the socioeconomic base. And, third, Malia puts ideology back at the center of causation. He

21 S. N. Eisenstadt, *Modernization: Protest and Change* (1966), quoted in ibid., p. 54.
22 Malia, *The Soviet Tragedy*, p. 4.

takes socialism, as he understands it, seriously and argues that consistently through Soviet history the leadership worked to implement full integral socialism, that is, full non-capitalism, the elimination of the market, private property and profit, which because it was fundamentally unrealizable led to the creation of a monstrous repressive regime. In one of his most redolent phrases, Malia concluded, "In sum, there is no such thing as socialism, and the Soviet Union built it."[23] Because the moral idea of socialism is utopian and unrealizable, the only way it could be "realized" on the ground was through the terroristic means that Lenin and Stalin used. Finally, he asserts, the collapse of the Soviet system was inevitable; the regime was illegitimate and doomed from the beginning; its end was inscribed in its "genetic code."

Malia's ambitions were considerable, much more than the trashing of Soviet studies and exposing the Soviet Union as a civilizational aberration. He aimed to show that the Soviet tragedy has a broader lesson for all of us, that no socialism is possible anywhere—at least not non-market socialism. While this large claim remains an inspiration throughout the book and, in my opinion, undermines his more compelling arguments, his actual achievements in this work deserve to be enumerated.

First, he took seriously, even when he was most critical of it, the profession of Soviet studies. In this, he differed from other conservative critics of Sovietology who largely ignored the arguments of their opponents. Second, he brought ideology and politics back to a field in which there was, at times, a regrettable reductionism to the social and economic, or what many of us called the material. Third, he offered a nuanced view of totalitarianism, the major paradigmatic understanding of Stalinism and the USSR during and immediately after the Cold War by rejecting the T-model and accepting a more limited concept of totalitarianism. Fourth, he rejected the so-called "continuity school," among whom might be listed Edward Keenan, Richard Pipes, and Robert C. Tucker, which drew parallels between Stalinism and Muscovy or late tsarism and tended to privilege a coherent, continuous authoritarian Russian political culture from which the Soviet Union appeared unable to escape. Malia points out that similarities are not continuities and still less are they causal explanations. Fifth, he places the Soviet project in the larger problematic of modernity from the Enlightenment on. The logic of the modern age, he claims, gave people the idea that history had a secular goal, or telos, namely progress, the rational, scientific mastery

23   Ibid., p. 496.

of nature and the creation of a rational egalitarian society. Socialism, the logical extension of the idea of democracy, was the highest form of this modernist illusion.

For all the suggestiveness of his critique of Sovietology, Malia's account has its own limitations. He admits regrettably that there could not be any value-free approach to the USSR. "Overall, one had to be either for or against the Specter."[24] His principal enemy, social history, was "an ideological effort to explain the Soviet system as the product of popular action, and hence as democratically legitimate."[25] It follows, then, that Malia's interpretation too must be full of values, but he stops short of the view that all is ideology, for his "ideology" is based on the "fact" that "the market is part of the social order of nature."[26] The idea that the market is natural, not the creation and creature of human beings, is never questioned.

A Perverse Alternative Modernity: Stalinism as Socialism

While post-Soviet historians differ among themselves, the failure of the socialist experiment was a setback to those who practiced social history and had preferred a détentist approach to the "Evil Empire." Many younger scholars had no stake in the conflicts of the Cold War generation and were intrigued by the insights that the modernity paradigm appeared to offer. "The modernity group, by contrast [with those who had gone before] with its powerful preoccupation with the ideological and political dimensions of twentieth-century history grew out of a rejection of the social history of the 1970s–1980s," writes Michael David-Fox. "Modernity scholars maintained other debts to their totalitarian grandfathers, as well, including a general tendency to see continuities rather than breaks from Lenin to Stalin."[27]

One of the most influential proponents of the modernity paradigm is a student of Malia's, Stephen Kotkin, who from the earliest days of his career was anxious to redefine Soviet historical studies. In a sweeping review article of the field of Soviet studies, which in many ways echoed Malia's attack on the old paradigms, Kotkin imagined his piece as a

---

24   Ibid., p. 19.
25   Ibid., p. 10.
26   Ibid., p. 518.
27   Michael David-Fox, *Crossing Borders: Modernity, Ideology, and Culture in Russia and the Soviet Union* (Pittsburgh: University of Pittsburgh Press, 2015), p. 39.

manifesto of a younger generation of historians who were "coming of age
in a world without the problem of Communism."[28] He dismisses older
views that saw "the Russian Revolution as the embodiment of a lost social
democracy, or, conversely, as a legitimation of Western society through
negative example." Instead, he likens "the Russian Revolution to a mirror
in which various elements of the modernity found outside the USSR are
displayed in alternately undeveloped, exaggerated, and familiar forms."[29]
He seems to argue that socialism represented a distinctive modernity
different from but certainly comparable to the modernities found in the
West, and he proposes a double research agenda: the discovery of what
"socialism—and hence the revolution—meant over time (all the way to
1991), for the regime and for the people" and the comparison of Soviet
practices with those of other modern countries.[30] "Understanding how
an Enlightenment ethos of scientific social engineering and accompanying modern practices of government mixed with a theocratic party-state
structure and quasi-religious systems of dogma is perhaps the principal
challenge facing interpreters of revolutionary Russia."[31] His conclusion
illustrates his thesis:

> ... an Enlightenment science of society, as well as revolutionary politics,
> originated in France; languages of class in England's pioneering fossil-
> fuel industrialization; conceptions of ethnofederalism in the Habsburg
> empire; worship of machines in Germany and futurist Italy; giant corpo-
> rate trusts in America; and welfare states everywhere. Combining all this
> and more, Soviet socialism forms an intimate part of Western history,
> however singular the Bolshevik "autocracy" and its "Orthodox" rituals,
> or the partly indigenous, partly Marxist-inspired struggle to transcend
> capitalism, may appear.
>
> To characterize these commonalities, I have employed the term
> "modernity" (not modernization). Today (and hence retrospectively),
> modernity may seem synonymous with parliamentary democracy and
> the market; but at the time of the Russian revolution and throughout
> the interwar period, experiments with nonparliamentary and at least
> partially nonmarket structures enjoyed great popularity.... To my
> mind, Soviet socialism is more than simply a matter of dictatorship

---

28   Stephen Kotkin, "1991 and the Russian Revolution: Sources, Conceptual Categories, Analytical Frameworks," *Journal of Modern History* LXX, 2 (June 1998), p. 386.
29   Ibid., p. 387.
30   Ibid., p. 400.
31   Ibid., p. 403.

and noncapitalism. It is a pivotal case for understanding the matrices of social welfare and thus of the early twentieth-century modernity and subjectivity that emerged transformed in the Great War.[32]

Kotkin takes a view of ideology similar to Malia's, arguing that "notwith-standing the frequent shifts, Bolshevik 'ideology' had a structure derived from the bedrock proposition that, whatever socialism might be, it could not be capitalism. The use of capitalism as an antiworld helps explain why, despite the near total improvisation, the socialism built under Stalin coalesced into a 'system' that could be readily explained within the framework of October."[33] Many of Kotkin's points are delivered telegraphically in his rambling review of recent works on Soviet history, but one can with profit look into his mammoth study of Magnitogorsk for the application of his research program.

Even as Kotkin accepts Malia's basic premise that the Soviet state is a radical application of modernist fantasies, he breaks with his mentor in his positive reconstruction of what Soviet socialism was. More than just non-capitalism, it was a new civilization, at least in its own terms (and in Kotkin's evaluation), that involved new social structures and property relations, the beginnings of a welfare system, a self-confident new culture, a new kind of strong-state politics, a language of its own, and convictions that a new, superior world was on the horizon. Kotkin positions himself differently from both Sheila Fitzpatrick, who argued that Stalinism was the restorative triumph of a new postrevolutionary elite, and Moshe Lewin, who saw that triumph as a betrayal of the initial promise of the revolution (preserved by Lenin) and a backward form of modernization but one not to be uncritically equated with socialism or modernity. For Kotkin, what Stalin built was socialism, the only real fully non-capitalist socialism the world has ever seen. Fitzpatrick and Lewin, the two major Western historians of the first generation to tackle the Stalin period, see Stalinism as "an end to the revolution and some-thing of a return, under conditions of great stress, to nonrevolutionary traditions."[34] For Lewin, socialism was an alternative modernity to capi-talism, a humanism yet to be realized, and Stalinism was a "blockage," a temporary "obstruction" to Russia's path to modernity.[35]

---

32   Ibid., p. 425.
33   Ibid., p. 400.
34   Stephen Kotkin, *Magnetic Mountain: Stalinism as a Civilization* (Berkeley: University of California Press, 1995), p. 5.
35   Ibid., p. 379, fn. 21. The 222 small print pages of footnotes are a parallel text to

Kotkin, like Malia, rejects the continuity theorists who link Stalinism back to Russian autocracy, serfdom, and traditional authoritarian political culture and agrees with him that the roots of Stalinism can be traced back to the seventeenth and eighteenth century in the West. "It is impossible to comprehend Stalinism," he writes, "without reference to the eighteenth-century European Enlightenment, an outpouring of impassioned public discussion that took as its point of departure the seventeenth-century innovation of modern science."[36] He argues that the Bolsheviks used a scientific vocabulary to achieve a rational social order, an urban, social welfare society that in many ways set a standard for the West in the interwar period.[37] Stalin had a modernist vision. "We are becoming a country of metal," he proclaimed to his comrades, "an automobilized country, a tractorized country. And when we have put the USSR on an automobile, and the *muzhik* on a tractor, let the esteemed capitalists, who boast of their 'civilization,' try to overtake us."[38] He planned to reverse the assessment of the Soviet Union as backward and the West as advanced.

The Soviet experience was about the building of socialism, and what socialism meant, Kotkin asserts, was clear to the Soviet leaders. "By socialism was meant the party's monopoly on power combined with the headlong expansion of heavy industry—carried out in a determinedly non-capitalist way."[39] The "chaos" of the market would be replaced by the order of planning. "Socialism represented nothing less than the full transcendence of capitalism."[40] But, rather than emphasizing how the Soviet project was radically different from what was going on in the capitalist world, which may be self-evident, Kotkin underlines how Marxism, like other Enlightenment projects, was developmentalist and self-styled science. Development was "the acclaimed universal goal of civilization" and science, "the supreme language of modernity."[41] The primary irony of Soviet development was that in order to become different from the West, to transcend capitalism, the country (its leaders believed) had to become more like the West; it had to industrialize, urbanize, mobilize its population, educate its people. Modernity seemed to be a condition that

the main narrative and the place where Kotkin engages in a barrage of criticism against other historians.

36   Ibid., p. 6.
37   Ibid., p. 20.
38   Cited in ibid., p. 29.
39   Ibid.
40   Ibid., p. 30.
41   Ibid.

was unavoidable, and modernization the necessary road to emancipation. A second irony is that by holding on to their vision of socialism "in any guise Bolshevik conceptions of the options before the country were narrowed considerably by their anticapitalist mission."[42]

Both Malia and Kotkin make the fundamental point that socialism in the Bolsheviks' understanding ultimately was to be non-capitalist, but they do not seem to allow whether this view would have prevailed or been modified under different conditions. Being anti-capitalist did not necessarily mean the immediate abandonment in conditions of poor peasant agriculture of all markets. It would be a mistake to confound the non-capitalist nature of the socialist end with a non-capitalist or at least non-market road to socialism. Lenin argued reluctantly but forcefully that Russia had to pass through a long period of state capitalism, of markets and marketeers. The market and the NEPmen, the petty merchants and entrepreneurs, were certainly suspect, but the debate in the 1920s was on whether (and when) to move decisively and completely into a coercive, non-market transition to "socialism," the path eventually adopted by Stalin. Kotkin has collapsed the method into the goal, the means into the end, and left out consideration of how means affect ends. Bukharin distinguished the two, and like Lenin and Trotsky emphasized the low level of development of the Soviet economy and the need to remain allied to the peasants as reasons for ameliorating the pace of development. The devil here is in the details, not in a stark choice between capitalism and non-capitalism as suggested by Malia and Kotkin. In a long footnote on Lewin, Kotkin tries to contrast his views with Lewin's, noting that "the Soviet industrialization debate of the 1920s was about the optimal path to socialism, which meant non-capitalism."[43] But Lewin is speaking about how to get from here to there and keeps open what socialism might have looked like after a different kind of transition. Ultimately, like Malia, Kotkin deduces Soviet practice from its ideological commitment to a certain idea of socialism, while Lewin sees ideas of socialism developing within the debates, successes, and failures of the first ten years of Soviet power.

As a product of both the Enlightenment project of social rationalization and the particularities of Russia's geopolitical, developmental, and cultural position, Kotkin argues that Lenin and Stalin's vision of Soviet socialism as complete non-capitalism ultimately tied them together

---

42   Ibid., p. 32.
43   Ibid., p. 395, fn. 14.

and therefore effaced alternative paths. Reconnecting Stalinism back to Lenin and the October Revolution, he concludes that the one necessarily led to the other. The difference between Malia/Kotkin and Lewin is in the openness of the possible understandings and strategies of socialism, and, in many ways, this has always been the great divide in Soviet studies—between those who have tied Lenin tightly to Stalin and therefore obliterated the possibility of an alternative socialism and those who have tried to uncouple Lenin from Stalin and kept open the possibility of another form of socialism. Given the former position, any evolution toward Social Democratic accommodations with market capitalism (which occurred in Marxist parties in the West) or the Gorbachev reforms would appear to be precluded. Stalin monopolized and identified socialism exclusively with his choices, limiting the range of discussion that had raged before 1930; adopted a non-market socialism at the given level of development in isolation from the rest of the world; and carried it out by the massive application of state violence. The result, which he, Malia, and Kotkin call socialism, was, for many Communists who perished at Stalin's hands, a grotesque parody of socialism. Kotkin, at one point, notes the difficulty for Soviet workers to draw a "principled distinction between the cause of socialism and the existing Soviet regime," but then he analytically does the same thing.[44] Kotkin reifies socialism, whereas Lewin sees it as an ongoing discussion and an open possibility offered by historical practices.

Reasonably enough, Kotkin is interested in what socialism meant to the peoples of the USSR, both in the pronouncements and agendas of the leadership and in everyday life. Socialism presented "the prospect of a quick leap, not simply into modernity but a superior form of modernity, the corresponding attainment of high international status, a broad conception of social welfare, and a sense of social justice that was built into property relations."[45] This "belief in Soviet socialism, as in all matters of faith, was never without ambivalence, confusion, and misgivings."[46] "Socialism addressed real problems and seemed to offer real solutions. As long as capitalism was mired in crisis, socialism retained a powerful appeal."[47] But socialism seen as a superior alternative to capitalist modernity

---

44   Ibid., p. 236.
45   Ibid., p. 358.
46   Ibid.
47   Ibid., p. 359.

turned out to be a crushing burden. Soviet socialism collapsed from within, but it did so because it existed as an anti-world to capitalism. It was from capitalism that socialism derived its identity and against which it constantly measured itself. Over the long haul, however, social-ism proved incapable of meeting the challenge that it had set itself of besting capitalism.[48]

Like other historians of the USSR, Kotkin looks to the Soviet past as a source about learning about politics and society, about the risks and possibilities of humanly initiated social transformations. The lesson he learns is that the USSR is part of European history, not merely an alien deviation. "Stalinism constituted a quintessential Enlightenment utopia, an attempt, via the instrumentality of the state, to impose a rational ordering on society, while at the same time overcoming the wrenching class divisions brought about by nineteenth-century industrialization."[49] This "urban-modeled, socially oriented utopia" has a long pedigree that Kotkin traces back to Tommaso Campanella's (1568–1639) City of the Sun of the early seventeenth century. Rather than marginalize or reject as foreign the Soviet experiment, Kotkin ends his rich and challeng-ing book by setting the USSR in the context of other modern industrial welfare states. The current crisis of post-socialism, rather than a cause for comfort or self-congratulation, "might better be seen as also our own."[50]

Thinking About Ideology: Dogma, Discourse, Subjectivity

Rather than material or cultural structures, ideology is at the center of Malia and Kotkin's approach. They see themselves righting Soviet his-toriography, turning over the inversion that was Sovietology. Yet in a more forthright way, they are reviving an older political, ideologi-cal orthodoxy that underlaid the totalitarian approach. Within Soviet historiography, modernization theory, with its emphasis on material-ity, economics, and social transformation, stood in stark contrast with ideocratic approaches that centered on the power of ideology. These two competing interpretative framings held radically different views on the nature and role of ideology. The ideocratic paradigm that many in the modernity school have adopted holds that ideology is relatively fixed,

48   Ibid., p. 360.
49   Ibid., p. 364.
50   Ibid., p. 366.

constant, and determinant; that Soviet social, political, and cultural practices flowed from an ideological project (what Malia identifies as "integral socialism," full non-capitalism); and, in fact, that Stalinism is the continuation, indeed the fulfillment, of ideas based in Leninism and even Marxism. One more irony is that this deeply conservative Western view almost exactly corresponds to the views of the Stalinists themselves, that Stalinism was socialism, that it had been achieved in 1936, and that Marxism-Leninism-Stalinism was a seamless synthesis. The obvious difference is that the valences are reversed—what was positive for the Stalinists was negative for Malia and Kotkin.

Those affiliated with the modernization paradigm, along with other social historians of the USSR, argue in contrast that ideology itself is part of a social process. It shifts, changes, adapts, is used and abandoned—and whatever socialism was in its earlier manifestations in Marx and Lenin, it became something quite different in official (post-Lenin) Leninism and Stalinism. In this view, socialism is preserved as an ideal or as a variety of ideals and actual manifestations, among which Stalinism is a peculiarly virulent form of repressive, undemocratic "state socialism." Somehow, Russia went off the track, and the usual explanation for that deviation is social backwardness and international isolation.[51]

Malia's account in *The Soviet Tragedy* radically substitutes an ideological reductionism for a socioeconomic determinism, and ultimately his work is deeply ahistorical. One does not really need history for his explanation, for Soviet history in Malia is the working out of a logic, an inevitability from beginning to end. If there were aberrations, they occurred when there were momentary deviations from the true socialism as Malia understands it. In other words, the New Economic Policy (NEP, 1921–28) was an aberration, as were the reforms of Nikita Khrushchev (1953–64) and certainly the revolutionary transformations of Mikhail Gorbachev (1985–91). Only so-called "War Communism" (1918–21) and Stalinism (1928–53) were true socialism in Malia's sense.

My own argument is that Soviet history should not be explained deductively or as the unfolding of a logic. Neither War Communism nor NEP nor Stalinism was the "true" Bolshevik program in action, but each was a contingent adaptation to circumstances, expedient, necessitated by limited choices, and to a large extent improvised—all within a framework of broad, inconsistent, contested ideas of what socialism might be.

---

51   This view, developed by the social historians, is most fully worked out in the writings of Moshe Lewin. As one deeply influenced by the work of Lewin, I should admit that I might be considered a Marxist–Lewinist!

Debate, discussion, and dissent were integral to the Bolshevik movement until Stalin ruthlessly eliminated them. For Communists, ideology was a framework, a prism through which the chaos of reality was perceived, understood, made sense of, but not something that could be applied in an unmediated way. There was little predictability about what would happen and much—here both Malia and Kotkin would agree—path dependency that limited future options once certain choices had been made. Nikolai Bukharin can be seen as an emblematic figure, someone who defended War Communism but changed his mind and became the chief ideologue of NEP and a key opponent of the breakthrough that led to Stalinism. People changed, as did ideas, even ideologies, certainly ideas of socialism. Learning took place even among Bolsheviks.

All of this is not to deny ideology but to take it very seriously. For, in the Soviet context, "ideology," that is the operative ideational frameworks, the symbolic and structural orders, operated even when people did not believe in the official ideology or want to participate in the system. In that society, people could only "speak" out loud within the dominant discourses or suffer exile or death.

If one follows Malia's commandment to take ideology seriously, one also has to get the ideology right. For instance, what was the relationship of collectivization of peasant agriculture to Marxism or Leninism? The forced requisitioning of grain was certainly a practice that Bolsheviks might engage in, and they did so during the Civil War to feed the cities and the Red Army in the life-and-death struggle with the enemies of Soviet Power. But forced collectivization or war on the peasantry contradicted the strictures of Engels on how to treat agricultural producers, as well as rejected Lenin's own NEP policies, as his widow Nadezhda Krupskaya uncomfortably reminded the party leaders late in the 1920s.[52] Fundamental to Marxism was the notion that socialism could only be built either on a highly advanced industrial capitalist society or with the help of a revolutionary regime in such a country. Neither of these conditions obtained in Soviet Russia, as Lenin and the Left Opposition repeatedly reminded the party. Much of Bolshevik rule was a compromise with a resistant reality in which there was no aid from abroad, the peasants resisted programs that would have supported industrialization, and increasingly difficult choices had to be made if they wanted to develop the country economically.

---

52   N. Krupskaia, "Lenin i kolkhoznoe stroitel'stvo," *Pravda*, January 20, 1929; discussed in Moshe Lewin, *Russian Peasants and Soviet Power: A Study of Collectivization* (Evanston, IL: Northwestern University Press, 1968), pp. 318–19.

While some historians have argued that the Bolsheviks were simply power-hungry opportunists who spoke one way but acted another, Malia sees the Leninists as dedicated fanatically to a single integral socialist project. In his highly determinist interpretation, he leaves little room for agency, even for Bolshevik agency. Stalin may have been a bad man, but for Malia it was not his evil that made the system but the system that made his evil. This is the story of a Logic with a capital L that prevails, a "reflex," something unconscious that has to be carried to the tragic end. The vicissitudes and contingencies of actual historical events are irrelevant to Malia's vision.

Still, Malia and Kotkin's suggestion to bring ideology back in remains salutary. Some years ago, a graduate student at the University of Chicago, who had been attentively listening to my course of lectures in Soviet history and politics, asked: "Why do you avoid the ideology? How can you talk about the Soviet Union without bringing in ideology?" I was somewhat taken aback, but I had an answer. Basically, from the time I had started teaching history in 1967, I had been struggling against the then-dominant causal arguments that explained Soviet policies and practices as derived from Marxism-Leninism. As a member of the emerging group of self-described "social historians" (in my case, "socialist historian" would have been a more accurate description—but this was the United States, not Britain), I was trying to understand the grander structures and processes, the underlying forces, what earlier had been called the substructure, that shaped the Soviet state and social experience. Deductions from Marx's *Capital* or Lenin's *What Is to Be Done?* could not, we believed, explain much more than the aspirations of leaders. They left out the actual social and economic constraints in which Bolsheviks found themselves, not to mention the unintended consequences of their choices and actions.

By the late 1970s, the twig, in the opinion of some, had been bent too far in the social direction, and historians—not me—were speaking of a "social history with the politics left out." Ideology still figured in more conservative readings and in popular formulations of Soviet history, but few of us anticipated that a younger generation would follow some of the most conservative writers on the USSR and revive the argument from ideology. In a fine review article in *Revolutionary Russia*, Stephen Smith gave three reasons why ideology had come back into Soviet studies with such strength: the opening of the archives, which showed that Soviet leaders actually took Marxism-Leninism quite seriously and "spoke Bolshevik" even in their internal communications; the limitations presented by a purely social explanation; and the cultural turn in social science and history, that is, the new emphasis on ideas, culture, meaning, and interpretation, the centrality of discourse.[53]

The problem remained, however: what do scholars and others mean when they speak about ideology? In what has become an essential starting text, Terry Eagleton provides sixteen different common uses of the word "ideology," everything from "false and deceptive beliefs" to something close to culture or discourse.[54] When Marx wrote *The German Ideology*, the word referred to false and misguided understandings of the real world that would have consequences in the world if not corrected or supplanted by accurate understanding. Ironically, as one of Marx's prominent critics within Russian studies, Malia had a similar view: ideology (in this case, socialism) was a false idea that would create a monstrous society and lead to its inevitable collapse. In common usage, Eagleton explains, the word "ideological" is always applied to the other guy; he or she has dogmatic or incorrect ideas, while we have science or objectivity or realism. As he puts it, with evident irony, "the Soviet Union is in the grip of ideology, while the United States sees things as they really are."[55] Indeed, when I was growing up, eminent former Marxists on their way to becoming neoconservatives were preaching the "end of ideology" in the West, anticipating what they later would proclaim as "the end of history," the triumph of liberal capitalism and its attendant ideas and political forms.

The stark dichotomy that positions ideology at one pole and realism, *realpolitik*, pragmatism, or objectivity at the other—juxtaposed opposite one another like passion and reason, religion and science, state socialism and market capitalism—is not very useful. For historians and social scientists, a more fruitful approach would be to suspend normative preferences for the moment and see political ideology or official ruling state ideology not as true or false but as a system of beliefs or even more broadly a discourse that legitimates a given arrangement of power and property. Ideology sustains certain relations of dominance. In Eagleton's words, "A dominant power may legitimate itself by *promoting* beliefs and values congenial to it: *naturalizing* and *universalizing* such beliefs so as to render them self-evident and apparently inevitable; *denigrating* ideas which might challenge it; *excluding* rival forms of thought, perhaps by

---

53   Stephen Smith, "Two Cheers for the 'Return of Ideology,'" *Revolutionary Russia* XVII, 2 (December 2004), pp. 119–35.
54   Terry Eagleton, *Ideology: An Introduction* (London: Verso, 1991).
55   Ibid., p. 4.

some unspoken but systematic logic; and *obscuring* social reality in ways convenient to itself."[56] Ideologies, both official or Ruling State Ideology, as in Stalin's USSR, or broadly accepted political discourses, as in the United States, are, among other things, about political mystification. The ideology of the United States, which takes private property, market economics, and liberalism as the highest stage of human possibility is as ideological as the more doctrinal formulations of fascism or Communism. In many ways, liberalism works far more effectively and subtly in the United States than Marxism-Leninism ever did in the Soviet Union, where it was generally ham-fisted and force-fed.

The conception of ideology to which so many social historians objected was the "recipe book" view of ideology, in which ideology is a set of dogmas or doctrines that can be ascertained by reading, teaching, and propagandizing. Not only is ideology doctrinal, it is also doctrinaire. Historians who saw ideology as doctrine made a simple deduction from text to intention and action. For historians like Malia and Kotkin the stated aspiration for a socialism that was full non-capitalism was sufficient explanation for both what the revolution intended and for the consequences of the actions of the Bolsheviks. Alternative views of ideology see ideology broadly as discourse or, more narrowly, as a frame or prism through which the world is apprehended and understood. Peter Kenez writes: "Marxist thought provided a prism, through which revolutionaries saw the world. It established an ideological framework within which the Soviet leaders operated, especially immediately after the revolution. Had they not been Marxists, at critical turning points, they would have made different decisions."[57] For historians like Moshe Lewin, ideology is one factor, albeit of great weight, which is then thwarted and distorted by social structures, limited political possibilities, personalities, and the impossibility of predicting the outcome of ones choices and actions.

Not only is it more helpful for a historian not to conceive of ideology as mere dogma, but it is important to notice that it is neither fixed nor unchanging. Ideology talks back to reality, and, more important, the real world talks back to it. Steve Smith writes:

> Throughout the period, the "real" world—whether in the shape of a railway system brought to paralysis, the ravages of typhus, or a military

---

56   Ibid., pp. 5–6 (emphases in original).
57   Peter Kenez, *A History of the Soviet Union from the Beginning to the End* (New York: Cambridge University Press, 1999), p. 279.

offensive by Denikin—had a nasty habit of sneaking up on the Bolsheviks from behind and throwing into confusion their best-laid plans. In
other words, the world in which the Bolshevik policy makers operated
had a recalcitrance that defied their efforts to impose meaning upon it.
It could force them to change direction radically (although, of course,
any such change of direction would immediately find an ideological
justification).[58]

Explicitly articulated political ideologies are quintessentially modern,
a product most immediately of the French Revolution, and from their
emergence were connected to mass politics and, later, democracy. Ideologies are tools for mobilizing populations, and like political parties
they function to coordinate diverse opinions and people.[59] When politics becomes less about obedience to divinely sanctioned monarchs and
becomes more about representative leaders persuading and negotiating
with their constituents, ideologies both in the narrow sense of doctrines
and the broader sense of hegemonic discourses become indispensable
as political tools of elites and political leaders. Despite our democratic
desires and fantasies, modern politics is less a free marketplace of ideas
and more like state capitalism in which a leading role—the commanding
heights—are held by groups with articulated ideologies.

In societies with a well-established, widely understood and accepted
discourse of politics, ideology is already diffused and internalized.
But, in other societies, those newly formed or emerging from revolutionary transformations, the aspirants to leadership must articulate
and diffuse their ideological premises. Here, ideology appears more
directed, a top-down project of ideologizing the population, as the histories of nationalism, socialism, liberalism, conservatism, and fascism
demonstrate. The master narrative has yet to be constructed, and not
surprisingly persuasion is likely to be more coercive. Bolshevik Russia

58   Smith, "Two Cheers for the 'Return of Ideology,'" p. 132.
59   Stephen E. Hanson makes the argument that ideologues can induce rational
individuals to cooperate with others sharing an ideology. Without successful party ideologies there cannot be effective political parties. The absence of coherent ideologies
in post-Soviet Russia helps explain the failure of political parties in that country. (See
his "Ideology and Party System Development," paper prepared for the 2006 Annual
Meeting of the American Political Science Association, August 31–September 4, 2006,
p. 7.) Hanson makes a strong case that ideology should be treated as an independent
variable and not explained away as "reflections of more fundamental social forces (be
these cultural, class-based, or strategic in nature)" as they have been by the three dominant social science paradigms—liberal modernization theory, Marxism, and rational
choice theory (p. 8).

during the Civil War and the NEP was such a society, but the ideology of the Bolsheviks was not yet coherent. Leninism was a post-Lenin phenomenon, a construction of his successors, and what constituted Marxism or Leninism or, indeed, the Soviet project remained a contested topic of discussion and fierce political infighting well into the early 1930s. After his imposed "revolution from above," Stalin's Soviet Union was in many ways a new country, one in which a radically restricted official ideology was both solidified and imposed. In such cases of revolutionary transformation, the process of deliberate construction of ideology is evident and does not flow from the bottom up. But the most effective and long-lasting ideologies are those that resonate in a given population, those that answer important questions, give direction to life choices, and bring rewards in this life or an anticipated one. If ideologies deviate too far from the way the world is operating or come into uneven conflict with competing ideologies, then ideologies must change or die, just like political systems. There is a Darwinian struggle that pits ideologies against one another, and adaptations (hybridizations) occur. Flexibility rather than rigidity is an advantage.

Ideologies are only in part rational, programmatic, and cognitive. In large part, the most effective ideologies are also affective: they are about emotions, feelings. They relate to lived experience or they become sterile and die. In other words, they cannot be force-fed for very long. Ideology is a way of simplifying and organizing the chaos and confusion of experience. Connected to identity, collective identity in particular, ideology informs people about who they are, and whom they think the "other" is. Ideology defines the dimensions and the qualities of the "we," which in politics means the *pays légal*, the politically relevant population.[60] Such senses of difference are not simply rational calculations but are also about preferences for those like oneself (homophily), however conceived, and those who are different. Ideologies influence how we sort out friends and enemies and perceive threats and opportunities. They shape our attitudes, our emotional dispositions toward others.

While ideology in the broad sense is often about maintaining the status quo, more pointed and articulated political ideologies, like Marxism, are transformative. While some ideologies build on pre-existing elements —folk religion, custom, nativism—and benefit from the emotional connections to the familiar and already accepted, revolutionary ideologies

---

60   Hanson argues "that ideologies can be best understood as involving proposals to define the formal criteria for membership in a proposed polity" (ibid., p. 13).

are more synthetic and require greater cognitive work. Finally, ideologies provide a view of history, of the past, and of destiny. This is immediately evident in nationalism and Marxism but is also built into the varieties of liberalism and conservatism.

The argument here is that ideology is a term that gravitates between two poles of meaning. At one end it is thought of narrowly as dogma or doctrine; at the other it is something closer to discourse or culture. The Stalinist period was the moment at which the regime audaciously attempted to systematize the doctrine, turn it into a dogma (in the *Short Course*), and explain entirely the world and how to think and act properly within it. But with the death of Stalin, the official ruling ideology became a desiccated and often meaningless ritualized expression, which over time lost its affective and cognitive hold over most people. The obligatory teaching and study of *Istmat* (historical materialism), *Diatmat* (dialectical materialism), and *Istoriia kompartii* (History of the Communist Party) withered into irrelevance by the last decades of the Soviet experiment. Yet ideology, in the sense of a broad hegemonic discourse within which ordinary people as well as the Soviet leaders thought about themselves and the world, continued to operate. Here, the hegemonic ideological construction of "us" and "them," of the potential of socialism and its disappointing, dispiriting actuality maintained a tenacious hold on the imagination, aspirations, and understandings of Soviet people until the rapid deconstruction of their worldview took place under Gorbachev, only to be partially replaced by borrowed formulations from the West.

Two major works of Western scholarship on Stalinism illustrate alternative ways of employing ideology in explanation. Amir Weiner in his study of World War II and its effects on Soviet society sees the Soviet experience as a product of modernity but in essence a particularly perverse alternative to Western modernity.[61] "The Soviet ethos," he writes, "was ingrained in the politics that shaped the modern era where states sought the transformation of societies with the help of scientific models and a myriad of institutions charged with managing all social spheres."[62] All modern states, he claims, whether liberal democratic, Communist, or fascist, are inspired by transformative ideologies, though totalitarian modernity carries Enlightenment impulses to unforeseen dimensions of violence. The aesthetics of socialism involve control and coordination, harmonization of society and expulsion of intruding elements.

---

61   Amir Weiner, *Making Sense of War: The Second World War and the Fate of the Bolshevik Revolution* (Princeton, NJ: Princeton University Press, 2001).

62   Ibid., p. 7.

Weiner gives us a neo-totalitarian model that turns social history on its head and locates the ultimate causal factor in ideology. In his view, the urge to perfect society is the essential key to understanding Soviet violence; the weeds must be torn out of the Soviet garden. Inspired by Hannah Arendt and Zygmunt Bauman, and following in the footsteps of Malia and Kotkin, Weiner argues that purification, whether the periodic expulsion of party members or the more vicious campaigns against various internal enemies, was fundamental to Soviet ideological practices. State action, even individual action in many cases, flows from the discursive environment in which people find themselves. While, in some ways, the Soviets took the pursuit of *chistota* (purity, cleanliness) more seriously than the Nazis, Weiner is careful to note that the Soviets were wary of moving all the way to the "zoological" racism of the Nazis. However, he allows that Stalinist practices were similar enough to invite comparison.

The explanatory thrust of Weiner's work comes from its employment of a notion of modernity as a relatively coherent set of responses to the imperatives of state-driven transformations that are shared by all modern polities to one degree or another. Modernity is asserted unproblematically, and practices as different as Nazi death camps and Leninist nationality policy follow from it. But the emphasis here is on consistency, for, if there is no essence to modernity, then deductions from it would be difficult to demonstrate. Yet many historians are convinced that the legacies of the Enlightenment (presumably the source of modernity) do not map very neatly but run in various, even contradictory, directions. Take, for instance, Weiner's assertion that resettlement, deportations, and unmixing of peoples (that is, ethnic cleansings and genocides) are quintessentially modern. While one might agree that an irresolvable problem of "minorities" and "diasporas" emerges with the idea of the nation-state, the solutions proposed by modern states have been quite different. After the Armenian Genocide of 1915 and the Turkish-Greek population exchanges of the early 1920s, the League of Nations institutionalized an innovative system of recognizing and protecting minorities in the new states of East Central Europe. That regime of minority rights in heterogeneous states stood, however unsteadily, until the Munich Agreement, when Hitler proposed to change it with an ethnic consolidation of the Germans of central Europe. These were very different policies, as were the decisions that led to the Holocaust, but to reduce them to a "universal axis of modernity" (whatever that is) homogenizes what should be distinguished.

The recent turn among scholars toward investigating Soviet subjectivity has led to the adoption of the broader discursive understanding of ideology. "Rather than a given, fixed, and monologic textual corpus, in the sense of 'Communist party ideology,'" Jochen Hellbeck claims, "ideology may be better understood as a ferment working in individuals and producing a great deal of variation as it interacts with the subjective life of a particular person."[63] Ideology was not only top down—in some sense the official dogma was dead ideology—but "a living and adaptive force" that operated "in living persons who engage their selves and the world as ideological subjects."[64] Soviet citizens had to reconcile their enthusiasms and convictions with the evident shortfalls and repression of everyday Stalinism. In Hellbeck's view, by "rationalizing unfathomable state policies," Soviet citizens became "ideological agents on a par with the leaders of party and state."[65] Hellbeck's Soviet man and Soviet woman, at least as evidenced by the diarists he investigates, were introspective in ways that historians hitherto may not have suspected; but their tortured efforts were directed, not toward forging an individual identity in a liberal mode, but toward remaking themselves into politically conscious citizens who fused with the cause of the revolution and the building of socialism. Soviet socialist subjectivity did not prize individual autonomy or private values; they were the signs of a bourgeois consciousness that needed to be eradicated.

For Hellbeck, Soviet subjectivity is never simply the imposition of an all-encompassing ideological formation. He moves away from the structuralist notion that much of the subject's subjectivity is, in fact, the effect of dominant structures, culture, or discourses. For a structuralist Marxist like Louis Althusser, what was obvious to the individual as subjectivity was merely the effect of ideology! And, for poststructuralists, the subject is not the one who does but the one to whom something has already been done. For Hellbeck, however, "Subjectivity thus subsumes a degree of individuals' conscious participation in the making of their lives."[66] Hellbeck sees this act of creation as quintessentially modern in the Foucauldian sense—the making of a self free of a higher power or abstract social forces, able to invent his or her individual life story—but, whereas Foucault seeks to demonstrate the illusory nature of liberal autonomy of

63   Jochen Hellbeck, *Revolution on My Mind: Writing a Diary under Stalin* (Cambridge, MA: Harvard University Press, 2006), p. 12.
64   Ibid., p. 13.
65   Ibid.
66   Ibid., p. 9.

the individual, Hellbeck proposes an illiberal, socialist subjectivity, an idealized form of personhood that people under Stalinism desperately tried to forge—in both senses of that word.

Hellbeck's diarists live in an environment structured by an authoritarian regime, enforcement of ideological conceptualizations, and a thick web of discursive constructions within which they were constrained to operate and think. Their search for an authentic Soviet subjectivity was sincere, he claims, but, as one critic of the Soviet subjectivity school argues, it was not carried out in a space full of alternatives. "They were sincere, but they were not free."[67] The more telling point, derived from Foucault (and implied in Hellbeck), is that neither are the liberal subjects of capitalist democracies. Certainly, poststructuralists have convinced many of us of the power of discourse and, in most modern societies, of official ideologies as well to limit and shape the fashioning of selves and collectivities. But that power is not total, not without fissures and self-contradictions that open space for variation in subjectivities. In Stalin's USSR, there were still people who had come of age before Bolshevism; there were religious believers of many stripes; millions who were untouched or only very slightly affected by the urban based, thinly stretched regime; criminals, dissenters, ornery outsiders, and principled opponents. Standing at the other end of the grocery store queue from Stepan Podlubnyi, the son of a kulak who desperately tried to transform himself into a true Soviet man, was the thirteen-year-old Nina Lugovskaia, the unreconstructed daughter of a Socialist Revolutionary father.[68]

Even Marx would admit that ideas and ideologies have effects, though the material, temporal, and structural contexts in which they are generated and deployed also had to be taken into consideration. An idea that seizes a person in power or a large number of people is equivalent to a material force. Ideologies that coordinate disparate people into a political movement have causal effect. The closer the ideology is to the dogma/doctrine pole, the more it has the potential to make things

67   Alexander Etkin, "Soviet Subjectivity: Torture for the Sake of Salvation?," *Kritika* VI, 1 (Winter 2005), p. 177.

68   Nina Lugovskaia, *The Diary of a Soviet Schoolgirl, 1932–1937* (Moscow: Glas, 2003). For this point, as well as other of my thoughts in this essay, I am indebted to conversations with and readings of reviews by Lewis Siegelbaum. For a sense of the variation of Soviet subjectivities, see the first-person narratives in Veronique Garros, Natasha Korenevskaya, and Thomas Lahusen (eds.), *Intimacy and Terror: Soviet Diaries from the 1930s* (New York: New Press, 1995); and Sheila Fitzpatrick and Yuri Slezkine (eds.), *In the Shadow of Revolution: Life Stories of Russian Women from 1917 to the Second World War* (Princeton, NJ: Princeton University Press, 2000).

happen. Discourses, however, are different, and modernity as an inclusive cluster of ideas and practices is more difficult to employ as explanation for action. An extraordinarily capacious term, modernity may be less a causal factor than a context, an environment within which certain ideas, aspirations, and practices are more likely to find support than others. Now that historians and other social scientists have taken the cultural or discursive turn, simple structural or material analyses are insufficient. Soviet historians who wish to "bring ideology back in" are making an important contribution to explanations of the Soviet experience, but modernity is so broad a concept that unless particular elements are specified and the causal links demonstrated it may obscure more than it illuminates. Reintroducing ideology into the explanatory mix is a fruitful methodological move, but "bringing modernity in" has been fraught with normative claims. Whereas the modernization school had positively evaluated the modern, the Foucault-inspired poststructuralists and postmodernists emphasize the dark side of the Enlightenment, the utopian aspects of attempts at reform and revolution, and their own pessimism about the possibility or desirability of "progress." Whether intentional or not, inherent in their anti-modernism is a deeply conservative acceptance of the way the world has come to be.

Modernities and Utopias

The high drama of Stalinism, with all its tragic excesses, its indiscriminate and pervasive terror, and its near-total isolation from the rest of the world is what most people in the West associate with the Soviet system, as if there had been neither a Leninist prelude nor a long denouement. But the age of wanton terror ended with the death of Stalin in 1953, and much of the last four decades of Soviet rule was marked by fitful attempts by Khrushchev and Gorbachev to reform the system and recover, at least in part, some aspects of the original socialist inspiration. The history of the Soviet Union is now (and probably forever more will be) written from a postrevolutionary (1991, not 1917) point of view. While more conservative scholars contend that the breakup of the USSR was inevitable, written into the genetic code of the revolution, others to their left argue that the Soviet collapse was highly contingent. Russia was the most inhospitable place in the world to try to build socialism—indeed, it seems it may be the most inhospitable place to build capitalism as well! Zygmunt Bauman, himself a kind of postmodernist "Marxist," believed that "the collapse of Communism was the final nail in the coffin of the modern ambitions which drew the horizon of European (or Europe-influenced) history of the last two centuries. That collapse ushered us into an as-yet-unexplored world: a world without a collective utopia, without a conscious alternative to itself."[69] In a 1990 interview, Bauman asserted: "I think that people who celebrate the collapse of communism, as I do, celebrate more than that without knowing it. They celebrate the end of modernity actually, because what collapsed was the most decisive attempt to make modernity work; and it failed. It failed as blatantly as the attempt was blatant."[70] This from a man who fifteen years earlier, in his *Socialism: The Active Utopia* (1976) saw socialism as the "counter-culture" of capitalism. In 1990, he was more concerned with "the counter-culture of modernity." Capitalism and socialism were both nineteenth-century modernities, a "family quarrel inside modernity."[71]

This chapter in general agrees with Bauman. Socialism was, and remains, an alternative imaginary of modernity and not an alternative to modernity. Russian leaders after 1991 chose the Western modernity of capitalism and subscribed to the view that Soviet socialism (and by extension all socialisms) failed because it could not produce an effec-tively competitive modernity. But after the collapse of self-proclaimed actually existing socialist regimes, as in its origins, socialism regained its utopian side. From its non-existence, it exists only as an ideal yet to be realized. Socialism, then, is both an alternative modernity and a utopia, not in Malia's sense of an unattainable goal, an impossible dream, but as a direction toward which to orient one's politics. Historian Geoff Eley distinguished usefully between two constructions of utopia. The first is a "kind of blueprint for an ideal society, with extremely detailed descriptions of the mechanisms and arrangements involved," that is, for example, the kind of ideal society associated with the so-called "Utopian Socialists" (Henri de Saint-Simon, Charles Fourier, Etienne Cabet and the Icarians) but more widely applied to a range of social planners. The second sense of utopia, which needs to be separated analytically from this model of the ideal, is "a kind of longing, or fantasy, of some-thing better, a projection of desire."[72] Included in this second sense of

---

69   Bauman, *Intimations of Postmodernity*, p. xxv.
70   Ibid., p. 222.
71   Ibid., pp. 221–2.
72   Geoff Eley, "What's Left of Utopia?: From the New Jerusalem to the Time of Desire," paper given at the Institute for the Humanities, University of Michigan, March 2, 1993, p. 3; published as "What's Left of Utopia? oder: Vom 'Neuen Jerusalem' zur 'Zeit der Wünsche'," *WerkstattGeschichte* IV, 11 (July 1995), pp. 7–18.

utopia are the political hopes and ends for which people are prepared to work.

In a sense, every politics seeking change contains within it a utopia, a place where if at all possible one would like to end up. The Left is by its very nature utopian in that it seeks to change and to reconstruct society along the lines of greater equality and social justice. Only conservatives content with the status quo avoid utopia. As the Polish philosopher Leszek Kolakowski once wrote (when he was still on the Left), "The Right, as a conservative force needs no utopia; its essence is the affirmation of existing conditions—a fact and not a utopia—or else the desire to revert to a state which was once an accomplished fact. The Right strives to *idealize* actual conditions, not to change them. What it needs is fraud, not utopia."[73] For Kolakowski, utopia implied an act of negation, a desire to transform an existing reality. But the political Right and Left are also defined by the direction of their respective utopias. Reactionary movements, like fascism, also want change, but change in the direction of institutionalized hierarchies, racially determined, the enshrinement of obedience to the Leader, celebration of violence, and imperial expansion. The vision of the Left—though not by any means the actual practice of many who have called themselves Leftists—has been characterized by a utopia based on the abolition of unearned social privilege, the end of racism and colonial oppression, the maximum expansion of freedom of expression, the secularization of society, and the empowerment of working people, that is, a radical embodiment of the ideals of the Enlightenment.

From the early nineteenth century, socialism, in its variety of specific meanings, has been the principal set of ideas and the principal social movement opposed to the form of modern human organization that arose to become the dominant system of production throughout the world, namely capitalism. From its origins, socialism has been a movement with the goal of extending the power of ordinary people, that is, of extending as far as possible the limits of democracy—not only in the realm of politics (which was the goal of democratic radicals and left liberals), but also in the economy as well. Indeed, socialists were always convinced that the utopia of liberal democrats, now so hegemonic as to have become a self-evident truth—of a representative political order

---

73   Leszek Kolakowski, "The Concept of the Left," in Carl Oglesby (ed.), *The New Left Reader* (New York: Grove Press, 1969), p. 149. The essay was originally published in Kolakowski, *Toward a Marxist Humanism* (New York: Grove Press, 1969), emphasis in original.

coexisting with the private ownership of the means of production and the potential accumulation of enormous wealth in the hands of a few—was fundamentally contradictory. The power implicit in property and wealth, they believe, would inevitably distort and corrupt the democratic political sphere. Therefore, socialists have searched for mechanisms of social control over or social ownership of the means of production. In the twentieth century, however, socialism went wrong. Soviet-style "state socialism" ended up with a "perversion of authentic social ownership," where a ruling elite of party chieftains and bureaucratic managers ran the country in the name of—and ostensibly in the interests of—the mass of the people.[74]

Even after losing its more experimental side, its utopia of new possibilities, and settling down in a more productionist program in the 1930s, the Soviet Union appeared a vision of alternatives to many both within and outside the country. Affection for the Soviet Union, many people would argue now, was ridiculously misplaced, but, for those who traveled there in hope, the Soviet Union was always more than just another state; it was a dream. Even when dream descended into nightmare, the expectation remained that prosperity or reform would fulfill the aspirations of the founders. In the end prosperity proved to be elusive and reform led to revolution. The casualty regrettably was socialism, which, like liberalism, was always making more promises than it could keep.

As modernities and postmodernities compete for possible futures, utopia appears neither a blueprint nor an illusion, but rather a goal toward which active citizens may work through politics and in their everyday lives. Utopia provides an inspiration and a direction, if not an ultimate end, for political and personal activity. The philosopher David Love put it this way: we may want and try to achieve perfect health, all the time aware that perfect health is ultimately unachievable. But does that mean that we stop eating healthily and going to the gym, that the effort is not worth it? Or in Bauman's words, Utopia is "something like the idea of the ideal experiment, which of course is never achieved, but unless you have it, you can't experiment at all."[75]

---

74   George Lichtheim, "What Socialism Is and Is Not," *New York Review of Books*, April 9, 1970.
75   Bauman, *Intimations of Postmodernity*, p. 217.

8

Gorbachev and History:
Why the Soviet Union Fell Apart

History is a discipline based on hindsight.[1] The farther away the events, the more confident historians are about their conclusions. Interpretations of the causes of the Soviet collapse are becoming as numerous as books on the subject, but even more than a quarter century later they must be considered provisional.[2] They range from fatalistic structural accounts at one extreme—the end of a utopian system already present in its DNA at conception—to highly voluntarist and contingent explanations that focus on key players—the Polish pope, John Paul II; Cold Warrior President Ronald Reagan; the determined but inconsistent reformer Mikhail Gorbachev; and an array of actors on both sides of the barricades from Lech Wałęsa to Nicolae Ceaușescu. But the events were so consequential for our own times that few are content to stop with

---

1   This chapter was first prepared for the conference Assessing the Collapse of the Soviet Union, Twenty Years Later, at UCLA, October 21–22, 2011. It also incorporates language from an unpublished paper on political elites in the South Caucasus.

2   See, for examples, Stéphane Courtois, Nicolas Werth, Jean-Louis Panné, Andrzej Paczkowski, Karel Bartošek, and Jean-Louis Margolin, *The Black Book of Communism: Crimes, Terror, Repression*, trans. by Jonathan Murphy and Mark Kramer (Cambridge, MA: Harvard University Press, 1999); François Furet, *The Passing of an Illusion: The Idea of Communism in the Twentieth Century*, trans. by Deborah Furet (Chicago: University of Chicago Press, 1999); Stephen Kotkin, with a contribution by Jan T. Gross, *Uncivil Society: 1989 and the Implosion of the Communist Establishment* (New York: The Modern Library, 2009); Constantine Pleshakov, *There Is No Freedom without Bread!: 1989 and the Civil War That Brought Down Communism* (New York: Farrar, Straus and Giroux, 2009); and Victor Sebestyen, *Revolution 1989: The Fall of the Soviet Empire* (New York: Pantheon Books, 2009).

narration, analysis, and explanation. Moral and political lessons must be learned. Judgments about socialism, capitalism, democracy, and the costs of social engineering that come with modernity are brought along with the stories of what happened and why.

The argument in this chapter is that the collapse of the Soviet Union was neither inevitable nor very likely in 1985. Yet six years later the USSR was gone as the result of a combination of structural flaws badly in need of reform; extraordinarily poorly planned policies to modernize the system; and a number of international pressures and contingencies. Among the principal factors leading to collapse was the program of *glasnost'*, which worked to undermine the ideological legitimacy of the system and the justification for a unified multinational, non-nationalist federation. One of Gorbachev's most ambitious goals was to turn what was essentially a pseudo-federalist empire into a democratic multinational federation. Later the possibility of federation gave way to confederation, but on the eve of signing the Union Treaty in August 1991, the putsch against Gorbachev changed the balance of power between the president of the Soviet Union and Boris Yeltsin, the elected president of the Russian Federation. Gorbachev's reforms led to the weakening of the principal instrument that held the USSR together, namely the Communist Party. In his democratizing zeal he was reluctant to use force to maintain order and compliance with the dictates of the center. In early December 1991, a few months after the attempted coup against Gorbachev, Yeltsin and the leaders of Ukraine and Belorussia conspired to dissolve the USSR. While there were many factors, domestic and international, structural and contingent, that have been used to explain the collapse of the Soviet system and the disintegration of the union, my conclusion is that overdetermination is not the same as predetermination.

An astute commentator at the time of the Gorbachev *perestroika*, Andrei Melville, asked whether everyone was prepared to pay the price of *glasnost'*:

> Glasnost is an intense, difficult process, and it has a price .... The cost of glasnost is the open expression by others of views and ideas that might be alien and unacceptable to you personally and that you may even find repulsive. Glasnost's cost means the protest of the Crimean Tatars, the activities of the chauvinistic society *Pamiat*, the demonstrations of the *refuseniki*, the meetings in Nagornyi Karabakh, and the outrageous behavior of our own primitive "rockers" and "punks." Glasnost applies

equally to the Stalinists and to those fighting Stalinism, for neither one nor the other is able to repress their opponents.[3]

About the same time, convinced that only transparency and the open airing of the faults of and problems with the Soviet system could transform the country into a democracy, Mikhail Gorbachev may be said to have answered that question: "We need glasnost as we need air."

Theories about the collapse of the Soviet system and the breakup of the Soviet Union fall into two distinct but related clusters: those that are primarily structural in emphasis and those that are primarily agent-centered. The first cluster of explanations tends to be quite inevitabilist, noting fatal structural flaws and an inability to change; the second cluster tends to emphasize contingency, accident, and just plain luck, while maintaining an openness to the possibility of successful transformation. The most extreme example of the inevitability school (some have called it the "totalitarian" paradigm) believes that the fall of Soviet socialism was already inscribed in the initial Bolshevik project, that is, in the genetic code of the revolution. In the more contingent, agent-centered cluster are an array of studies centered on the pivotal figure of Mikhail Sergeevich Gorbachev, either applauding him for his valiant attempt to reform Communism, end the Cold War, and create greater democracy and freedom or condemning him for losing that struggle and bringing down his own regime and destroying the Soviet state.

The classic statement of the inevitability position is Martin Malia's *The Soviet Tragedy*, though more generally conservative scholars have subscribed to similar views. Malia wrote, "The most fundamental cause was the economic decline and its repercussions for the Soviet Union's superpower status." To deal with "this crisis of performance" Gorbachev launched *perestroika*, followed quickly by his attack on the party and "the suicidal risks of *glasnost*' and then of democratization." Economic decline precipitated a cascade of crises: it "discredited the claims of the ideology, and *glasnost*' made it possible to proclaim this fact, thereby delegitimizing the system and, ultimately, depriving it of the will to coerce." Minority nationalities revolted, and the people's democracies of East Central Europe collapsed. "Finally, we may include in the chain of causation various tactical errors of Gorbachev, such as pushing democratization faster than economic liberalization, or, at

---

3 Andrei Melville, "A Personal Introduction," in Andrei Melville and Gail W. Lapidus (eds.), *The Glasnost Papers: Voices on Reform from Moscow* (Boulder, CO: Westview Press, 1990), p. 12.

the end, surrounding himself with conservative enemies of his own reforms."[4]

Few analysts would deny that structural factors were important, that the system itself had become the problem of further development, both economic and political. But this is not the same as saying that the system would inevitably fall, that choices made by leaders and opponents did not contribute fundamentally to the collapse. Political scientist Peter Rutland makes the essential point that the interference by party officials was both a principal cause of the economic stagnation of the Brezhnev era (1964–82), as well as a major obstacle to the efforts of Gorbachev to reform the economy. "Efforts to expand the scope for market-like forces, even on a modest scale, came to naught. This was not simply because of political opposition from conservative elements. It was more a case of the whole body politic rejecting the foreign cells of marketization, however modest, which local experiments or central reforms sought to inject."[5] Here deep structure and long-term practices proved to be major obstacles to successful reform. Whether they could have been overcome by a different approach—perhaps sequencing economic reforms first and political reforms only when the economy had shown improvement— remains an open question.

The most telling introduction to an agent-centered, contingent approach to the end of the Soviet Union came with an essay by political scientist/historian Alexander Dallin, where he argued against an array of essentialist arguments—the doomed-from-the-beginning argument (Malia); the fatalism of Russian political culture argument (Richard Pipes); and even certain Marxist arguments that the USSR was a distortion of socialism and a deviation from history and that it could never be reformed to become either real socialism or capitalism.[6] In place of these views, he lists six necessary but not sufficient causes for the collapse: the loosening of controls; the end of terror and decentralization; the spread of corruption; the erosion of ideology (the withering of utopianism); the impact of social changes on values and attendant social pathologies; the growing impact of the international environment on Soviet politics and society (which included growing pessimism of young people, a kind of

---

4   Martin Malia, *The Soviet Tragedy: A History of Socialism in Russia, 1917–1991* (New York: The Free Press, 1994), pp. 492–3.

5   Peter Rutland, *The Politics of Economic Stagnation in the Soviet Union: The Role of Local Party Organs in Economic Management* (Cambridge: Cambridge University Press, 1993), p. 218.

6   Alexander Dallin, "Causes of the Collapse of the USSR," *Post-Soviet Affairs* VIII, 4 (1992), pp. 279–302.

progressive disenchantment); and the consequences of economic constraints. Despite all these structural flaws and problems, Dallin concludes that the system was reformable, but it needed to be reformed gradually, something like the "Chinese option." The *razpad* [disintegration] of the union in turn was made possible by the failed reforms, which allowed for the rise of Boris Yeltsin, the key catalyst to the breakup of the USSR.

A similar agent-centered view can be found in two major studies by Archie Brown and Jerry F. Hough, particularly interesting because of their differences.[7] Whereas Brown admires Gorbachev's restraint in resorting to police or military force as he implemented his reforms, Hough concludes that the union fell apart because Gorbachev "refused to use enough force to ensure obedience to Soviet laws and to suppress separatism." Moreover, "his failure to oppose Yeltsin's attack on the treasury and to defend the central government's power of taxation created serious doubts within the military and bureaucracy about the desirability of supporting him against Yeltsin."[8] Hough's ultimate point is that, whereas the "revolutionary" change from communism to market democracy was the natural product of the forces of modernity, the dissolution of the USSR was a very avoidable accident caused by the mistakes and weakness of a single individual.

Stephen Kotkin's long essay on the Soviet collapse—*Armageddon Averted: The Soviet Collapse, 1970–2000*—can be read in a variety of ways. A reader could come away convinced that the fall was triggered by Communist ideology, by the attempt to create a "socialism with a human face."[9] The agents of the Soviet demise were Gorbachev himself and his generation of *shestidesiatniki* [people of the 1960s] who believed in a democratic Communist Party and the possibility of renewing the Soviet system. They were simply wrong, says Kotkin, to think they could make the socialist project work. In his universe, for better or worse, there is no alternative to liberal modernity. In order to achieve effective reform the general secretary had to draw clear lines of acceptable behavior and be willing to use force. But even then it might not have worked. His very goal of humane socialism both destabilized the system and made him reluctant to accept the human costs necessary to restabilize it.

---

7   Archie Brown, *The Gorbachev Factor* (Oxford: Oxford University Press, 1996); and Jerry F. Hough, *Democratization and Revolution in the USSR, 1985–1991* (Washington, DC: Brookings Institution Press, 1997).

8   Hough, *Democratization and Revolution*, pp. 498, 501.

9   Stephen Kotkin, *Armageddon Averted: The Soviet Collapse, 1970–2000* (New York: Oxford University Press, 2001), p. 2.

Another reader might come to a different conclusion. At the same time that he emphasizes agency, Kotkin also pays due attention to structural factors: the geopolitical competition between the USSR and the United States; the failure of the Soviets to convert from an economy founded on heavy industrial production to a more flexible consumer economy in the decades when the capitalist West rose from the Great Depression to affluence and consumerism; the time-bomb constitution that gave potential power to union republics in a pseudo-federation but could not survive without the firm hand of the Communist Party; and the lack of the indispensable liberal institutions that make markets work and without which real economic reform and the transition to a market economy are impossible. In addition, he notes how *glasnost'* undermined the popular allegiance to socialism and raised illusions about an affluent welfare society in Russia like those imagined to exist in the West. Take your pick. Whether inevitable or contingent, at the end we should all be relieved that the collapse did not result in the bloodbath that many predicted. Armageddon was averted because "reform socialism meant breaking with anything that resembled Stalinism or Brezhnevism, including domestic military crackdowns."[10]

Kotkin's account borrows liberally from a number of different, even contradictory, analyses of the fall of Soviet socialism. As he considers both context and contingency, his various explanations coexist in unresolved tension. What is euphemistically referred to by Western analysts as the "transition to democracy and the market economy," or more accurately and ironically as "privatization," was actually the "chaotic, insider, mass plundering of the Soviet era, with substantial roots prior to 1991."[11] With little more than lip service paid to the public good, "Russian officials used their positions of public power to pursue their private interests."[12] This "squalid appropriation of state functions and state property by Soviet-era elites" could not have been helped, however.[13] Rather than the fault of self-important Western advisors or ambitious Russian policymakers, the "underlying cause" of the Russian failure to establish a dynamic economy "was the Soviet bequeathal"—the industrial "white elephants" and the larcenous state officials.[14] But one is left to wonder whether the Soviet legacy is the cause of the failed transition or the background

10   İbid., p. 183.
11   Ibid., p. 124.
12   Ibid., p. 126.
13   Ibid., p. 116.
14   Ibid., p. 141.

condition within which a different strategy might have worked better. The Chinese example, quickly dismissed by Kotkin, comes to mind: similar though hardly identical conditions but a political strategy of maintaining a single-party state authority and direction while undertaking a planned, gradual marketization.

Both Malia and Kotkin argue that Gorbachev was trying to do the impossible: reform Marxism-Leninism and a system that was fatally rigid. Rigor mortis had long set in, but the doctors had not yet noticed that the patient had passed on. Yet one could more plausibly argue the reverse. Marxism and Leninism had been constantly reforming; the decades of Soviet power had seen one set of improvisations after another—state capitalism (1917–18); war communism (1918–21); the New Economic Policy (revived state capitalism, 1921–28); Stalinist command economy (1928–53); economic and social liberalization under Khrushchev (1953–64); social transformation, economic internationalization, and political stagnation under Leonid Brezhnev and Konstantin Chernenko (1964–82, 1984–85), with tentative, aborted reforms by Yuri Andropov (1982–84); and radical reform leading to revolution under Gorbachev (1985–91). When Gorbachev came to power, the system was stagnating and needed to be reformed. But there was no serious foreign threat; there was no rebellion from below. The Soviet system could have muddled along for decades had Gorbachev not embarked on his wildly ambitious, largely improvised program.

Gorbachev's reforms were overwhelmingly destructive rather than constructive, in the sense that he was far more effective in tearing down than building up. As with Marx and Lenin, there were no blueprints for what the future political structure and social supports would be. This was building the ship at sea, while the seas were roiling and helping to tear the vessel to pieces. Or as my Soviet friend Vahan Mkrtchian said to me regretfully, one does not dismantle the old house when you have not yet secured the plans, the brick, the mortar, or the roofing for the new house you wish to build.

Gorbachev was confronted by a double defection: from conservatives who worked hard to undermine reforms and ultimately carried out a coup d'état to overthrow him; and from reformers and democrats who wore away at his credibility as a reformer and attempted to move faster toward liberal democracy and market economics. Both the right and the left undermined the very supports that made gradual reform possible. Gorbachev tried and failed to hold a centrist coalition together, tacking first to the left, then to the right, and then back to the left. In a sense he desired to be both Martin Luther and the Pope, both radical reformer and preserver of what might be maintained. Ultimately he could not be both the opponent of the existing system and the head of the church.

Political Elites and the Test of *Perestroika*

Whether one adopts the language of the classical theorists of elites—Gaetano Mosca, Vilfredo Pareto, Robert Michels—or the rival conceptualizations of the Marxist tradition, it is difficult in this post-Communist period to avoid the obvious: that political elites have been and still are an omnipresent and most potent part of the social structure of power. Whether we refer to the dominant political and economic actors in the Soviet Union and the post-Soviet republics as an "elite" or a "ruling class," the terms should not suggest a tight unity among the rulers but involve an appreciation of the heterogeneity and internal distinctions within any dominant group. Indeed, as a ruling class establishes and maintains its claim to rule, it must constantly engage in the difficult work of constituting itself as a dominant class, maintaining a degree of group identity and solidarity, and struggling against the internal and external forces that threaten to break down its distinctiveness and undermine its right to rule. At the same time, rulership is seldom merely a matter of exercising naked power but ultimately of creating legitimate authority by creating a hegemonic political culture that justifies the ruling class's dominant position.

Within the Soviet Union, successive generations of the ruling elite—Leninist, Stalinist, and post-Stalinist—not only transformed society and the economy but simultaneously unleashed processes and structures that accelerated the ultimate decay and disintegration of the system and left a particularly barren legacy for successive political actors. The party/state elite of the Soviet period was a highly integrated group of leaders, who effectively monopolized almost all influential positions in state administration, the economy, and intellectual and cultural life. Marked by a high degree of stability, the "ruling class" in the USSR from the late 1930s until the mid-1980s was basically the one formed after the Stalinist purges of the 1930s. At the moment of initiation into power, it made up the youngest ruling elite in Europe. By the time of its demise, it was the oldest. Only the aging process brought a generational shift and a belated turn toward radical reform. The Soviet elite displayed a high degree of solidarity, particularly in the late Stalinist period, and remained intact until greater internal divisions appeared in the 1960s and 1970s. Maintaining an extraordinarily tight control of recruitment into the elite through the *nomenklatura* system, the Soviet elite restricted access to political power and privilege. Making a career depended on the good will and support of already established people higher up in the hierarchy. Success depended on pleasing those above; being competent in your tasks; displaying loyalty and discretion; developing personal bonds; showing caution in criticism; being generally careful, even secretive.[15] Unlike many elites in more democratic, representational systems, the Soviet elite did not so much look to the population for support but to those who sat above them in the political pyramid. For nearly seven decades, Communists worked to eliminate all rival sources of authority. When through the actions of its top leaders, the Communist Party of the Soviet Union undermined its own claim to legitimate power, turning the reform movement begun by Gorbachev into a revolutionary transformation, both the acquired legitimacy of the Communist Party as well as the authority of almost all state structures throughout the empire were eliminated.

Focusing on the agency of Gorbachev but placing him within the larger context of the Soviet system, his most thorough biographer, William Taubman, shows how a well-meaning reformer who believed in socialism undermined both himself and his regime.[16] Mikhail Gorbachev grew up in a stern but loving family divided between two grandfathers, one the chairman of a collective farm, the other an individualistic farmer who spent time in the gulag. When the chairman also was arrested, detained for fourteen months, and tortured, young Gorbachev was shunned by his playmates. He worked in the fields as a boy in the absence of the older men during World War II, through a brief German occupation, until his father returned, wounded at the front. What he saw tempered him and probably influenced his future reluctance to use violence when he had the power to do so. Taubman speculates that such experiences gave Mikhail a balanced view of the Soviet experiment and a keen understanding of the injustices of the system.

As a teenager Mikhail was an extraordinarily hard worker, a medal-winning combine driver, physically strong and intellectually curious. He performed in plays and gained confidence in his abilities. But the greatest change came when this provincial peasant spent five years studying

15   Jeffry Klugman, *The New Soviet Elite: How They Think and What They Want* (New York: Praeger, 1989), pp. 56–7.

16   William Taubman, *Gorbachev, His Life and Times* (New York: W. W. Norton, 2017).

at the most prestigious university in the Soviet Union, Moscow State, trained as a lawyer (in a country without the rule of law), and "began the long process of rethinking [his] country's history, its present, and its future."[17] Like many talented people from the bottom of society, his story is a Soviet version of the log cabin to the White House story, an improbable career formed by a socialist affirmative action program. Gorbachev imbibed the values of Soviet-style socialism: egalitarianism, contempt for wealth and anything considered bourgeois, along with strong doses of Soviet patriotism.

Ambitious, he rose in the Komsomol and at age twenty-one, in the last year of Stalin's life, entered the Communist Party, even though he was already having doubts about many Soviet practices. He returned to Stavropol province with his wife, Raisa, and steadily climbed the party ladder. In the Soviet system who you knew and who could favor and promote you were keys to advancement, and throughout this career Gorbachev was skilled or lucky enough to attract important patrons, most consequently Yuri Andropov, then KGB chief and later General Secretary of the Communist Party. Thanks to his connections, he was called to Moscow in 1978 to become the youngest Central Committee secretary. Seven years later, after the death of three aged first secretaries in succession, his desperate comrades chose him leader of the Soviet Union. His comparative youth (fifty-four) was a major asset.

Taubman sees Gorbachev as "a true believer—not in the Soviet system as it functioned (or didn't) in 1985 but in its potential to live up to what he deemed its original ideals. Gorbachev believed in socialism, the faith of his beloved father and grandfather."[18] Like his university friend, the Czech reformer Zdenek Mlynar, he was a convinced Communist in the sense that he believed in the project of building a more just and egalitarian society called socialism. Faithful and optimistic as they were, the two comrades were not blind to how far removed Soviet reality was from their ideals and the original projections of Marx and Lenin. Gorbachev was not disillusioned by Khrushchev's 1956 revelations about the crimes of Stalin because he had already seen the consequences of collectivization and the purges in the lives of his own family. Unlike most of his fellow Soviet leaders, he knew his Marx and Lenin and was inspired by the courageous example of Lenin, who dared to seize power and extend the revolution.

---

17   Ibid., p. 44.
18   Ibid., p. 215.

As society became more mobile after the death of Stalin, more highly educated, more exposed to diverse influences from the West, pressure for change in the system increased, both within the elite and from ordinary people. At the same time, the limits on upward mobility and the restrictions on expression—in a time of growing social diversity and a slower rate of economic development—led to frustration and dissent on the part of the intelligentsia. With the end of Stalin's terror and hypercentralism, the post-Stalin elites made a greater effort to rule through persuasion and "delivering the goods" to the population. In national republics and regions this meant more concessions to ethnic feelings, expanded permissiveness (within enforced limits) of national expression, and, often, increased acceptance of extra-legal economic practices. The greater tolerance of somewhat autonomous decision-making in regions and non-Russian republics led to a regional and ethnic fragmentation of the Communist elite, which in turn necessitated the exercise of a kind of coalition politics. The evident need to deal politically with a variety of interests in the more open political world of the post-Stalin system led some Western social scientists to talk about a "conflict model" of Soviet politics and others to imagine a nascent pluralism.[19]

Diversity of interests and attitudes, however, did not threaten Soviet oligarchic rule from above. Only the academic and literary intelligentsia remained somewhat autonomous in some republics, along with courageous but marginalized dissidents. Then when the dominant elite lost its ideological conviction and its political will was weakened (from the top) during the Gorbachev revolution, the alternative elites that emerged proved to be extraordinarily weak and without broad social bases in many republics. One considerable source of strength was the ability of some intelligentsias to express their aspirations in the language of national revival or survival, but in many republics the old elites quickly attempted to appropriate the now-hegemonic discourse of nationalism.

On becoming General Secretary in 1985, Gorbachev embarked, at first cautiously, on a "revolution by evolutionary means," refusing violence or the brutal means that would taint his democratic socialist ends.[20] To the detriment of his intended reforms, he rejected the Chinese path of decollectivization and promotion of peasant agriculture, which might have

---

19   On the conflict model, see H. Gordon Skilling and Franklyn Griffiths (eds.), *Interest Groups in Soviet Politics* (Princeton, NJ: Princeton University Press, 1971); on pluralism in the Soviet system, see Jerry F. Hough, *The Soviet Union and Social Science Theory* (Cambridge, MA: Harvard University Press, 1977).

20   Taubman, *Gorbachev*, p. 218.

fueled economic prosperity and gained popularity for the reforming government. Instead, frustrated by the slow pace of change, he embarked on a multipronged frontal assault: political democratization, economic liberalization, decentralization of control of non-Russian republics, emancipation of Soviet satellites, and ending the costly Cold War. The first great shock, after the ill-fated and unpopular prohibition campaign, was the explosion of the nuclear reactor at Chernobyl, "an evil augury of what was to come."[21] The deep rot in the system was exposed more glaringly than ever.

A persistent underlying thread running through Taubman's interpretation of the Gorbachev phenomenon is what might be called "the dilemma of Soviet reform." Changing the system in the Soviet Union could only come from the top, from the regime itself; there was no crisis in society that could bubble up into a revolution. Control by the state, party, police, and army was secure, and dissent had largely been channeled or crushed. But having learned a peculiar lesson from the Hungarian Revolution of 1956 and the potential of the Prague Spring of 1968, party officials feared that weakness or division at the top might unleash massive forces from below that could rip apart the Soviet structure. Thus, many resisted reform, while others understood that it could proceed only gradually, with great caution, and if controlled from above. Andropov notably "dreaded the prospect that freedom could get out of hand, while Gorbachev turned out to be far less cautious."[22]

Though it began as one more state-directed campaign to mobilize the population toward greater economic effort (*uskorenie*, acceleration), the reform program of Mikhail Gorbachev from its inception involved an explicit and radical critique of the relationship of the political elite to the people they ostensibly represented. As early as the April 1985 plenum of the Central Committee, Gorbachev elaborated his assessment of the status quo. The party and state were not accountable to the people; the system was too highly centralized; information was constantly being manipulated and falsified; and the deep, chronic problems of society were being ignored. He introduced new emphases into the existing official discourse: the systemic nature of the problems and the need "to speak with people in the language of truth" and to deepen "socialist democracy, the self-government of the people." Gorbachev was convinced that economic development required political restructuring in an environment of

---

21   Ibid., p. 242.
22   Ibid., p. 144.

reduced international competition. By raising the specter of a fundamental breakdown of the system and the need for radical, even revolutionary transformation, Gorbachev borrowed from the Leninist tradition, but in his concerted attack on "stagnation" and bureaucracy he introduced elements that undermined the party's exclusive claims to leadership.

At the end of 1986 and the beginning of 1987, Gorbachev pushed his closest advisors to begin to think of more radical changes in the political structure of the country, even flirting with the idea that the Communist Party should give up its monopoly of power and compete with other parties. At the Central Committee plenum in January 1987, he cautiously presented his thoughts on democratization. Much of the party elite was cool to the suggested changes, vague as they still were. Again, in June, another plenum adopted Gorbachev's moderate economic reforms that slightly loosened the controls of powerful state ministries over enterprises. His Martin Luther hoped to reform the system, his Pope not to destroy it. But in his centrist position he created opposition on both the Right and the Left. And in a real sense, as Taubman shows painfully, he created his own nemesis, the ambitious, impulsive radical, Boris Yeltsin. "Gorbachev was instinctively democratic, Yeltsin an authoritarian populist."[23]

By 1987, the reform leadership had mobilized the intelligentsia as the spearhead of the anti-bureaucratic movement. Thousands of party and government officials were demoted, shifted, and replaced. Beginning with the removal of Dinmukhamed Kunaev in Kazakhstan in December 1986 (unwisely replaced by an ethnic Russian), the entrenched national elites in the non-Russian republics were threatened. They demonstrated remarkable resistance to the center's dictates, however, and those under the top leadership stayed intact. Both non-Russian Communist elites and their opponents found in Gorbachev's rhetoric of democracy and decentralization a language to justify their own political activities.

Sympathetic to Gorbachev's aspirations, Taubman's overall vision is not that reform was impossible but that indecision, confusion, hesitancy, compromise, misjudgments about personnel, and ultimately lack of clarity about goals and methods on the part of Gorbachev doomed *perestroika* and the Soviet Union. By 1988 Gorbachev was prepared to take his country further on the road to greater democracy. He intended to shake up the Communist Party, which had become the principal obstacle to further reform of the economy and political order, and to revitalize the

23   Ibid., p. 333.

moribund soviets. "It was as if the tsar had turned Bolshevik and decided to overturn his own regime."[24] As the leader of the Soviet Bloc, he had no strategy for change in the Soviet satellite states in East Central Europe, letting each state work it out on its own without Moscow's interference. In negotiating with West Germany over unification with East Germany and with a recalcitrant Reagan administration over reduction of inter-mediate range missiles, he gave away the store with little in return. At home as well as abroad, the General Secretary was reluctant to use force, the police and the military, even when faced by riots and rebellion. "Most important, by gutting the [Communist] party's ability to run the country, he was undermining his own power."[25]

The elections of May 1989, fostered by Gorbachev, were the freest that Russia had experienced since 1917, and the results shook the hard-liners in the Communist Party as liberals and more radical reformers surged to prominence in the now open politics. Excited by the possibilities pre-sented for further reform, Gorbachev proved to be far less skilled in a democratic arena with a critical media than he had been for most of his life in the closed, top–down patronage system of the Soviet Union. In 1989 he was overwhelmed by cascading trends and events: disastrous economic decline; ethnic conflicts in the Baltic republics and the South Caucasus; the fall of the Berlin Wall and the defection of East European states from Communist rule; massive public protests; miners' strikes; and deepening divisions within the elites desperately trying to hold on to some semblance of power. As the union itself began to pull apart, he reiterated that "the use of force is out of the question."[26]

The Subversive Force of *Glasnost'*

The Russian word *glasnost'* has its own contradictory history and was used both in tsarist and Soviet times to mean making things public, public disclosure, openness, and truthfulness. Autocrats and dictators as well as reforming liberals and democrats deployed the term until its meanings were a complex alloy of progressive intentions and rational-izing spin. For Gorbachev *glasnost'* at first was a strategy to improve the Soviet economy and society. Openness, admission of problems, and free discussion would accomplish what secrecy and cowardice had failed

24   Ibid., p. 355.
25   Ibid., p. 373.
26   Ibid., p. 436.

to do: identify problems and find solutions. *Glasnost'* was never about abandoning socialism but about its improvement in a democratic and participatory direction. The initial discussions were largely in the discursive arena of understandings of socialism, and much of the early debate was between different conceptions of socialism.

Because that openness was a threat to those who held unaccountable power, *glasnost'* was attacked from two sides simultaneously: not enough *glasnost'*, too much *glasnost'*. There was no perfect equilibrium of just the right balance of openness; the limits and constraints on public disclosure and an uncensored media were being worked out at the same time as the whole society was undergoing radical change and the necessary laws were either not in effect or were not being obeyed. As the economy worsened and the criticism of the Soviet system and Gorbachev personally intensified, *glasnost'* steadily undercut the legitimacy, not only of the old Soviet system, but of all forms of socialism, leaving the field open to a single, seemingly viable alternative—western-style capitalist democracy of the neo-liberal variety, which at the time was the program of the Reagan administration in the United States and the Thatcher government in Great Britain.

By 1990 much of Gorbachev's domestic and foreign program had been realized: the radical transformation of the Soviet system into a more democratic, more market-oriented, more pluralistic system; contested elections; an uncensored press; the end of the political monopoly by the Communist Party; the legitimation of various forms of ownership. The Cold War was coming to an end; negotiations were proceeding on arms limitations and nuclear weapons; the Soviets had withdrawn from Afghanistan; and the countries of East Central Europe had been allowed to abandon their Communist governments and establish more democratic and capitalist systems. Yet the unintended consequences of the Gorbachev reforms effectively eroded the "vertical of power" within the USSR. Moscow's hold over the peripheries of what had been its empire grew weaker by the day. The first cracks appeared in the South Caucasus, in Karabakh in February 1988, and almost simultaneously in the Baltic republics. The economy was a hollow shell marked by empty shelves and long, aimless lines. The beginning of the collapse of the union began in 1988–89 and accelerated in 1990–91.

After enduring suspicions both at home and abroad when he first came to power that he was simply a wolf in sheep's clothing, an insincere reformer though a genuine communist, Gorbachev over time managed to convince the skeptics, at least abroad, that he was an authentic dismantler of the Stalin–Brezhnev command system. The withdrawal from Afghanistan and East Central Europe in 1989 and the declaration that a multiparty system was possible in the USSR persuaded even the professional Cassandras of academic Sovietology to change their tune from worry about Gorbachev's sincerity to anxiety about his survival. Gorbachev's dilemma was how to maneuver between the ends of democratization and the means to achieve it. Would the use of force in Georgia or Lithuania end progress toward democracy? Could the USSR be turned from an empire, in which Moscow dominated over subordinate peoples, into a genuinely democratic confederation of equal nations? Was Lenin's oft-stated goal of national self-determination (which included secession) to be treated, as it had been for so many decades, as mere rhetoric, or put into practice for the first time in seventy years?

Gorbachev's cautious, phased revolution-from-above had from its beginning been dependent on social forces outside the ruling circles to prevent the conservative *apparatchiki* from undermining his reforms. Most important, intellectuals were mobilized through *glasnost'* to deconstruct the rhetorical facades that had propped up Brezhnevism. But in unleashing the pent-up resentments and discontents festering in Soviet society, Gorbachev underestimated the ability of a state that itself was being torn asunder to control a growing revolution-from-below. Striking miners, incensed consumers angry at privileged party potentates, and the suppressed hostilities of non-Russians shook the foundations of the Soviet state and endangered the gradualist "revolution from above." Democracy stimulated separatist nationalisms that threatened to break up the USSR. Yet in Gorbachev's mind a brutal crackdown from Moscow would mean the end of *perestroika*.

Violence by the state would be used—but reluctantly, hesitantly, and inconsistently. Brutal suppression of demonstrations and protests and even pogroms occurred in Georgia, the Baltic republics, and Azerbaijan, but the use of the police or army was intermittent, hesitant, and usually followed by concessions or apologies. Gorbachev was looking the other way, at problems at home, as Communist rule over the "satellites" evaporated with hardly a shot fired—except in Rumania, where the Ceauşescus were executed by their own people. In the last few years of Soviet power, he was not only unwilling to use force to hold on to the East European states but extremely reluctant to use coercion against recalcitrant and rebellious Soviet citizens. Just as holding on to the empire in Eastern Europe needed a measure of force, so keeping the Soviet state together required coercion to compel people to obey the existing laws and prevent separatism. But Gorbachev, it turned out, did not have the "iron teeth" that Andrei Gromyko, in nominating him to the highest post in the land, had promised he would show. Revolutions are always accompanied by violence and often followed by civil wars. Lenin unhesitatingly called for civil war when he was struggling for power. Terror was one of his tools for state building. Unlike that other state preserver, Abraham Lincoln, Gorbachev was reluctant to use the instruments at hand to keep his union intact.

From his office in the Kremlin, Gorbachev waited in vain for help, material and diplomatic, from the United States, but after the overtures by Ronald Reagan, his successor, George H. W. Bush, offered very little to a floundering Gorbachev. The Chinese, led by Deng Xiaoping, were wary of the reforms in the Soviet Union, even as they carried out serious changes in their economic policies and maintained firmly the grip of the Communist Party over politics and society. Deng smashed the students protesting in Tiananmen Square after Gorbachev's visit. In China state and party would not permit democracy to undermine the unity of the country and its gradualist path toward a more market-oriented economy.

Nineteen-ninety was the year that both the Soviet Union and Gorbachev himself began to come apart. His now increasingly formidable rival Yeltsin was elected chairman of the Russian Republic's parliament. Continually underestimating his erratic opponent, Gorbachev, exhausted and without clear ideas about how to proceed, fell back on his usual incantation, "Everything will be alright. You'll see."[27] In the summer he tried to compromise with Yeltsin and the more radically inclined economists who wanted to move rapidly toward a market economy (the so-called "500 Day Plan"). In the end he tried to marry the radicals with the doubters, like his prime minister Nikolai Ryzhkov, only to fracture his temporary alliance with Yeltsin, who then essentially declared war on Gorbachev. The leaders of Russia and other Soviet republics were by the fall of 1990 looking toward independence from the USSR. In September Gorbachev moaned to his close advisor Anatolii Cherniaev, "Tolya, what should we do? Where is the way out?"[28]

That year also saw Gorbachev's greatest and most inexplicable concession to the West. As its economy faltered, and the East German state was collapsing, the Soviet Union was increasingly vulnerable to US and West German pressure to allow unification of the two Germanys. East

27   Ibid., p. 515.
28   Ibid., p. 529.

Germans wanted to unite with their wealthier, freer compatriots in the Federal Republic. Taubman relates the bizarre story of Gorbachev agreeing to German unification without written guarantees—merely verbal promises from the Americans and Germans—that NATO would not expand eastward. George H. W. Bush and Secretary of State James Baker were incredulous when Gorbachev conceded that the German people could themselves decide which military alliance they would join. Top Soviet military officers and diplomats shared their bewilderment. Gorbachev's pleas for desperately needed economic aid were gently, repeatedly rebuffed. His foolish—and from a strategic perspective, irrational—decisions seriously and negatively impacted the future security of Russia, as Vladimir Putin would later repeatedly assert, and prefigured both the 2008 war with Georgia and the subsequent crisis with Ukraine.

By 1991 Gorbachev could no longer ride the tiger he had unleashed. The hard-liners who feared that his program would lead to the breakup of the country proved to be correct. But their clumsy attempt to overthrow him in August 1991 lasted only three days, unbalancing the scales of power in favor of Yeltsin. Democratic Russia required a different kind of politician. Gorbachev talked too much, changed his mind too often, and was unwilling to use power when he had it to punish his opponents. Yeltsin, on the other hand, was "a master of passive aggressiveness as well as the more active kind."[29] Reflecting on their differences, Gorbachev sadly, bitterly recognized Yeltsin's ambitions and abilities: "Such ... a simpleminded yen for the scepter! I'm at my wit's end to understand how he combines this with political instinct. God knows, maybe this is his secret, maybe this is why he is forgiven everything. A tsar must conduct himself like a tsar. And that I do not know how to do."[30]

Taubman's Gorbachev is a decent, moral man who aspired to create a democratic Russia, convinced that there was no real socialism without democracy (and no real democracy without socialism). He had moved from being a critic of "actually existing" Soviet "socialism" to attempting to revive what he took to be the essence of Leninism only to eventually abandon what was left of "communism," that is the remnants of Stalinism, to become a social democrat. Heroically he accomplished a true revolution, brought greater freedom to millions. Yet he remains a tragic figure. He had never intended to destroy the Soviet Union but ended up

---

29   Ibid., p. 625.
30   Ibid., p. 581.

tearing apart his beloved country and leaving in its wake a weak Russia at the mercy of a global hegemon, the United States. Betrayed by many of his comrades, by the Soviet intelligentsia, and by the Great Power allies he hoped to enlist in his cause, Gorbachev was set adrift, a president without a country on December 25, 1991. The red flag came down over the Kremlin, and his hopes that he could revive socialism as an alternative to actually existing capitalism appeared quaint and irrelevant to most of his compatriots.

Taubman's story is about the personal limitations of Soviet actors. He deftly demonstrates the many sides of Gorbachev's personality, his abilities, and his limitations, but without condescension or imposing superfluous judgments. Personal flaws, most important among them overconfidence and even arrogance, are key to explaining the ultimate failure of his democratic and market-oriented reforms. This is a Western, even a US, take on the successes and ultimate failure of the man at the center of the story. Liberalism is the dominant frame through which Taubman understands history and current politics. When Gorbachev and his allies thought and wrote like Westerners, they were on the side of history; when they used Marxist phrases or concepts they were stuck in the past. "The fact that he himself was still wedded to at least some old orthodoxies also held him back," Taubman concludes.[31] Still, his book is even-handed, critical when it must be, and free of the kinds of anti-Soviet biases that so often mar foreigners' views of the USSR. Geared to a wide readership—there is a lot of attention paid to clothing and footwear—what is lost is a deeper-level analysis that more conventionally scholarly books would provide. There is little investigation of the conflicting readings of the weaknesses of the Soviet system, how they were understood at the time and since. Complex debates are flattened into sound bites. Antonio Gramsci, whom Gorbachev read, for example, is summed up in a sentence: "His notion of 'cultural hegemony' replaced cruder conceptions of how capitalism maintained its hold over society."[32] One is left to wonder about the ideas expressed by the repressed Fadim Sadykov, a philosopher from Stavropol, in his banned book, *The Unity of the People and the Contradictions of Socialism* (1968), a work that Raisa approved and Mikhail was forced to denounce. The pivotal discussion in 1990 about transition to a market economy is reduced to a clash of personalities rather than elucidated with reference to the complex imperatives of such

31   Ibid., p. 542.
32   Ibid., p. 128.

a fundamental transformation. But engaging in such explorations would require a different book for a different audience.

Bringing together structure and agency, as Taubman does, it appears that Gorbachev's own policies were contradictory, attempting to coordinate complex programs of transformation from the center through the instrumentality of the party while actually eroding central state and party power and authority and permitting regional and republic elites to grow more independent. The Gorbachev reformers had both raised new political and material expectations and proved unable to satisfy them. Political mobilization far outstripped the glacial pace of economic development, and the party lost the ideological conception of its right to rule (what Mosca called the "political formula"). In a particularly strong formulation of the "abdication" of power, political scientist Judith Sue Kullberg shows that in contradiction to the image prevalent in the West at the time, the Communist Party was not forced by popular pressure or mass resistance to give up power. Rather its decline is a story of its own consent to a reduced role, a voluntary abdication of its control over both the political system and the society.[33]

Rather than claiming that the disintegration of the Soviet system was the inevitable, delayed effect of a wrongly conceived political project, this chapter posits that the Soviet Union suffered from its successes as well as its failures. In the area of nationality policy, the contradictions of the Soviet system and its policies both created new, coherent nations within the pseudo-federal structure of the union and undermined the sources of nationality and nationalism. And in the political sphere the very programs that over seven decades had created a more urban, educated, articulated and articulate society eroded the need for a vanguard party monopolizing all decision-making.[34] As Kullberg argues:

> To a certain extent the Party's self-destruction in the perestroika period is a continuation, although expanded in size and compressed in time, of the long path the party had taken to self-elimination. Because its end goal was the modernization of society, which was seen as inextricably intertwined with the construction of socialism, it set about creating the

33   Judith Sue Kullberg, "The Origins of the Gorbachev Revolution: Industrialization, Social Structural Change and Soviet Elite Value Transformation, 1917–1985," PhD dissertation, University of Michigan, 1992, pp. 163–87.

34   This is essentially the argument of Moshe Lewin, *The Gorbachev Phenomenon: A Historical Interpretation*, expanded edition (Berkeley: University of California Press, 1991).

social groups and organization of society that would eventually make it superfluous.[35]

As Gorbachev must have eventually realized—and as the successor elites would discover—political elites may react to, initiate, shape or even inhibit larger historical processes, but they cannot control them. Political elites may make history, but not just as they please; they do not make it under circumstances chosen by themselves, but under circumstances given and transmitted from the past.

A Test for *Perestroika*: Conflict in the Caucasus

Along with ending the Cold War, liberalizing the command economy, and democratizing the state, Gorbachev offered to end the imperial relations between Moscow and the non-Russians in the former satellite states. Few states in history have survived such a radical reformation. Determined to prevent the breakup of the Soviet Union, Gorbachev repeatedly made it clear that "independence" and "sovereignty" for the non-Russian nations were not precluded outcomes. The precise meaning was to be worked out. The broadest cultural, political, and economic autonomy for the republics was promised, but with foreign policy, military security, and certain budgetary decisions retained by the center. Decolonization was to be the ultimate "test of *perestroika*," a test that Gorbachev failed in the Karabakh conflict.

Both in the tsarist and Soviet empires, the peoples of the South Caucasus lived intermingled in the towns, villages, and countryside of what would in Soviet times become more ethnically homogeneous republics. The single most volatile territorial issue among Soviet Armenians was without doubt the question of Karabakh, the autonomous region heavily populated by Armenians but lying within the Azerbaijan Soviet Republic. Mountainous Karabakh (*Lernaiyin Gharabagh* in Armenian, *Nagorno-Karabakh* in Russian, abbreviated NKAO) had been contested between the independent republics of Armenia and Azerbaijan in 1918–20 and was formed as an autonomous region within Soviet Azerbaijan shortly after the establishment of Soviet power. At the time, 94.4 percent of the 131,500 people in the district were Armenian (124,000) and only 5.6 percent (7,400) were Azerbaijani. By 1979 Armenians made up just

---

35   Kullberg, "The Origins of the Gorbachev Revolution," pp. 412–13.

under 76 percent (123,000), a net decline of 1,000 people, and Azerbaijanis had increased five times to nearly 24 percent (37,000).[36] Armenians
were fearful that their demographic decline would replicate the fate of
another historically Armenian region, Nakhichevan, which had been
placed under Azerbaijani administration as an autonomous republic.
There Armenians, a significant minority in the 1920s, had declined from
15 percent (15,600) in 1926 to 1.4 percent (3,400) in 1979, while Azerbaijanis, with in-migration and a higher birth rate, had increased from 85
percent (85,400) to nearly 96 percent (230,000).[37] Besides fears of losing
their demographic dominance in Karabakh, Armenians were resentful
about restrictions on the development of the Armenian language and
culture in the region. Although they lived better than Azerbaijanis in
neighboring districts, the Armenians saw that their standard of living
was not as high as Armenians in the Armenian republic.[38]

Hostile to the Azerbaijanis whom they blamed for their social and
cultural discontents, the Karabakh Armenians preferred to learn Russian
rather than Azeri in a ratio of eight to one.[39] Beginning in the 1960s,
dissidents reported open friction and clashes between the Karabakh
Armenians and the Azerbaijanis. But under the Soviet system, open
protest was impossible; petitions went unanswered; and Karabakh Armenians either emigrated or acquiesced to Azerbaijani rule. But they did not
assimilate; they maintained their Armenian identity, even while being
considered by the Armenians of Armenia somewhat ersatz Armenians,
akin to hillbillies or rubes. Indeed, except for some nationalist intellectuals, until February 1988 there was very little interest in Karabakh among
the Armenians of Soviet Armenia.

Gorbachev and *glasnost'* created a new political playing field with new
rules in the Soviet Union. The possibility now existed, if people were courageous enough to try, for an open politics: public appeals, articles in the
press, mass protests, and street demonstrations. Igor Muradian, a very
savvy young activist from Karabakh who was working in Erevan at the
time, understood that the game had to be played by the new rules before
the rules of the game could be changed. The movement had to appear to
be pro-Soviet, loyal to the regime, working in tangent with *perestroika*.

---

36   Anatolii N. Yamskov, "Ethnic Conflict in the Transcaucasus: The Case of
Nagorno–Karabakh," Working Paper, no. 118, Center for Studies of Social Change, New
School for Social Research (New York, May 1991), p. 11.

37   Ibid.

38   Ibid., pp. 7–9.

39   *Vestnik statistiki*, no. 10 (1980), p. 70.

In February 1986, Muradian secured the signatures of nine Armenian Communist Party members and scientists on a draft letter on the Karabakh problem. He took it to Moscow and there convinced Gorbachev's economic advisor, fellow Armenian Abel Aganbekian (after he drank about two liters of vodka), to affix his name to the letter. At the same time Muradian secretly provided Czech weapons for Komsomol (Communist Youth League) members and other young activists in Karabakh.[40]

Tensions between the two ethnicities rose in 1987, reflected in a petition to unite Karabakh with the Armenian Soviet Republic signed in the summer of 1987 by 75,000 people. It was reported in the French Communist newspaper *L'Humanité* that Aganbekian revealed that he had proposed that Nagorno-Karabakh be united with Armenia and hoped the issue would be resolved in the context of *perestroika* and democracy. Early the following year, a delegation of Karabakh writers and artists went to Moscow to discuss the issue. Organizers back in the Karabakh capital, Stepanakert, prepared for their return with a mass demonstration. Leaflets were stuffed in mailboxes; party officials and the KGB were fully informed about what was going on.

Azerbaijanis in the autonomous region were not part of this preparation. As Muradian told Tom de Waal, author of *Black Garden*, a stunning account of the Karabakh crisis, "I will tell you the truth. We weren't interested in the fate of those people. Those people were the instruments of power, instruments of violence over us for many decades, many centuries even. We weren't interested in their fate and we're not interested now."[41] Armenian activists seemed unconcerned that along with the 123,000 Armenians in NKAO, there were almost three times as many Armenians (350,000) in Azerbaijan outside of the Autonomous Region. Armenians were a majority in NKAO, but Azerbaijanis were a significant minority (24 percent). In the rest of Azerbaijan Armenians were a minority and Azerbaijanis an overwhelming majority, and the exact reverse was true in Soviet Armenia.

Both sides in the conflict were able to make credible historical claims to the territory of Karabakh. They simply had to emphasize different historical periods and events and willfully efface others. Armenians could argue in favor of national self-determination, since they have been for at least a century the majority population in the region, while Azerbaijanis could appeal to the international law principle of national territorial

---

40   Thomas de Waal, *Black Garden: Armenia and Azerbaijan through Peace and War* (New York: New York University Press, 2003), pp. 16–18.

41   Ibid., p. 21.

integrity, since Nagorno-Karabakh has been an integral part of the Azerbaijani republic since the early 1920s and continues to be so recognized by the international community.

Muradian's thinking, and the organizational work of him and his associates, resonated with the cognitive and emotional dispositions of Armenians, both in Karabakh and Armenia proper, about Azerbaijanis. Armenians saw Azerbaijanis as inferior, less civilized, *vaireni* (wild, savage), and akin to the Turks of Anatolia who had carried out the Genocide of 1915. Azerbaijanis had their own affective disposition toward Armenians, whom they saw as arrogant, condescending toward Azerbaijanis, well connected to the outside world and to Moscow, and as people who took advantage of Azerbaijani vulnerability. Even though both peoples had lived in relative peace for almost seventy years of Soviet power, the structural situation, which included the perceptions of the other and the sense of potential threat if the imperial state faltered (or favored the other side), heightened the possibility of the conflict turning violent.[42]

Given the appeals of *glasnost'* and *perestroika* to democracy, social activism, humane behavior, and the avoidance of force and violence, it was very difficult for the state to respond vigorously (and especially difficult for it to use armed force) to quell violations of older norms or even disorder. Officials, including top leaders in Baku and Moscow, were unsure about what they were allowed to or supposed to do in the new environment. Hesitation only encouraged further expansion of demands, new forms of public behavior, and violence. On February 13, 1988, the first mass demonstration was held in Stepanakert. Two days later the prominent poet Silva Kaputikian spoke to the writers' union in Erevan about supporting the demands of the Karabakh Armenians. Small demonstrations followed in Erevan, not directly concerning Karabakh, but around the far safer subject of environmental degradation. At first little attention was paid to the Karabakh issue, and only toward the last week of February was the environmental issue linked to the "national" issue.

Groups of Azerbaijani students, workers, and intellectuals reacted with their own demonstration on February 19, and the next day 30,000 people responded with a demonstration on Theatre Square in central Erevan. Demonstrations escalated from day to day until on February

---

42 For an account of the Karabakh conflict and a proposal for resolution, see David D. Laitin and Ronald Grigor Suny, "Armenia and Azerbaijan: Thinking a Way Out of Karabakh," *Middle East Policy* VII, 1 (October 1999), pp. 145–76.

22, as many as 100,000 flooded into the square. In an unprecedented move, the legislature of NKAO, the regional soviet, voted to transfer Karabakh to Armenia. Moscow immediately removed the Armenian Boris Kevorkov from his post as party secretary of NKAO. On February 25, a million people demonstrated in a kind of euphoria in Erevan.

Armenians hoped that Gorbachev would act and resolve the crisis in favor of Armenia. But Gorbachev was not prepared to intervene on the side of one republic against another, and in his "Appeal to the Workers of Armenia and Azerbaijan" on February 26, he called for calm. The journalist Zori Balayan and Silva Kaputikian met with Gorbachev in Moscow. The General Secretary was extremely upset. "What is happening around Karabakh," he told the Armenian representatives, "is a stab in the back for us. It is hard to restrain the Azerbaijanis, and the main thing is that it is creating a dangerous precedent. We have several dozen potential sources of conflict on ethnic grounds in the country, and the example of Karabakh can push those people, who have not so far risked resorting to violence, into impulsive action." The writers appealed to history, showed Gorbachev a Turkish map that painted vast swaths of the Soviet Union in green. Gorbachev pushed it aside: "This is some kind of madness." Zori Balayan pleaded: "Mikhail Sergeevich, mad ideas sometimes become realities." Gorbachev commented, "Now we have to put out the fire." Kaputikian asked, "Good, but what with? Give us water. Some kind of promise, some kind of hope. I will go [to the crowds] but what will I tell them?" Gorbachev's adviser, Georgii Shakhnazarov, an Armenian, replied, "Tell them there will be a conference devoted to the nationality question. That is where a decision will be taken." At this point Gorbachev refused to transfer NKAO but promised that reforms would enhance the cultural and economic life of the region, a "little renaissance." The writers agreed to ask the Erevan demonstrators to call off their protests for a month.[43]

Within a few days the crisis escalated from peaceful demonstrations into wanton killing. Azerbaijani refugees fled from Armenia to Azerbaijan, and the Baku party secretary Fuad Musaev attempted to relieve tensions in the capital by restricting movement of Sumgait workers into Baku and sending the refugees to two villages on the edge of the dreary industrial town of Sumgait. Azerbaijani protestors were incensed by stories of Azerbaijani refugees forced from their homes. It was reported that two Azerbaijanis had been killed in the town of Agdam. On February

43   De Waal, *Black Garden*, pp. 27–9.

27, with several hundred gathered on the central square in Sumgait, the atrocity stories became more vivid. Women, it was rumored, had had their breasts cut off. A second secretary of the party, Bairamova, called for the expulsion of Armenians from Azerbaijan. People clashed in a movie theater and at a market. That evening Alexander Katusev, a military prosecutor of the USSR, who was in Azerbaijan, appeared on national television and radio and confirmed that five days earlier two men had been killed in Askeran. The Communist authorities were rapidly losing control. Azerbaijani party chief Kamran Bagirov was sick and, as a protégé of ousted party boss, Heidar Aliev, was not in favor in Moscow. The local Sumgait party secretary Jehangir Muslimzade tried to calm the crowd and called on the demonstrators to allow the Armenians to leave the city. He tried to lead a march along *Ulitsa druzhby* (Friendship Street) to the seashore, but people broke off, looking for Armenians, and killings started. When that evening Moscow officials arrived in Sumgait, they witnessed dismembered corpses, bodies mutilated by axes and set afire. A mob threw Molotov cocktails and attacked a regiment of troops from the Ministry of Internal Affairs with sharpened metal casings. One hundred soldiers were wounded. The slaughter continued the next day, as five thousand Armenians huddled terrified in the Palace of Culture on Lenin Square, protected by marines. They took Moscow's representatives hostage and demanded that a plane be brought in to take them to Russia (not Armenia!).[44]

The Politburo met in Moscow on February 29. Gorbachev was enraged by the events in Sumgait:

> I should say that even when there were half a million people on the streets of Erevan, the discipline of the Armenians was high, there was nothing anti-Soviet .... For my part, I see two causes: on the one hand, many mistakes committed in Karabakh itself, plus the emotional foundation, which sits in the people. Everything that has happened to this people in history remains, and so everything that worries them provokes a reaction like this.[45]

His military chief, General Dmitrii Iazov, called for strong measures: "But Mikhail Sergeevich, in Sumgait we have to bring in, if you want—it may not be the word—but marital law." Gorbachev suggested a curfew.

---

44   On the events in Armenia and Azerbaijan in February 1988, see ibid., pp. 11–45.

45   Ibid., p. 26.

Iazov went on: "We have to pursue this line firmly, Mikhail Sergeevich, to stop it getting out of hand. We have to send in troops and restore order. After all, this is an isolated place and not Armenia with millions of people. Besides, that will surely have a sobering effect on others." Gorbachev demurred. Even though there had been some mild disturbances in the Azerbaijani city of Kirovabad, "We have to bear in mind that they did not yet know what happened in Sumgait, but that this is growing like a snowball." His foreign minister Edvard Shevardnadze worried that this was "like a connecting vein. If they find out about the casualties in Armenia, then it could cause trouble there." Another Politburo member, the liberal Alexander Iakovlev, declared, "We must announce quickly that criminal cases have been opened in Sumgait and criminals have been arrested. We need that in order to cool passions. In Sumgait itself, the city newspaper should say this firmly and quickly." Gorbachev was reluctant to use military force. "The main thing now," he concluded, "is we need to send the working class, people, people's volunteers into the fight with the criminals. That, I can tell you, will stop the hooligans and extremists. As happened in Alma-Ata [where in December 1986 there had been demonstrations by Kazakhs]. It's very important. Soldiers provoke hostility." Only after much hesitation did Gorbachev agree to send a limited military force to Sumgait and enforce a curfew.[46] After the killing subsided, it was discovered that between twenty-six and twenty-nine Armenians had been killed in Sumgait. Hundreds had been wounded; and almost all the 14,000 Armenians in the city had fled. Six Azerbaijanis were killed. Of those arrested, eighty people were convicted of crimes, and one man executed.

Glasnost' contributed to the Karabakh conflict and the pogrom in Sumgait in two seemingly opposite ways. Too much *glasnost'* and too little both contributed to the crisis. The conflict between Armenians and Azerbaijanis over the mountainous district of Karabakh was not the result of "ancient tribal hatreds" or strongly felt religious differences, but a struggle of two peoples for a piece of what they consider to be their historical homeland. At the moment of the outbreak of the conflict in February 1988, the intense sense of attachment and commitment to Karabakh had to be created, and it was created almost instantaneously. Armenians and Azerbaijanis had much more diffuse and less passionate feelings about Karabakh before February 1988, but when the possibility for open expression arose and mobilization and coordination by activists

46   Ibid., pp. 38–40.

began, the emotional disposition of Armenians, first in Karabakh, then in Armenia, intensified. The visible threat of loss at the hands of Armenians then caused reaction among Azerbaijanis, first among refugees from Armenia, some intellectuals, and then more broadly in the population. Both sides felt and expressed hostility toward the other based on fear of potential endangerment, loss of land and status. Both resented the experience and future possibility of political or social subordination to the other. For Armenians the war with Azerbaijan over Karabakh was and is framed in the most powerful of all frames, that of genocide, the fear of total extermination at the hands of traditional enemies. For Azerbaijanis the Armenians are an inherently aggressive, rapacious people, who initiated the conflict, victimized the Azerbaijanis, and used their privileged position in the world community (and with Russia) to perpetuate the humiliation of Azerbaijan.[47]

At the same time, the Soviet press and electronic media did not report what happened in Sumgait in real time. Instead it showed riots in Israel, South Africa, and Panama. Later the violence was labeled "acts of hooliganism" and not ascribed to interethnic hostilities. In February 1988, there was too little real *glasnost'* just as there had been two years earlier at the time of the Chernobyl explosion. Problems could be aired; demonstrations held; and information passed around. Yet the mass media limited what could be known. In that vacuum rumors operated freely, escalating what might have been true, exaggerating the sense of danger because of what was not known. Armenians believed that hundreds had been killed in Sumgait. The newspapers did not officially announce the death totals until weeks later. At the same time officials were constrained, confused about what was now the appropriate response. Force was needed, but there was fear about the consequences of its use. In this toxic mix the state appeared weak, indecisive, but also partisan. Inaction led to both sides believing the Soviet government was on their opponents' side. The

47 Examining the Karabakh case, Stuart J. Kaufman concluded: "Prejudice, fear, and a hostile myth-symbol complex can create a contest for dominance and an interethnic security dilemma even in an apparently stable country, which the Soviet Union was in 1988. There was no previous hint of emergent anarchy, so theories about 'structural security dilemmas' based on anarchy do not work in this case. The Armenians flatly rejected Moscow's generous economic package, proving that economic benefit was not their central goal. And nationalist mobilization occurred against the efforts of incumbent leaders to squash it, showing that elite-led explanations cannot account for the conflict. Ethnic politics and war are sometimes driven by hate and fear. No theory focused primarily on elite calculations, material interests, or 'structural' security dilemmas can capture that dynamic." *Modern Hatreds: The Symbolic Politics of Ethnic War* (Ithaca, NY: Cornell University Press, 2001), pp. 82–3.

conflict over Karabakh exploded at the moment when the very ideological foundations of the Soviet system were being widely questioned. A few weeks later, the schoolteacher Nina Andreeva's infamous letter appeared in *Sovetskaia Rossiia* (March 13, 1988). The letter, published without the imprimatur of the General Secretary, signaled that there was serious disagreement about *perestroika* and *glasnost'* within the highest levels of the Soviet party. Someone, evidently Gorbachev's more orthodox nemesis, Pavel Ligachev, had sanctioned the publication of the letter to weaken the more liberal supporters of reform.

The Karabakh crisis was a major turning point in the trajectory of the Soviet Union. The US ambassador to the USSR at the time, Jack Matlock, remembered:

> In 1988 ... there was no substantial independence movement in either of these republics. Each was seeking Moscow's support for its territorial claims, and neither, at this point, questioned its status in the Soviet Union or its commitment to "socialism." ... [Gorbachev] then, and subsequently, ... reacted with extreme irritation to all Armenian requests: he was invariably harsher in dealing with the Armenians than with the Azeris, but for a while the Armenians continued to nourish the hope that he could eventually accept their position.[48]

Although he "found Gorbachev's refusal to change the constitutional structure understandable," Matlock was perplexed by Gorbachev's caution. The General Secretary refused to do anything effective. The party bosses of Azerbaijan and Armenia "had no freedom of action. They were trapped between Moscow's passivity and political passions at home. Attitudes in both Armenia and Azerbaijan continued to harden, and old hatreds took on new life."[49]

In January 1990 violence erupted again, this time in the Azerbaijani capital, Baku. While militant Muslim nationalists tore down border posts between Soviet Azerbaijan and Iran, crowds rampaged through the streets of Baku killing Armenians. To many it appeared as if the Soviet state was dissolving right before the television cameras. Some predicted a second Afghanistan within the Soviet Union, and Gorbachev appeared to be a sheep in wolf's clothing. After nearly a year of reluctance to use military force—following the April 9, 1989, killings in Tbilisi,

---

48   Jack F. Matlock, Jr., *Autopsy on an Empire: The American Ambassador's Account of the Collapse of the Soviet Union* (New York: Random House, 1995), p. 166.
49   Ibid., p. 168.

Georgia—the Soviet state attempted to demonstrate that it retained the muscle to act as the final arbitrator in ethnic clashes. Despite the interpretation by Azerbaijanis of the Russian invasion and wanton killing of Azerbaijanis in January 1990 as "Black January," and later as a "genocide," Gorbachev's decision to restore order was precipitated by several days of Azerbaijani pogroms against local Baku Armenians. The measured but forceful response of the Soviet military in Azerbaijan brought the most dangerous phase of the Caucasian crisis to a temporary halt. Whatever the role of Azerbaijani officials was in 1988 and 1990—and that remains murky—it is clear that the key actors in the pogroms, particularly those in Baku in 1990, were Azerbaijani refugees forced out of Armenia in the previous few years. As horrific as the killings of Armenians in Sumgait in February 1988 and in Baku in January 1990 were, it should be noted that the initial tragic events in Sumgait and Baku were affairs of a few days and ethnic violence did not spread from city to city, village to village. There was no overall Azerbaijani plan to rid Azerbaijan of Armenians, certainly not to murder them systematically. There was no genocide on either side. The riots, Sumgait and Baku, the invasion (one of the few times that Gorbachev resorted to military force), and the subsequent killing of Azerbaijanis by Soviet troops created two mutually exclusive—Armenian and Azerbaijan—understandings of the nature of the opposing nation. A kind of "civil war" within the USSR became an "ethnic war" and eventually an interstate war that continues to the present time.

Events both in Moscow and Karabakh demonstrate that the fall of the Soviet Union was largely the result of an overly ambitious reform program initiated by Gorbachev without adequate preparation and determined leadership. He simultaneously undermined the power of the Communist Party, which was the skeleton and nervous system of the Soviet order, and opened the floodgates of free speech and assembly that permitted more radical elements to seize his podium. Both structural factors and the personal aspirations, indecision, and reluctance to use what instruments of power he possessed steadily weakened Gorbachev and his small cohort of reformers who wanted a more humane society based on democracy, human rights, and personal dignity. The problem was that the aim required measures (more control, even force by the government) that Gorbachev was unwilling to employ. He allowed too much freedom too rapidly and did not control the process. The Soviet Union did not disintegrate because of popular nationalist revolts from below, though in the Caucasian and Baltic republics such movements found wide support. As late as March 1991 over three-quarters of the Soviet people voted to preserve the Soviet Union, albeit in a new, less imperial form.

The end of the Soviet Union was a moment of liberation for millions, particularly in East Central Europe and the Baltic states. But it was also a triumph for global capitalism and US hegemony and a tragedy for their possible alternatives. As flawed, repressive, and bloody-minded as Soviet state socialism had been, it was the space in which "socialism" held state power. With the failure of its reform in a democratic direction, the Left, having lost its burdensome anchor in Russia, was set adrift. Unable to unburden itself from the Soviet, particularly Stalinist, past, socialists moved to the margins of politics; Communist parties dissolved; and nationalist, anti-democratic populist, religious, and authoritarian substitutes occupied the void left by the Left.

In the West political scientists were faulted for failing to predict the collapse of the Soviet Union, even in its last days. But in hindsight it was not reasonable to think that Gorbachev would act so irresponsibly, to try to carry out a revolution without using the enforcement power he had. Gorbachev was neither a Lenin nor a Lincoln. He was a well-intentioned man with truly humanistic ideals, but not the will to do what was necessary to preserve his country. Read in the West as the failure of socialism, the Soviet disintegration was much more immediately a failure of democratization, so essential to what Soviet socialism might have been. Even as millions of people celebrated new freedom, tragedy followed for millions of others. Violence and bloodshed continued for the next several decades in Tajikistan, Uzbekistan, the North and South Caucasus, and Ukraine. The unraveling of the Soviet Union only began in 1991. Empires do not simply fade away.

Index

workers), 91n84, 156, 163–4; and workers, 145–6, 162–3, 166

socialism: aid for, expected from West, 10, 68–9, 139, 147, 159, 162; as alternative modernity, 226; and capitalism, 64; as non-capitalism, 209–13; conflated with Soviet tragedy, 205–6, 228; conflated with Stalinism, 15, 60, 64, 80, 150, 197, 209–10; and culture, 139; and democracy, 15–6, 150, 201, 207, 227, 246; enemies of, as Soviet threat, 81; and *glasnost'*, 243; and Gorbachev, 238; and international proletarian revolution, 69n12; Kotkin on, 60; Lewin on, 147–8, 150; as modern project, 203; opposition to Stalin's negation of, 83; and Soviet disintegration, 259; Soviet studies divided over, 212; and Stalinism, 38, 43, 60, 81, 83, 214; and West, 208. *See also* revolution

society: lacks capacity for resistance, 193; and state, 137, 149, 188

The Soviet Bloc (Brzezinski), 102

The Soviet Century (Lewin), 149–50

The Soviet Citizen (Inkeles & Bauer), 102–3, 105–6, 109–12

The Soviet Middle East (Nove & Newth), 114–5

Soviet studies: academic professionalization of, 116; and archives, 189; and Cold War, 102–3; and Cold War consensus, 184–7; Columbia University's Russian Institute, 185; crisis in, 101; divide in, 104, 147, 212; Harvard Project on the Soviet Social System, 78n40, 105, 110; and ideology, 159–61, 165, 216–9; Institute for the Study of the USSR in Munich, 106–7; and Lewin, 131, 134–5, 148–9; Malia trashes, 206; and Marxism, 160; nationality as constructed category, 122–30; non-Russian nationalities, 104–11; and non-Russian peoples, 116–22; revisionism, 165, 168; Russian Research Center of Harvard University, 102n3; and Stalinism, 167–70; two schools of, 195; in United States, 184–5. *See also* archives; totalitarian model

The Soviet Tragedy (Malia), 205–7, 214, 231

Soviet Union (USSR): as argument against alternatives to capitalism, 195, 197; citizens as spectators, 89; concentration of power, 66–9; conflated with socialism, 205–6, 228; destalinization of, 186; disintegration of, 121, 149, 182, 194, 199, 205, 225, 229–30, 257–9; disintegration of, agent-centered explanation, 231–5; disintegration of, and elites, 236–7, 239–40, 249; disintegration of, and *glasnost'*, 230–1, 243–8; disintegration of, structural explanation, 231–4; dominant understanding of, 197; elections of May 1989, 242; and empire, 3–4, 6, 14, 109, 115; as empire of nations, 129; end of, 247, 259; and Enlightenment, 159; foreign policy, 53–4, 65; formation of, 69, 109; and Great Purges, 97; and imperialism, 3, 6, 107, 116, 129; isolation of, 99–100; military purge, 94–5, 97; referred to as Russia in West, 126; reform of, 191–2, 240–4; threatened by enemies domestic and

foreign, 86, 93–7, 100; threatened by enemies of socialism, 81

Sovieticus: American Perceptions and Soviet Realities (Cohen), 182

Sovietphobia, 184–6, 192

soviets, weakening of, 67

Spanish Civil War, 93–4

Stalin: A Political Biography (Deutscher), 28–9

Stalin: An Appraisal of the Man and His Influence (Trotsky), 27, 29

Stalin: Breaker of Nations (Conquest), 44–5

Stalin: Man and Ruler (McNeal), 22, 39

Stalin: Triumph and Tragedy (Volkogonov), 27n21, 42–4

Stalin and the Struggle for Supremacy in Eurasia (Rieber), 53–6

Stalin as Revolutionary (Tucker), 31–4, 41

Stalin in October (Slusser), 20n2, 22, 40–1

Stalin in Power (Tucker), 46

Stalin, Joseph: authority of, and authoritarianism, 65, 68; and Bolshevism, 33, 49, 70, 83, 215; central mystery in Soviet Union, 19–20, 22, 44, 64; childhood of, 26–7, 29–30, 32, 34, 47–8, 57; conflated with Soviet history, 100; cult of, 31, 80, 188; death of, 148, 225, 239; on democracy, 73; and foreign policy, 53–4, 65; as great actor, 43, 47, 49; and Great Purges, 13, 41–5, 52–3, 60–1, 65–6, 91–2, 95–7; and Hitler, affection for, 34; and Hitler, alliance, 62; and Hitler, comparison, 55–6, 60, 97; insecurity/unhappiness of, 93; as Ivan the Terrible, 46, 52, 66, 91, 167; and Lenin, influence of, 31–2, 38, 43, 46, 58; and Lenin, revision of, 78, 80; and Lenin, threatened by, 59, 142; and loyalty, 90–1; and Marxism, 32, 44, 50, 58–9; modernist vision of, 210; as murderous egomaniac, 48, 62; and October Revolution, 40–1; as people person, 50, 58; proclivity toward use of force, 84–5; rise to power, 49, 70–5; Stalin revolution destroys worker-peasant relations, 76; threats to, internal and external, 93–7, 100; and Trotsky, 57, 71; as womanizer, 48, 51; and World War II, 97–9

Stalin, Joseph, biographies, 19–64; by Bychowski, 29–30; and collectivization, 46–7, 51; by Conquest, 44–5; by Deutscher, 28–9; fictional portraits, 20; first biographies, 21; as history of Soviet Union, 21, 23, 44; by Kotkin, 56–63; by McNeal, 39; by Medvedev, 36–9; proliferation of, 22; and psychoanalysis, 20n3; and psychohistory, 23–36, 63; by Rancour-Laferriere, 33–4; by Rieber, 53–6; by Sebag Montefiore, 47–53; by Slusser, 40–1; by Trotsky, 27, 29; by Tucker, 31–4, 41, 46; by Ulam, 36; by Volkogonov, 42–4

Stalin (Kotkin), 56–63

Stalinism: alternatives to, 138; antithetical to revolution, 209; and Bolshevism, 188; Bukharin as alternative to, 183, 188–90; and bureaucracy, 142, 146–7; and class, 81, 170; Cohen on, 167, 188; and collectivization, 144;